THE ULTIMATE RULE OF LAW

The Ultimate Rule of Law

DAVID M. BEATTY

OXFORD
UNIVERSITY PRESS

OXFORD
UNIVERSITY PRESS

Great Clarendon Street, Oxford OX2 6DP

Oxford University Press is a department of the University of Oxford.
It furthers the University's objective of excellence in research, scholarship,
and education by publishing worldwide in

Oxford New York

Auckland Bangkok Buenos Aires Cape Town Chennai
Dar es Salaam Delhi Hong Kong Istanbul Karachi Kolkata
Kuala Lumpur Madrid Melbourne Mexico City Mumbai Nairobi
São Paulo Shanghai Singapore Taipei Tokyo Toronto

Oxford is a registered trade mark of Oxford University Press
in the UK and in certain other countries

Published in the United States
by Oxford University Press Inc., New York

© D. Beatty, 2004

The moral rights of the author have been asserted
Database right Oxford University Press (maker)

First published 2004

British Library Cataloguing in Publication Data
Data available

Library of Congress Cataloging in Publication Data
Data available
ISBN 0-19-9269807

3 5 7 9 10 8 6 4

Typeset by Kolam Information Services Pvt. Ltd, Pondicherry, India
Printed in Great Britain on acid-free paper by
Biddles Ltd., King's Lynn, Norfolk

For Ninette, Erin, and Sam

Preface

This is a book about one way of solving disputes and settling differences. It is known to lawyers and laypersons alike as the 'rule of law', although these words have become a term of art that seems incapable of yielding a single, comprehensive definition. Its ambiguities notwithstanding, the rule of law has come to represent an ideal around which systems of government should be organized. It is the primary purpose of this book to explain why that is; what law and its rule really mean.

Although its subject is the resolution of conflict, the book was conceived and nurtured in a corner of the world in which harmony and co-operation prevail. I live and work in a faculty where collegiality is valued as highly as whatever job is being done and the office of the dean is an oasis of friendship and support. I am also blessed to be surrounded by family and friends whose selflessness and generosity are ironclad guarantees that all conflicts and disagreements are settled fairly and peacefully.

In contrast with best practice in the culinary arts, this book is undeniably better for its having passed through many hands Although none can be held responsible for what follows there are a lot of people who have helped in its production. Kamil Ahmed, Becky Allen, Gwen Booth, Alan Brudner, Sugit Choudry, Guy Davidov, Ron Daniels, Rajeev Dhavan, Sara Ferris-Childers, Charles Fried, Cheryl Fung, Miranda Gass-Donnelly Angus Gibbon, Sylvia Jaffrey, Ninette Kelley, David Klacko, Trevor Knight, Don Kommers, John Louth, Patrick Macklem, Marylin Raisch, David Schneiderman, May Seto, Shikha Sharma, Kathy Tam, Ted Tjaden, and Beth Woods deserve special thanks. Funding for the research was generously supported by the Social Sciences and Humanities Research Council of Canada and by the Robert Prichard and Ann Wilson Chair in Law and Public Policy. As always, the Institut Suisse de Droit Comparé provided a welcoming home away from home.

The heroes of this story are the jurists of our generation who have, day in, day out, shown the world how law can give government more integrity than it is has ever had. The jurisprudence they have written demonstrates how timeless ideas of justice and fairness can be guaranteed in the everyday lives of ordinary people. As a snapshot of their work, this book simultaneously bears witness to moral truths of long standing and challenges future generations not to repeat the mistakes we have made. To have been able to chronicle how judges in our time have come to understand their part in government, in Rousseau's own backyard, is testimony to how good a life in the law can be.

D.M.B.

Pays de Gex
21 June 2003

Contents

Contents

Table of Cases

Court of Appeal of Botswana

Court of Appeal of New Zealand

Court of Appeal of Singapore

European Court of Human Rights

European Court of Justice

Supreme Court of India

Supreme Court of Ireland

Supreme Court of Israel

Supreme Court of Japan

Supreme Court of the United States of America

1

The Forms and Limits of Constitutional Interpretation

1. JUDICIAL REVIEW AND DEMOCRACY

Conflict is everywhere part of everyday life, and, if Darwin is right, it has always been and must always be that way. Even in the most developed and enlightened societies, ideas and ideologies clash and compete for recognition and rewards. Religious and ethnic minorities resist assimilation and the forces of globalization that threaten their identities. Women struggle for emancipation from the bonds that male-dominated assemblies have imposed and, in some communities, still insist be maintained. The poor and downtrodden groan against the injustice of a world in which they are left malnourished and cold.

If conflict is endemic to the human condition its resolution (or at least regulation), is essential for the species to survive. At different times and in different places, various methods have been tried. Physical force has usually been the default rule for the most difficult and deeply felt disagreements. Spiritual inspiration, divine revelation, and religious codes have also been timeless sources of authority to settle all manner of conflict and controversy. Negotiation and strategies of compromise and give and take are universal solvents of discord and dispute that have come to play an increasingly prominent role in the modern era, both in local conflicts and on the international stage. And, over the course of the last two hundred years, democratic decision-making has almost completely displaced the divine authority of the clerics and the kings.

Recognizing that the people were sovereign, and establishing democratic forms of government, were undoubtedly enormous improvements on the monarchies and theocracies of times gone by, but it was far from a perfect solution as the fascist and 'people's' democracies of the last century tragically attest. Majorities can abuse their authority just like Hart's highwayman whose power, like theirs, stems from the barrel of a gun.[1] Left on their own, democracies can strip people of their belongings and their dignity and, where capital punishment is legal, even kill them on the spot. The defining events of the twentieth century confirmed the truth of Blackstone's observation, more than two hundred years ago, that there is no power that can control politicians bent on acting 'contrary

---

[1] H. L. A. Hart, *The Concept of Law* (Oxford: Oxford University Press, 1961), 6.

to reason' in democracies in which the sovereignty of the majority's rule is absolute and unconditional.[2]

How to ensure that the atrocities that have been committed in the name of the people don't happen again is a global problem. It is a challenge that more and more countries around the world have had to face. Remarkably, many communities, at the moment of their liberation from despotic and arbitrary regimes, have looked to the courts for help. Over the course of the last fifty years, more and more judges have been given the power to review the way in which the two elected branches of government exercise the coercive authority of the state. Whether the politicians and their officials have crossed the line has been left to the judiciary to say. They are expected to provide answers to the most controversial and contested political and moral dilemmas; to tell the people who is right and what they can and cannot do.

The faith that so many people have placed in the judiciary is one of the defining characteristics of our age. In an era of intense globalization, making judges responsible for testing the legitimacy of laws passed in the name of the people, against rules and principles that are embedded—more or less explicitly—in a constitutional text, has flourished as never before. The idea of a 'higher law' that could tell people whether their own rules and regulations are legitimate has been around for a long time. The concept of law in Greek and Roman times included a hierarchical structure and theories of natural law have been part of Europe's political and legal tradition for hundreds of years.[3] But until now the idea that the courts should be given the final say on how a society's most controversial social conflicts should be resolved has not been widely shared. Even in Europe large pockets of resistance remain. In France the arbitrariness of the courts (known as *parlements*) during the *ancien régime* permanently discredited the idea of judicial review in 'la Republique', and in England Edward Coke's famous claim for the supremacy of the judiciary and the common law[4] was never the reigning orthodoxy and was repudiated by the time of Blackstone, if not long before.[5]

Until its unprecedented proliferation over the last fifty years the idea of looking to the courts to be the ultimate arbiters of social conflict had for a very long time been exclusively an American idea. In the United States, where law was first proclaimed to be the king,[6] judicial review was a matter of simple logic.

---

[2] W. Blackstone, *Commentaries on the Laws of England* (Chicago: University of Chicago Press, 1979), vol. 1, 91.

[3] Edward S. Corwin, *The 'Higher Law' Background of American Constitutional Law* (Ithaca: Cornell University Press, 1965); Mauro Cappelletti, *The Judicial Process in Comparative Perspective* (Oxford: Clarendon, 1989), ch. 3; Dennis Lloyd, *The Idea of Law* (London: Penguin, 1991), ch. 3; Carl J. Friedrich, *Constitutional Government and Democracy* (Boston: Ginn & Co., 1964), ch. 1.

[4] *Dr. Bonham's Case*, (1610) 77 Eng. Rep. 646, 652.

[5] Gordon Wood, 'Reply', in Antonin Scalia, *A Matter of Interpretation* (Princeton: Princeton University Press, 1997), 129–30. See also Corwin, *Higher Law Background*, 84–7; Friedrich, *Constitutional Government*, chs. 6, 12.

[6] Thomas Paine, *Common Sense*, in B. Kuklick (ed.), *Political Writings*, Rev. Student Edn. (Cambridge: University Press, 2000), 27–8.

Once it was decided to adopt a written constitution with a federal structure and an entrenched Bill of Rights, there really was no other choice. Having established limits on what majorities could and could not legitimately do, neither the legislative nor executive branches could be given the job without violating the principle of impartiality which forbids anyone being the judge and a litigant in the same case. To have a fair and neutral resolution of disputes between majorities and those over whom they rule, it was necessary that the decision-maker be independent and have no direct interest in the case.

John Marshall, the first great Chief Justice of the US Supreme Court, saw the Court's responsibility very clearly. 'It is emphatically the province and duty of the judicial department', Marshall wrote in the seminal case of *Marbury* v. *Madison*, 'to say what the law is . . . So if a law be in opposition to the constitution . . . the court must determine which of [the] conflicting rules governs the case. This is the very essence of judicial duty.'[7] Nor did he have any doubt that, because constitutions are the supreme authority in all legal systems—the mother of all laws, some might say—where an act of government is 'repugnant' to the constitution it cannot, any more than can a highwayman, have any legal force or effect.

In the rest of the world it was the legacies of the fascist and socialist states in the second half of the century that led to the proliferation of constitutions in which courts were given the power of reviewing the work of politicians and other public officials. The practice was picked up first by the Austrians and Germans following the First World War and then by all the defeated powers, as well as India and the members of the Council of Europe, after the Second.[8] After the fall of the Berlin Wall, judicial review spread into central and eastern Europe, Africa, Asia, and the Middle East.[9]

Making politicians justify their behaviour in court offered a way to curb the excesses and abuses of majoritarian models of democracy in which legislative power is absolute and unbridled. Again and again, as new states were built on the ruins of authoritarian and dictatorial regimes, people looked to the law and the courts to ensure the horrors of their histories would never haunt them again. By the end of the twentieth century, constitutional democracies had taken root on every continent, giving credence to the claim of one of its leading theorists that the idea of judicial review and enforcement of basic human rights is the single most important contribution the United States has made to political theory.[10]

---

[7] *Marbury* v. *Madison* (1803) 5 US 1 Cranch 137, 177–8.

[8] Mauro Cappelletti, *Judicial Review in the Contemporary World* (Indianapolis: Bobbs-Merrill, 1971), 25–42; Hans Kelson, 'Judicial Review of Legislation', 4 Journal of Politics (1942) 83.

[9] For a review of the globalization of constitutional rights see Ran Herschl, 'The Political Origins of Judicial Empowerment Through Constitutionalization . . . ' (2000) 25 Law and Social Inquiry 91. For an up-to-date compilation of constitutional texts see A. P. Blaustein and G. H. Flanz, *Constitutions of the Countries of the World* (loose-leaf) (Dobbs Ferry, NY: Oceana). For a comparative assessment of the globalization of constitutionalism see C. Neal Tate and T. Vallinder (eds.), *The Global Expansion of Judicial Power* (New York: New York University Press, 1995); Donald Jackson and C. Neal Tate (eds.), *Comparative Judicial Review and Public Policy* (Westport, Conn.: Greenwood Press, 1992).

[10] Ronald Dworkin, *Freedom's Law* (Cambridge, Mass.: Harvard, 1996), 6, 71.

The American juggernaut has not, however, been welcomed everywhere. Although there is a logic and justice in giving judges the job of drawing the borders between the reach of a majority's legitimate lawmaking authority and the domain of individual and minority rights, even in the United States there remains a very serious concern about its compatibility with bedrock principles of democracy and the ultimate sovereignty of each person to govern him- or herself.[11] For many, a process in which unelected judges oversee the activities of the elected branches of government fits uneasily in communities committed to a democratic form of government in which the general will of the people—not the legal opinion of a judge—is sovereign. Especially when a constitution is written in the lofty and inspirational style of the American Bill of Rights, the power of judicial review risks running roughshod over the principle of separation of powers and replacing the threat of a tyranny of the majority with an oligarchy of the courts. While white South Africa, almost to a person, was in favour of empowering a Constitutional Court to oversee the politicians and their officials when the country became truly democratic, many black South Africans questioned why, at the moment of their liberation, they should shackle their freedom in this way.

The problem is that constitutional exhortations proclaiming the inviolability of life, liberty, and equality, that are the centrepiece of virtually all bills of rights, actually tell judges very little about how to solve the hard, real-life disputes they are called upon to decide. The great majestic phrases characteristic of all constitutional texts provide little practical guidance on such controversial questions as whether women have a right to abort a foetus or whether gays and lesbians have a right to marry. Whether religious communities have a right to establish and seek state support for separate schools and whether those schools can refuse to admit and/or employ people whose morals and/or religion are different than their own, cannot be answered just by reading words such as 'Congress shall make no law respecting an establishment of religion or prohibiting the free exercise thereof.'[12] Similarly, when constitutions contain positive guarantees of, for example, 'emergency medical treatment' or 'access to adequate housing'[13] the text doesn't tell the court whether a person dying of kidney failure has a right to receive dialysis treatment[14] or a person who is homeless has a right to shelter from the cold;[15] at least, not in so many words.

---

[11] The critical, sceptical literature on judicial review is enormous. See e.g. J. Waldron, *Law and Disagreement* (Oxford: Clarendon, 1999), pt. III; M. Walzer, 'Philosophy and Democracy' (1981) 9 *Political Theory* 391; M. Tushnet, *Red, White and Blue: A Critical Analysis of Constitutional Law,* (Cambridge, Mass.: Harvard University Press, 1988); M. Mandel, *The Charter of Rights and the Legalization of Politics* (Toronto: Wall & Thompson, 1989).

[12] Constitution of the United States of America, 1st Amendment (1791) in Blaustein and Flanz, *Constitutions of the Countries of the World.*

[13] Constitution of the Republic of South Africa, Articles 26–7, in Blaustein and Flanz, ibid.

[14] *Soobramoney* v. *Ministry of Health* (Kwazulu-Natal) [1998] 1 SA 765; (1997) 4 BHRC 308.

[15] *Grootboom* v. *Republic of South Africa* [2001] 1 SA 46.

It is the fact that constitutional texts almost never provide direct answers to the cases that are taken to court that makes the idea of judges being able to tell people they cannot decide for themselves whether to recognize a right to abortion or gay marriage so problematic. If judges are free to define such words as 'life', 'liberty', and 'equality' anyway they please, their supervision of the elected branches of government doesn't make any sense. If the job of the judge is to mark out the boundaries of legitimate lawmaking on the basis of what he or she thinks is fair and just, there can be no reason why a judicial opinion should ever 'trump' judgements of the people and their elected representatives. If the limits of legitimate lawmaking are just a matter of personal opinion, majorities can claim a moral authority in the sovereignty of the people that judges and minorities lack.

To reconcile the practice of judicial review with the sovereignty of people to govern themselves, it is necessary to show that courts do not resolve conflict and judge the way those in government exercise the powers of the state on the basis of their own personal opinions of what is right and wrong. One needs a theory about the way in which judges should exercise their powers of review that tells them how they can distinguish laws that are a legitimate expression of the coercive powers of the state from those that are not without being influenced by their own biases and personal points of view. Theory, as Oliver Wendell Holmes once said, is as foundational to the integrity of the law as the architect is to the building of a house.[16]

2. CONTRACT THEORY

In the earliest years that judicial review was practised in the United States, there does not seem to have been a lot of discussion about how the judges ought to read and think about their new constitution. It apparently was not (and for some still isn't)[17] thought that there was (is) any need for a grand theory of constitutional adjudication. It seems it was just taken for granted that the constitution should be read the way those who were responsible for its entrenchment, and those whose lives it was meant to control, understood it. For judges and commentators alike, 'the first and fundamental rule in the interpretation of all instruments is to construe them according to the sense of the terms and the intention of the parties'.[18]

Preserving the original meaning of the constitution was a natural thing for the first generation of judges to have done. Adopting an 'originalist' approach to constitutional interpretation made for a simple and straightforward account that was easy for ordinary people to understand. It coincided with the belief that

[16] Oliver Wendell Holmes, 'The Path of the Law' (1997) 110 Harv. L Rev. 991.

[17] Richard Posner, 'Against Constitutional Theory' (1998) 73 NYUL Rev. 1; *The Problematics of Moral and Legal Theory* (Cambridge, Mass.: Harvard University Press, 1999), 144.

[18] Story J, *Commentaries on the Constitution of the United States* (New York: Da Capo, 1970), at s 400.

constitutions were addressed to 'the common sense of the people' rather than codes that required 'logical skill or visionary speculation' to be fully understood.[19]

The approach fitted naturally with the American instinct for practical, commonsense reasoning. Like Rousseau, the early American jurists thought of their constitution as a social contract and interpreted it as such. As with the enforcement of any agreement, judges were expected to give the words of the text the meaning that those who wrote and consented to be governed by them understood them to have.[20] So, for example, if it was the common understanding at the time of its adoption that the Fifth Amendment (that no person can be deprived of their life or liberty without due process of law) did not restrict the people's right to pass laws that made sodomy and abortion illegal, that is the meaning it must always have unless and until it is changed. Similarly, if it was never intended that the equal protection clause of the fourteenth amendment would have any application to the state's treatment of women or gays, it could still not be of any help to them today.

Ensuring the words of the constitution retain their original meaning also conforms with the common understanding that constitutions are supreme or basic laws that articulate foundational, long-term, political settlements. Constitutions are expected, as John Marshall famously observed, 'to endure for ages to come'.[21] They are solemn pacts in which communities commit themselves to their deepest values and highest aspirations. They are supposed to stand above and be immune to the passion and prejudices of politics. Unlike ordinary legislation and commercial agreements, constitutions are intended to be resistant to change and typically are much more difficult to amend. Reading the words of a constitution the way they were originally understood allows it to function as a moral 'centre of gravity' and provide a measure of certainty and stability that is essential for the effectiveness and integrity of any legal system.

The logic of reading the American constitution as it was originally understood made a lot of sense in the years immediately following its adoption and for many people, including William Rehnquist, Antonin Scalia, and Clarence Thomas, who currently sit on the US Supreme Court, it still makes good sense today. For them, originalism solves whatever contradiction or tension exists between judicial review and democracy in a way that respects the distinct authority of each. Judges ensure politicians and public officials operate within the rules and constraints that are laid out in the constitution. If the constitution is silent on a question, the judge has no role to play and majorities are entitled to do whatever they want. Courts must defer to the choices made by the legislature unless they clearly contradict some provision of the constitution. In the extreme, where a

[19] Story J, *Commentaries on the Constitution of the United States* (New York: Da Capo, 1970), Preface. p. viii.

[20] See e.g. *Slaughter-House* cases (1872) 83 US 36; *Reynolds* v. *US* (1878) 98 US 145.

[21] *McCulloch* v. *Maryland* (1819) 17 US 316, 415. See also *Marbury* v. *Madison* (1803) SC 137, 176.

constitution is wholly unwritten, as in the United Kingdom, the judges have no authority to impose any substantive limits on the powers of the elected branches of government whatsoever.

In addition to its maximizing the sovereignty of each new generation to fashion the character of the communities in which they live, originalists also claim the historical method of interpretation is able to constrain judicial discretion, and counter any temptation a judge might have to decide cases on the basis of his or her own values, better than any other approach. Originalist theories, they say, have a neutrality about them that no other theory can match. They make historical facts the test of whether a law is constitutional or not and so purport to avoid questions of politics and morality altogether.

The story modern originalists tell is of judges applying principles and rules settled at the moment when a constitution comes to life without regard for their own personal and political views. Like high priests preserving the integrity of a sacred text, by remaining faithful to its original ambition their neutrality is preserved. The derivation, definition, and application of the principles that distinguish laws that are legitimate from those that are not all lie beyond their control. The impartial application of historical principles determines the outcome of every case.

Originalists say their theory allows each case to be presented and analysed as a syllogism.[22] The major premise is a rule or principle—such as 'Congress shall make no law respecting an establishment of religion' or 'no State shall . . . deny to any person . . . the equal protection of the laws',[23]—that was part of the original understanding. The minor premise requires the judges to determine whether that principle or rule is threatened by the law or state action they have been asked to review. (Laws making sodomy a crime do (or do not) deny gays the equal protection of the law.) If a judge thinks the law is in conflict with the constitution, she or he must declare it to be invalid even if sympathetic to what it is trying to do. By contrast, laws that a judge personally thinks are offensive and/or ill advised must be allowed to remain on the books unless it can be shown that they violate one of the constitution's prescriptions in some way. The conclusion follows inevitably from the way the minor premise is phrased.

The distinction that originalists draw between judges doing politics and enforcing the law is always sharp and often very painful to apply. So, for example, originalists say it is just not possible to find welfare rights in the American constitution if it is interpreted to give effect to its original understanding, even though those who are least well off can make a very powerful moral claim for their community's assistance and support.[24] For the same reason originalists think judges would do wrong and distort the original meaning of

---

[22] Robert Bork, *The Tempting of America* (New York: Free Press, 1990), 162–3.

[23] Constitution of the United States of America, *supra* n. 9, 1st and 14th Amendments.

[24] Robert Bork, 'The Impossibility of Finding Welfare Rights in the Constitution' (1979) Wash. ULQ 695; 'The Constitution, Original Intent and Economic Rights' (1986) 23 San Diego LR 823.

the Eighth Amendment (outlawing cruel and unusual punishments) if they declared capital punishment to be unconstitutional because they were convinced America would be a more just society if it were never allowed to take another person's life.[25] On the originalists' account of judicial review, gays can never claim the protection of the Fourteenth Amendment (guaranteeing every person the equal protection of the law) because, at the time of its entrenchment at the end of the American Civil War, it was understood only as the legal recognition of the emancipation of the blacks who had previously been enslaved.[26]

Originalists say judges lose their neutrality and act illegally when they add or subtract rights from what was initially agreed to and claim an authority to dispense justice according to their personal beliefs of what is right and wrong. If abortion, capital punishment, and sodomy laws are not among the subjects which the constitution puts beyond the reach of the democratically elected representatives of the people, then judges must accept their legitimacy. Judges must defer to the value choices of the people and the representatives they elect to act on their behalf. Legislators can claim a moral authority based on the sovereignty of the people that no one who sits on the Bench can match. The golden rule of originalist interpretation is that if a judge can find nothing in the constitution that limits what a democratically elected majority can do, she or he must stand aside and allow the will of the people to prevail.[27]

Originalists insist that if Americans want to make capital punishment and laws that single out and disadvantage gays and lesbians unconstitutional, they must follow the procedures the constitution provides for its own amendment. Abolitionists and gay activists cannot ask the court to issue rulings it has no constitutional authority to make. To permit a court to override the intention of those who created a constitution on the basis of what it thinks is just and fair amounts, from an originalist's perspective, to authorizing those who have been put in charge of guarding the constitution to carry out an endless series of mini *coups d'état*.[28]

As it has been developed and defended in the United States over the course of the last two hundred years, the originalist account of how judges should address the moral and political conflicts that their communities find most difficult to resolve makes a very persuasive case. The theory has been embraced by some of the most articulate and intellectually rigorous judges in the country and, at the same time, it is easy for ordinary people to understand. There is an inescapable logic in grounding the Court's authority in the ambition of those who were responsible for and directly affected by the entrenchment of the constitution

---

[25] Scalia, *Matter of Interpretation*, 132, 145–6; Bork, *Tempting of America*, 213–14.

[26] Bork, ibid. 149–50, 249–50. Bork, 'Constitution, Original Intent and Economic Rights' 827–8; see also Scalia's judgment in *Romer v. Evans* (1996) 517 US 620; ('Since the Constitution . . . says nothing about [homosexuality] it is left to be resolved by normal democratic means').

[27] Bork, *Tempting of America*, 166–7. Michael McConnell, 'The Importance of Humility in Judicial Review: A Comment on Ronald Dworkin's "Moral Reading" of the Constitution' (1997) 65 Fordham L Rev. 1269.

[28] Bork, *Tempting of America*, 265.

and the role it anticipates judges will play imposes the narrowest possible limits on the power of each generation to govern itself democratically. It would be natural to expect that, as other countries put written bills of rights into their constitutions, judges and commentators in other parts of the world would find originalism equally persuasive. But it hasn't turned out that way. Although historical references to the founding moments of a new constitutional order can be found in the jurisprudence of every court, originalism has generally not played well in other parts of the world.[29] Even in the United States, originalism is now decidedly the minority view. In fact, in professional journals and judicial opinions, originalism has been subjected to sharp and sustained criticism from commentators and fellow judges alike.[30]

The problem with originalism is that, no matter how good it sounds in theory, in practice it can't meet the standards it sets for itself. Directing judges to resolve the flashpoints of social conflict in their communities against the understandings of people who lived as long as two hundred years ago, leaves them, it turns out, free to come down on whatever side of a case their consciences tell them is right. There is in originalism, in fact, no neutrality in the derivation, the definition, or even the application of the law.

Originalist theories of judicial review fail their own standards of legitimacy because they are based on empirical assumptions that are factually false and normative claims that are logically flawed. Their take on the understandings surrounding the entrenchment of the American Bill of Rights fits awkwardly at best with the actual historical events and their claims of neutrality are circular and question-begging. The fact of the matter is that originalist orthodoxy is entirely the creation of the legal imagination, wholly a matter of myth. There never is or was only one, single, common understanding of what the great guarantees of life, liberty, and equality were intended, let alone understood, to mean. Constitutions are where each community's great political compromises are made so that the intention that animates them is invariably multiple, often conflicting, and always complex.

Telling judges they must give effect to the original understanding of the constitution doesn't provide them with any guidance or direction and imposes no constraints because there are countless understandings from which they can choose. Quantitatively, the number can be huge. The hard, empirical reality is that, given the number of people it takes to bring a constitution to life, let alone the number who acknowledge it as the supreme law in their lives, it is never

---

[29] See e.g. W. Brugger, 'Legal Interpretation, Schools of Jurisprudence and Anthropology: Some Remarks From a German Point of View' (1994) 42 Am. J Comp. Law 395, 401; D. Beatty *Constitutional Law in Theory and Practice* (Toronto: University of Toronto Press 1995), 64–5.

[30] See e.g. Ronald Dworkin, *A Matter of Principle* (Cambridge, Mass.: Harvard University Press, 1985), ch. 2; Cass Sunstein, *The Partial Constitution* (Cambridge, Mass.: Harvard University Press, 1995), ch. 4; 'What Judge Bork Should Have Said' (1991) 23 Connecticut L Rev. 205; Richard Posner, 'Bork and Beethoven' (1990) 42 Stanford L Rev. 1365; John Hart Ely, *Democracy and Distrust* (Cambridge, Mass.: Harvard University Press, 1980), ch. 2; Paul Brest 'The Misconceived Quest for the Original Understanding' (1980) 60 Boston UL Rev. 204.

possible to speak of a single collective intent. As Larry Alexander, one of America's leading constitutional theorists once put it, 'if there are no group minds, how can there be group intentions?'[31] For Alexander and many others the question is rhetorical because constitutional intentions are the product of hundreds, sometimes thousands of individual wills and so the most that can ever be said of collective activities, such as the decision to adopt a constitutional bill of rights, is that there has been a vague and ill-defined convergence of many minds.

Even in those parts of a constitution where it is possible to speak of a general understanding of what certain words were meant to guarantee, it is usual to find more than one intention at work. For example, in interpreting the words of the Fourteenth Amendment of the US constitution that guarantees every person 'the equal protection of the laws' it is possible to speak about an intention to use that particular set of words and a separate intention to bring about certain specific results. So, even though the basic purpose of the amendment, which was adopted in 1868, was to guarantee the blacks who had been freed from slavery after the Civil War the same legal status and civil rights as whites, the words that were chosen to reach that result were not limited to the emancipation of African Americans or even to the elimination of racial discrimination more generally. In effect, the Fourteenth Amendment can be said to contain what Ronald Dworkin has called both a 'semantic' intention and an 'expectation' intention[32] which, in cases alleging discrimination against Muslims or women or lesbians and gays or the poor, would lead to opposite results. Read literally, the words of the Fourteenth Amendment are equally intolerant of discriminating against people because of their race or religion or sex or social position. From the perspective of those living in the United States in 1868, the thought that law-makers could no longer pass laws that might incidentally disadvantage women and gays and certain religious groups would have never crossed their minds.

Originalists can never supply definitive answers in such cases as these because the words and the political motivation underlying the Fourteenth Amendment point to very different meanings that can reasonably be ascribed to the text, and originalism has nothing to say about which one a judge ought to choose. Both can be said to be part of the document's collective intent. After all, if the equal protection clause of the Fourteenth Amendment was always and only about discrimination against blacks, Congress and the states could have said just that.

Originalism suffers from the problem of there being too many different understandings from which each judge is free to choose. Even common understandings about abstract principles of justice that everyone accepts can be articulated at different levels of generality.[33] Depending on the level of generality

---

[31] Larry Alexander, 'Originalism or Who is Fred' (1996) 19 Harv JL and Pub. Pol, 321. See also Dworkin, *A Matter of Principle*.

[32] R. Dworkin, *Law's Empire* (Cambridge, Mass.: Harvard University Press, 1986), chs. 9, 10. 'Comment' in Scalia, *A Matter of Interpretation*, 116–27.

[33] Dworkin, *A Matter of Principle*, ch. 2.

a judge prefers, originalism can be 'hard or soft',[34] 'strict or moderate'[35] in what it recommends and has to say and originalism again provides almost no guidance as to which level of generality is uniquely correct. As a practical matter, judges on the US Supreme Court are on their own when they decide whether to read the Fourteenth Amendment as a proscription against discrimination against blacks, or all races including whites, or women or gays, or invidious discrimination of all kinds.[36] Instructing the judge to choose the 'level of generality that interpretation of the words, structure and history of the Constitution fairly supports'[37] is no answer because the words, structure, and history of the text point in different directions. Where the plain words of the Fourteenth Amendment are easily wide enough to stop governments discriminating against people because of their sex, the history that lies behind them is not.

The fact that there are invariably multiple intentions and understandings caught up in the entrenchment of a constitutional Bill of Rights means originalism can never be as neutral as it claims constitutional theory must be. Because it is not possible to identify a single, dominant rule or criterion for each case, judges can justify just about any result that they want. Faced with the question of whether the Fourteenth Amendment protects women and gays against sex discrimination, originalist judges are free to privilege that part of the original understanding that leads to the result that they believe is morally right.

Originalists do recognize that establishing the original meaning of different parts of a constitution can be a difficult and uncertain task but they resist the conclusion that this means originalism does not qualify as a neutral theory of law. Some say the uncertainty and difficulties of determining original understandings are not as great as those that plague rival theories. Antonin Scalia has tried to make the case for originalism in this way, but without much enthusiasm or conviction.[38] Claiming originalism is less partial than rival theories is to try to salvage it with an apology rather than an argument. Even if it were true, it would not establish its neutrality. The most it can prove is that other ways of interpreting the constitution are illegitimate as well.

Others maintain the neutrality of originalism ultimately resides in the fact it was the method that those who were responsible for the entrenchment of the constitution intended judges to use. Robert Bork, one of the most prominent

---

[34] C. Sunstein, *Legal Reasoning and Political Conflict* (New York: Oxford University Press, 1996), 173.

[35] Brest, 'The Misconceived Quest', 222.

[36] The extent of the judges' freedom to define for themselves how broadly or narrowly the words of the constitution should be read is especially evident in the Court's recent judgment in *Lawrence* v. *Texas* (2003) 123 S. Ct. 2472 in which Scalia, Rehnquist, and Thomas dissented from their colleagues' ruling that sodomy laws are unconstitutional because rather than interpret the guarantee of liberty (that is also part of the 14th Amendment) expansively to include a right of personal privacy as the majority did, they read it very rigidly as not marking off a private domain of 'deviant sex'.

[37] Bork, *Tempting of America*, 150; see also McConnell, 'Importance of Humility'.

[38] Antonin Scalia, 'Originalism: The Lesser Evil' (1989) 57 U Cincinnati L Rev. 861; *A Matter of Interpretation*, 45.

exponents of originalism, has defended its neutrality in this way.[39] Originalism, Bork claims, is the only interpretative theory that can be derived from the original understanding and not the legal philosophy of each judge. However, Bork's attempt to defend the originalist approach to judicial review on the basis that it was the interpretative part of the original understanding has elicited mostly derision and scorn.[40] Bork's defence was dismissed as being seriously mistaken both in its logic and on the facts. On the empirical side, the critics pointed out, Bork never provided any hard evidence that originalism was actually understood to be the preferred interpretative strategy when the Bill of Rights was entrenched. He offers no proof that originalism was, as a matter of historical fact, part of the original understanding. In fact, what evidence exists on the way people thought about how legal texts should be interpreted, as well as the broad and sweeping style of the text, suggests just the opposite.[41]

More importantly, Bork's opponents made the point that it wouldn't have mattered even if his argument was based on good history. Even if the expectation in 1791 and 1868 had been that the American Bill of Rights would always be interpreted to give effect to its original meaning, that isn't a good enough reason, by itself, for it still to be interpreted that way today. Everyone, including originalists, recognizes that had the Bill of Rights been strictly interpreted according to the understandings that prevailed when it was entrenched, America would be a very different place than it is today. It is widely accepted that if the US Supreme Court had remained faithful to originalism as the only legitimate way to read the American constitution, many of the rights and freedoms that are cherished most by Americans would be lost. Freedom of speech and religious liberty, for example, would enjoy much less protection because when they were adopted everyone thought the First Amendment only applied to the federal government ('Congress shall make no law . . . ') and had absolutely no application to the states. Similarly, opportunities for inequality and discrimination would be greatly expanded because no one understood the Fourteenth Amendment to bind Congress in any way ('no state shall . . . '). If the US Bill of Rights meant today what it did to those who witnessed its birth, privacy would no longer be recognized as a fundamental right, gender stereotyping would be widespread, forced sterilization of people convicted of a criminal offence would be legal, and interracial marriages could still be banned.[42]

---

[39] Bork, *Tempting of America*, 177.

[40] Ronald Dworkin dismissed it as 'wholly circular' (*A Matter of Principle*, 54), Cass Sunstein described it as a 'rallying cry' that wasn't an argument at all. As far as Sunstein is concerned, anyone who denies that originalism is itself based on substantive values and principles of politics and morality is 'without self-consciousness': 'What Bork Should have Said', 211, 215.

[41] H. Jefferson Powell 'The Original Understanding of Original Intent' (1985) 98 Harv. L Rev. 888; see also Brest, 'The Misconceived Quest', 215.

[42] Richard Posner, 'Bork and Beethoven' (1990) 42 Stanford L Rev. 1364; Cass Sunstein, 'What Judge Bork Should Have Said' (1991) 23 Connecticut L Rev. 205; see also W. Eskridge, *The Case for Same-Sex Marriage* (New York: Free Press, 1996), 125, 153, 174. And see Ruth Bader Ginsburg, 'Sexual Equality under the Fourteenth and Equal Rights Amendments' [1979] Wash. ULQ 161 ('Boldly dynamic interpretation departing radically from the original understanding is required to

In extending the reach of the American Bill of Rights no one says the US Supreme Court exceeded its authority or acted illegally. Everyone, originalists included, recognizes that the judges who actually sat on the cases that raised these questions all faced a choice. They could have been governed by the generally accepted understandings of the First, Fifth, and Fourteenth Amendments that prevailed when they were made part of the constitution. Or they could, as they did, read the words as expressing a deeper and broader moral principle that better reflects how we understand such words as 'life', 'liberty', and 'equal protection of the laws' today. In order to do justice to the people who pleaded for their help, they decided to follow the logic of the text and extend its protection in ways that had never been contemplated when it was originally being debated and discussed.

Moreover, even if (contrary to the evidence), the judges had been told that an originalist approach to constitutional interpretation was an integral part of the original understanding when the Bill of Rights was adopted, the outcome almost certainly would have been the same. The judges would still have had to decide which method of interpretation they should employ. The fact that it was expected that judges would always and only enforce the original meanings of the constitution would not be persuasive for a judge like Holmes, who believed cases should 'be considered in light of [their] whole experience and not merely . . . [on] what was said a hundred years ago'.[43] For Holmes, and like-minded judges, the question would be why shouldn't current understandings supersede original meanings if we now know the latter to be arbitrary and unjust, and for that question the answer that they were not part of the original understanding wouldn't cut any ice. In the great, pivotal cases that mark the growth and development of American constitutional law, the fact that those who were responsible for the entrenchment of the Bill of Rights believed that future generations should read its words as they were originally understood can never by itself be conclusive. It doesn't explain why the constitution must always be read looking backwards, with an eye to the past, rather than with full knowledge of the present. What is needed is an independent reason, some separate principle or value that would justify the serious costs that the originalist interpretation would entail. In all these cases there is a contest between several possible meanings that could only be settled by reasons and arguments that are independent of the methods of interpretation that lie behind each.

Both Bork and Scalia acknowledge that there are occasions when it is legitimate for judges to adopt meanings that depart from and even contradict original understandings. Each recognizes that original meanings may have to give way, for example, to prior decisions of the Court, even if there is good reason to think they are wrong, where they have become so embedded in current practice that to

tie to the Fourteenth Amendment's equal protection clause a command that government treat men and women as individuals equal in rights, responsibilities and opportunities.'

[43] *Missouri v. Holland* (1920) 252 US 416, 433.

overturn them would threaten stability and settled expectations in the country.[44] Both would also abandon original meanings when the words of the text or even their own moral scruples told them that was the right thing to do. Bork, for example, seems open to reading the words of the Fourteenth Amendment that guarantee everyone 'the equal protection of the laws' literally, so as to cover discrimination on the basis of sex even though originally they were only aimed at ridding the country of certain especially egregious forms of discrimination that targeted blacks.[45] Scalia has admitted that for him the limits of originalism would be reached if a government ever passed a law that authorized public lashings or branding for certain criminal offences. Even if it could be shown these were not regarded as 'cruel or unusual' punishments in 1791 (and even though he personally believes a challenge to capital punishment couldn't 'pass the laugh test'[46]), Scalia is confident that no thoughtful judge would allow any government to engage in such brutality and 'originalism as a practical theory of exegesis must somehow come to terms with that reality'.[47]

The fact that an originalist theory of interpretation cannot provide answers in very basic cases that are satisfactory to its strongest supporters shows that it is not neutral in the way its defenders claim. It cannot be derived neutrally from within the four corners of the constitution nor is it capable of providing neutral definitions which will enable judges to decide cases impartially and without giving in to their own personal preferences and priorities. That originalism is incapable of meeting its own standards of legitimacy has been known for a long time. Its inadequacy as a theory justifying judicial review became especially acute, however, during the 1950s and 1960s when Earl Warren was Chief Justice of the US Supreme Court. The Warren Court is famous in the annals of American constitutional law because it constituted one of the most active, interventionist periods in its history. In its most celebrated ruling in *Brown* v. *Board of Education*,[48] it said segregated schools denied black Americans equal protection of the law. In other major decisions it defended the rights of those accused and/or convicted of a criminal offence,[49] insisted on the principle of one person, one vote[50] and began to mark out the boundaries of a fundamental right of privacy.[51] Many of its decisions were very controversial and many scholars were highly critical of the Court's jurisprudence, including *Brown*,[52] because, even though they were sympathetic with the outcomes of the cases, they thought the judges

[44] Scalia, *A Matter of Interpretation*, 139–40; Bork, *Tempting of America*, 158.

[45] Bork, ibid. 150, 330, cf. 'Neutral Principles and Some First Amendment Problems' (1971) 47 Indiana LJ 1.

[46] Scalia, *A Matter of Interpretation*, 46, 132, 145–6.

[47] Scalia, 'Originalism: the Lesser Evil', 861.

[48] *Brown* v. *Board of Education* (1954) 347 US 483.

[49] See e.g. *Gideon* v. *Wainright* (1963) 372 US 335. *Miranda* v. *Arizona* (1966) 384 US 436.

[50] See e.g. *Baker* v. *Carr* (1962) 369 US 186; *Reynolds* v. *Sims* (1964) 377 US 533.

[51] *Griswold* v. *Connecticut* (1965) 381 US 479.

[52] Herbert Wechsler, 'Toward Neutral Principles of Constitutional Law' (1959) 73 Harv. L Rev. 1; A. Bickel, *The Supreme Court and the Idea of Progress* (New Haven: Yale University Press, 1978).

had exceeded their powers of review. Originalists were especially critical of the jurisprudence of the Warren Court. They accused the Court of reading its own values into the constitution in all its landmark rulings on equality, privacy, due process, and free speech. Even *Brown* v. *Board of Education*, the Court's landmark ruling ordering an end to segregation in American schools, was not easy to justify on historical grounds.[53] At precisely the moment when the American idea of judicial review needed it most, there was no theory that could account for or support it.

In time, and within a few short years of each other, two new theories were offered to explain and defend the reasoning, if not all the results, of the Warren Court and the practice of constitutional review more generally. One made policing the procedures and processes of politics the primary function of the judiciary; the other called on judges to make political philosophy the ultimate source of all the really important rules of constitutional law. Process theorists argued that the best way to reconcile judicial review with the democratic character of modern government is for courts to focus all their energies ensuring that the institutions and processes of politics work fairly and effectively rather than worrying about outcomes and results. The theory that calls on judges to give a moral reading to their enforcement of the constitution, by contrast, asks them to formulate the best description of the moral principles that fit the broad contours of a country's constitutional experience and that does the most credit to the nation. Each approach has been endorsed by some of the world's foremost scholars and commentators of constitutional law. Both present attractive pictures of how courts can reconcile law and politics effectively and in a way that does justice to both. Neither, however, has been able to withstand the criticisms of the other and so the stalemate, and absence of a credible theory, endures.

3. PROCESS THEORY

John Hart Ely, one of America's most respected legal scholars, provided the first, full-length account of a procedural model of judicial review in 1980 in his book *Democracy and Distrust*.[54] He was especially stimulated by the jurisprudence of the US Supreme Court during Warren's tenure as Chief Justice. Ely's project was to address the controversy surrounding the Warren Court and give it a sympathetic interpretation. Ely read the Court's major judgments as being animated by the idea that, in reviewing the acts of the elected branches of government, the Court's overarching concern should be to help those who could not protect

---

[53] See e.g. Ronald Dworkin, *Life's Dominion* (New York: Vintage Books, 1994), 138–43; Alexander Bickel, 'The Original Understanding and the Segregation Decision' (1953) 69 Harv. L Rev. 1; Michael Klarman, 'Brown, Originalism and Constitutional Theory . . . ' (1995) 81 Virginia L Rev. 1881; Posner, 'Bork and Beethoven'; Sunstein, 'What Judge Bork Should Have Said', 214 n. 40, cf. Michael McConnell, 'Originalism and the Desegregation Decisions' (1995) 81 Virginia L Rev. 947.

[54] Ely, *Democracy and Distrust*.

themselves politically. Rather than testing the laws that are enacted in a legislature or decreed by the executive against substantive moral values, Ely saw the
leitmotif of the Warren Court as ensuring everyone could participate in and
benefit from the processes of politics on more or less equal terms. Judges, Ely
said, should take their cue from the Warren Court's agenda of guaranteeing that
the ordinary institutions of politics worked fairly, remained open to change, and
did not systematically exclude or work to the disadvantage of particular groups.
In Ely's view, all the broad and open-ended guarantees of the American constitution should be interpreted with this overarching orientation in mind.[55]

Ely argued that his theory of how judges should think about exercising
their powers of review was consistent with and made proper sense of the most
important parts of America's constitution including the Bill of Rights. A process-
based theory of judicial review was, he said, 'entirely supportive of the American
system of representative democracy' and 'assigns judges a role they are conspicu-
ously well situated to fill'.[56] Making value determinations and establishing the
moral character of their communities was for the people, not the courts, to do.
The job of the judge is to supervise and act as guardian of the processes of politics
and government to ensure they are not weighted unfairly in anyone's favour and
so not 'deserving of trust'. In Ely's mind, the unique contribution that courts can
make to government, based on the principle of representative democracy, is to
prevent 'the ins [from] choking off the channels of political change to ensure that
they will stay in [power]' and from 'systematically disadvantaging some minority
out of simple hostility or . . . prejudice . . . '.[57] Judges certify the integrity of the
processes of democracy by guaranteeing that everyone's political and civil rights
of speech and assembly and voting are respected and in particular making sure
that society's habitually unequal and poorly represented groups, like racial
minorities and individuals caught up in the criminal justice system, are not
prejudiced by their inability to negotiate the labyrinths of politics. By contrast
groups such as women, who actually constitute a majority of the electorate and
have the capacity to look after their own interests are expected to do so; and
substantive issues of morality and public policy, such as abortion, are left to the
people, through their elected representatives, to resolve.

Ely's book got rave reviews. It was hailed as a 'work of outstanding merit',[58] a
'dazzling intellectual performance',[59] and for at least one commentator, 'the
single most important contribution to the American theory of judicial review
written in the century'.[60] In a postmodern age of radical pluralism in moral and
political theory, the idea of seeking consensus on fair procedures touched a chord
that resonated with a lot of people. On further reflection, however, few thought
Ely had made out his case.

[55] Ely, *Democracy and Distrust*. ch. 4.   [56] Ibid. 102.   [57] Ibid. 103.
[58] Richard Posner, '*Democracy and Distrust* Revisited' (1991) 77 Virginia L Rev. 641.
[59] Gerald Gunther, book jacket, *Democracy and Distrust*.
[60] Henry P. Monaghan, book jacket, *Democracy and Distrust*.

Many different criticisms were made of the book. In different ways most reviewers challenged Ely's attempt to separate process from substance. A constitution such as the American Bill of Rights, they said, which guarantees people the freedom to follow the religion of their choice, for example, self-evidently contains both. Even those sympathetic to a process-based model of judicial review recognized that Ely hadn't been able to deliver on his promise of a theory in which judges would be able to decide whether laws were constitutional or not without having to evaluate the political and moral trade-offs they make.[61] If, as he insisted, the American constitution required the moral character of the community to be constructed by the people through their elected representatives and not by the courts, Ely's own theory couldn't pass the test. Reviewer after reviewer told Ely that any judge who tried to follow his advice would have to make the very kind of choices about fundamental values that his theory said judges must avoid.

The commentators were relentless in their criticism that, by itself, Ely's theory of judicial review was 'radically indeterminate and fundamentally incomplete'.[62] They showed how, in innumerable ways, the concept of representative democracy was too vague, capable of supporting too many different arrangements, to be able to tell judges how they should exercise their powers of review. It didn't give them any guidance on what kinds of rights of participation and representation they should defend or who the beneficiaries of their protection should be.[63] It didn't even determine the most basic rules of representation, such as how votes should be counted or how electoral districts should be drawn.

Telling judges their primary responsibility is to ensure that the way politics is conducted is fair and all inclusive doesn't give them a clear picture of what the process must look like if it's going to measure up. As Ronald Dworkin pointed out, it doesn't even provide any direction on basic rights such as free speech which for proceduralists are regarded as fundamental and deserving vigorous protection from the courts.[64] The aphorism that the judges should help those 'who can't help themselves politically' doesn't identify the circumstances in which it is legitimate for majorities to limit people's freedom to say what they want and those in which it isn't. How, it was asked, are judges, who are committed to the idea that their role is to ensure the political system remains open to change through peaceful persuasion, to decide whether lifestyle choices, such as same-sex marriages, that seek to convince by demonstration and example, qualify as the kind of speech that the constitution guarantees?[65] However they rule, the participation and representation of some people will be

---

[61] See e.g. Patrick Monahan, *Politics and the Constitution* (Toronto: Carswell, 1987); Jürgen Habermas, *Between Facts and Norms* (Cambridge, Mass.: MIT Press, 1996); Cass Sunstein, *Designing Democracy: What Constitutions Do* (New York: Oxford University Press, 2001).

[62] Laurence Tribe, 'The Puzzling Persistence of Process-Based Constitutional Theories' (1980) 89 Yale LJ 1063.

[63] Ronald Dworkin, *A Matter of Principle*, 57–71; Bork, *Tempting of America*, 196.

[64] Dworkin, *A Matter of Principle*, ibid.

[65] Tribe, 'Puzzling Persistence', 1078.

advantaged while others will be affected adversely. Even speech rights that conform to more traditional modes of political participation simultaneously impose limits on the power of democratically elected legislatures and the people they represent. Thinking strictly in terms of process doesn't tell you how to resolve conflicts of this kind and where the line should be drawn.

The incapacity of Ely's process-based theory to identify what types and modes of expression warrant constitutional protection was highlighted by many commentators as illustrative of its incompleteness and indeterminacy. It showed judges needed something more, something other than procedural criteria, to distinguish cases in which the political system was not working fairly from those in which those who lost out in the legislative or regulatory process could not be said to have a legitimate cause to complain.[66] Ely understood the problem and he recognized that, in a representative democracy where 'value determinations' were the responsibility of the people's elected representatives, just because a group felt aggrieved—even intensely—about a law that denied them a benefit or disadvantaged them in some way didn't invariably mean government was malfunctioning or that the courts should intervene.[67]

Ely argued the courts should come to the aid only of those who were systematically disadvantaged by majorities acting out of prejudice and crude hostility but, as the commentators were quick to reply, that solution could be defended only on substantive moral grounds, which his theory was supposed to avoid. Allegations of prejudice, as Laurence Tribe pointed out in an especially effective critique, inescapably involve making judgments on issues of substantive morality.[68] When someone says that a law that denies them benefits it makes available to others or seeks to disadvantage them in some other way is motivated by prejudice and hostility, they usually mean that they disagree with the reasons given for their selective treatment. For example, no one, including Ely,[69] thinks that burglars (a group that is certainly the focus of widespread hostility) are being punished, by laws making theft a criminal offence, out of prejudice. To the contrary, virtually everyone thinks it is perfectly legitimate to treat thieves as pariahs precisely because of the importance most people attach to their property and physical security. So too with laws making sodomy an offence, or denying same-sex couples the civil status of being married, that discriminate against lesbians and gays. Whether a judge concludes these laws are examples of prejudice or are based on a substantive moral vision of what constitutes proper behaviour (like the laws against burglary), depends on fundamental moral choices about whether sexual identity is part of what it means to be a person and so, unlike burglary, can be characterized as a fundamental human right.

That Ely had not succeeded in constructing a theory of judicial review in which judges could avoid having to make value judgements about complex and controversial moral issues, the reviews were unanimous. But not everyone

---

[66] Bork, *Tempting of America*, 199. [67] Ely, *Democracy and Distrust*, 103.

[68] Tribe, 'Puzzling Persistence', 1072–6. [69] Ely, *Democracy and Distrust*, 154.

thought that it followed from Ely's failure that the process model of judicial review was inherently flawed. Some theorists argued that even though Ely was mistaken in thinking judges who stick to process need not make decisions on issues of substantive political morality, a model that was dedicated to making democracy work better was still the best alternative around.

These theorists conceded, even celebrated, the substantive morality of the process model of review. In their minds there is no higher value than a community that governs itself rationally and fairly. If politics is rid of all its inequities and imperfections, the individual and the community of which she or he is a part can flourish simultaneously. Indeed, they say the process model of judicial review is not only consistent with the noblest aspirations of individuals and communities alike, it is uniquely capable of 'creat[ing] the preconditions for a well-functioning democratic order, one in which citizens are genuinely able to govern themselves'.[70] By directing judges to take an aggressive role in policing the procedures and processes of democracy, courts work co-operatively with politicians and other public officials to establish structures and institutions of government that are just and fair rather than having to act confrontationally by drawing boundaries beyond which the sovereignty of the people and their representatives does not reach.

The idea of defending a process-oriented theory of judicial review on a republican vision of a community of people who are encouraged and able genuinely and fairly to govern themselves has appealed to a number of prominent theorists. In the United States, Cass Sunstein has pressed the logic of the process model the furthest. Sunstein believes a good constitution should create an environment in government that combines 'political accountability with a high degree of reflectiveness and a general commitment to reason-giving'[71] and a responsible court should interpret it with these ideas in mind. Sunstein has no doubt of the Court's importance in a community's quest for what he calls 'the ideal of deliberative democracy', but he is equally emphatic that its role is for the most part a secondary and supportive one.

Like Ely, Sunstein believes the case for a vigilant and aggressive judiciary is strongest when it is alleged that the institutions and processes of government are defective in some way.[72] Beyond that, he is nervous about courts becoming entangled in 'managerial issues'—such as poverty, health care, or discrimination against gays—where considerations of substantive morality and public policy are at stake. In cases of this kind Sunstein believes the appropriate role of the judiciary is 'catalytic' rather than 'preclusive'.[73] He argues the virtues of a deliberative democracy and cautions judges to work through their dockets 'one

---

[70] Sunstein, *Designing Democracy*, 6.

[71] Ibid. 7.

[72] Cass Sunstein, *Legal Reasoning and Political Conflict* (New York: Oxford University Press, 1996), 179.

[73] Sunstein, *Designing Democracy*, 9–11, 205–6.

case at a time'[74] and avoid the construction of large, overarching frameworks of analysis. Except when democratic rights such as the vote or political speech are at stake, or when politically vulnerable groups are at risk, judges should defer to decisions of the politicians and their officials. On controversial moral issues such as abortion and same-sex marriage he thinks it is best for courts to move incrementally.[75] He is critical of the way the US Supreme Court carved out a broad and categorical right to an abortion in *Roe* v. *Wade* because in his view it intensified and exacerbated divisions that already fractured American society. Even when a court believes a case of discrimination has been made out, Sunstein thinks there will be instances when it ought to tolerate laws and regulations that are arbitrary and unjust. In order to maximize the values of deliberation and self-government, it is neither inconceivable nor inappropriate that sometimes constitutional rights go unenforced.[76]

Sunstein was not the first to follow Ely's lead and make 'democratic deliberation' the central value in a theory of constitutional review. Patrick Monahan, one of Canada's leading constitutional law scholars, advanced the same argument almost fifteen years earlier. Indeed, Monahan argued that the theory that a constitution should be interpreted as an embodiment of democratic ideals is even more fitting for Canada's Charter of Rights and Freedoms than it was for the American Bill of Rights.[77] It was, he said, more in keeping with the country's political traditions and the emphasis in the Charter on government support of community and group rights.

For Monahan, like Sunstein, defending judicial review in the name of democracy means the judiciary's mandate operates within very specific and narrow boundaries. Because judicial review hosts an 'elite debate in which only elite voices are heard'[78] it can never be a substitute for democratic dialogue and discussion. So, like Ely and Sunstein, Monahan is instinctively opposed to the judicial enforcement of social and economic rights because they would significantly reduce the scope for political dialogue and deliberation. On Monahan's theory, after a court has satisfied itself of the fairness of the basic infrastructure of democracy and maximized its openness to the 'revisionary potential of politics', its authority will have run its course. Like all proceduralists, Monahan thinks the court's primary role is to 'protect the basic infrastructure of liberal democracy', including rights of assembly, debate, and free elections, in order to ensure that access to and participation in the political process is roughly equal. Beyond that, the authority of the judge is limited. It is up to the people, through the representatives they elect, to decide what the moral character of their communities and the rules of social co-operation will be. '[I]f the collective morality of the

---

[74] Cass Sunstein, *One Case at a Time: Judicial Minimalism on the Supreme Court* (Cambridge, Mass.: Harvard University Press, 1999).

[75] Sunstein, *Legal Reasoning and Political Conflict*, 180; *Designing Democracy*, ch. 8.

[76] *Designing Democracy*, 193, 204, 208; *Legal Reasoning*, 178.

[77] Monahan, *Politics and the Constitution*, 99–120.

[78] Ibid. 137.

community is to become more informed,' Monahan concludes, 'this will be achieved through more rather than less democracy.'[79]

Both Monahan and Sunstein are public lawyers and, as advocates of a process model of judicial review, the accounts they offer are, like Ely's, lean and generally devoid of large theoretical claims. They declare their biases in favour of democracy and self-governing communities and are essentially content to leave it at that. They make no effort to refute the claims of Ely's critics that it is impossible to derive a process-based model of judicial review from neutral sources of politics or law.

Their ambition for their treatises is professionally modest and to the point. Their project is to explain how the process model of judicial review can 'lend structure and intelligibility to legal analysis'.[80] Both aim to help judges identify the types of argument (doctrinal, analogical, textual, etc.) they should use when interpreting a constitution and they spend little time trying to fit their ideas about legal reasoning into larger theories of politics and law. Sunstein, in particular, is emphatic that large-scale theories of politics and moral philosophy are alien to legal reasoning. Law is an intermediate, 'mid level' method of reasoning that is based on 'incompletely theorized agreements'.[81] In his view, and Monahan's as well, high theory is a subject for the elected branches of government and not for the courts. For both of them, doing theory is playing politics, not practising the law.

Not everyone who endorses a process model of judicial review, however, is averse to reflecting about it abstractly and in very philosophical terms. Jürgen Habermas, one of Europe's leading social scientists, has written a huge and highly theoretical book, *Between Facts and Norms*, in which the democratic conception of constitutional adjudication is grandly defended as being both neutral as between positivistic and moralistic theories of law[82] and as uniquely capable of justifying the coercive powers of the state.[83] In Habermas's terms, 'in complex societies, law is the only medium in which it is possible reliably to establish morally obligated relationships of mutual respect even among strangers'.[84] Law occupies a space between morality and reality and brings about their mutual reconciliation within the parameters of a single case. It serves, like a bridge, as a link between the real and the ideal without privileging or disadvantaging either.

Like all proceduralists, Habermas assigns the judiciary the responsibility of certifying the legitimacy of law by ridding the processes of democracy—indeed all social structures—of their inequities and arbitrariness. The idea is that if judges do their job properly, democracy offers an ideal way for resolving conflict and reconciling competing ideologies and visions of life. When it functions perfectly, all communication and consent is uncoerced and nothing but 'the force of the better argument' wins the day. The test, for Habermas, of whether

---

[79] Ibid. 138.   [80] Ibid. 125.   [81] Sunstein, *Designing Democracy*, ch. 2.
[82] Habermas, *Between Facts and Norms*, 107, 121.   [83] Ibid. 263.   [84] Ibid. 460.

a law is legitimate, is whether 'all possibly affected persons could agree [to it] as participants in rational discourses'.[85] He calls it a 'discourse principle' and claims it is neutral with respect to morality and law. It neither relies on a set of higher, overarching moral principles nor rubberstamps the preferences and prejudices of the people whenever they are expressed in a politically acceptable way. As a practical matter the discourse principle is presented as simultaneously conferring 'a legitimating force on the legislative process' and giving rise to 'a logical genesis of rights'.[86] Conceptually 'the genesis of rights' is said to be 'a circular process' in which the legal code (of judicially protected rights) and the principle of democracy are 'co-originally constituted'.[87]

On Habermas's understanding of what makes law legitimate, the role of the court is to ensure everyone enjoys all those rights and freedoms that are required to be a 'participant in rational discourses'.[88] Judges gauge the legitimacy of law by examining the rationality of the democratic procedures through which it must pass. To ensure participation is fully rational, the judiciary must guarantee not only that the traditional political, civil, and legal rights are respected, but that social and economic rights are provided for as well. Habermas is clear and unequivocal that there can be no legitimate law if people don't enjoy the full range of both positive and negative rights.[89]

Habermas believes the judiciary is uniquely well suited to perform this task because of the 'superior rationality of its professional discourse'.[90] He describes legal reasoning as a process involving the application and concretization of general rules and principles to particular facts, which is a different method of argumentation than the usual terms of engagement in political debate.[91] Law is a way of communicating between the moral and empirical. It creates a space in which it is possible to engage in social mediation 'between facts and norms'. It is the unique logical structure, which distinguishes what Habermas calls 'discourses of application', that gives law its exceptional capacity for rationality.

Habermas is familiar with Ely's and Sunstein's writing and generally is very sympathetic to what they have to say. His orientation, however, is focused more on clarifying the neutral premises from which a process model of judicial review can be derived and less on how it actually works. His ambition, unlike theirs, is to demonstrate how understanding the role of the judiciary the way they do grows out of the most basic conceptions of democracy and the law. Habermas wants to show that a process model of judicial review can be derived from concepts that transcend individual constitutional texts. His idea is that a process model of judicial review guarantees the integrity of both democracy and law simultaneously. It is the fulcrum around which the internal relation between law and democracy is organized. Law and democracy are both preconditions and products of each other. Law satisfies the discourse principle only if it is enacted within

---

[85] Habermas, *Between Facts and Norms*, 107.   [86] Ibid. 121.   [87] Ibid. 122.
[88] Ibid. 107, 263.   [89] Ibid. 123, 125, 247, 263, 415–17.   [90] Ibid. 266.
[91] Ibid. 172, 217–19, 229–32, 265–6.

a democratic process, which in turn is only legitimate so long as it operates within the parameters of the law. Courts are uniquely situated to supervise and oversee the dialectic between the two.

Whether Habermas's attempt to provide a 'neutral derivation' of a process model of judicial review comes to be understood as a 'considerable theoretical advance', as has been suggested,[92] remains to be seen. It seems unlikely, however, that it will ever be regarded as having opened up a 'new paradigm of law'. Habermas's orientation is too abstract and his presentation too dense to be of much assistance to the judge who must translate the discourse principle into practical rules of constitutional law.[93] Indeed, when he does turn his mind to real concrete questions—such as what rights people can claim from their governments and how vigorously judges should exercise their powers of review—his reflections show just how unprincipled and open to manipulation the process model can be. Even if it can claim a neutrality in its conceptual derivation, the discourse principle cannot come close to the standards of neutrality that constitutional theories are expected to meet.

For Habermas, the logic of 'ensur[ing] that the process of lawmaking takes place under the legitimating conditions of deliberative politics'[94] means the judiciary's supervision of politics must be 'active' and 'far reaching', even 'bold'.[95] To guarantee rational participation in all the processes through which communities organize their affairs, rights must protect people from all abuses of power, not just those committed by the state. For Habermas, the logic of a democratic theory of judicial review requires 'economic power and social pressure . . . to be tamed by the rule of law no less than . . . administrative power'.[96] 'Basic rights to the provision of living conditions' are implied as well.[97]

Habermas's interpretation of what rights judges should recognize and how they should exercise their powers of review is exactly the opposite of what the process theorists in North America have had to say. Ely, Monahan, and Sunstein, as we have seen, all think a process model contemplates a much more modest role for the judiciary, and in particular that it would—and should—not do much, if anything, for the poor.[98] The idea that courts should read in and/or enforce welfare rights in order to promote the political participation of people disadvantaged by economic insecurity makes Sunstein 'nervous'.[99] For Monahan, social and economic rights are both illogical and undesirable. Their recognition would make unelected judges rather than politicians responsible for setting welfare

[92] William Rehg, 'Translator's Introduction', in Habermas, *Between Facts and Norms*, p. xxiv.

[93] Bernhard Schlink, 'The Dynamics of Constitutional Adjudication' (1996) 17 Cardozo L Rev. 1231. See also Robert Alexy, 'Basic Rights and Democracy in Jürgen Habermas's Procedural Paradigm of the Law' (1983) 7 Ratio Juris 227.

[94] Habermas, *Between Facts and Norms*, 274.

[95] Ibid. 244, 280.

[96] Ibid. 263.

[97] Ibid. 123.

[98] Ely, *Democracy and Distrust*, 162.

[99] Sunstein, *Designing Democracy*, 10, 205–6.

budgets and the tax schedules that are required to fund them and so 'would vastly limit the scope for democratic debate and dialogue rather than expand it'.[100] Such a result, Monahan argues, is precisely what the democratic conception of judicial review was designed to avoid.

The fact that a process model of judicial review can support two completely contradictory conclusions, on issues as important as these, undercuts any claim of neutrality that may be made on its behalf. Process theorists cannot even come to a common understanding among themselves about what democracy looks like and what rights it guarantees. Moreover, other conflicting opinions could be added to the mix. Frank Michelman, for example, another leading process theorist in the United States, has staked out a position—in support of a limited range of social and economic rights—somewhere between Habermas and the others.[101]

Even Ely, Monahan, and Sunstein see things differently when it comes to issues of sex discrimination.[102] Ely believes that because all the legal barriers that used to block women's participation in politics have been removed, it is no longer credible to claim they are incapable of being able to advance their own interests politically. In systems of government that recognize the right of majorities to rule, women have the power in their numbers to protect their position fully. As a result, Ely says, except in rare cases of blatant prejudice, there is no justification for courts to invalidate laws that disadvantage women on the ground that they discriminate on the basis of sex.

For Patrick Monahan, the logic of the democratic model of judicial review is exactly the opposite. The formal, legal equality of men and women in politics is not as significant for him as it is for Ely. In his view the really critical fact of modern politics is that women continue to participate politically much less extensively than men. For Monahan, the fact of women's unequal influence means that whenever they are not treated as well as men by the state, courts have a constitutional obligation not simply to intervene but to subject such decisions, as the products of a tainted process, to a 'heightened standard of review'.[103]

Cass Sunstein's position on what role courts should play in confronting laws and government policies that disadvantage women is characteristically ambivalent and seems to fall somewhere in between. Like Monahan, he knows that women are still vulnerable to being discriminated against because of their sex notwithstanding the fact that the political influence they can exert is potentially very large.[104] However, because he thinks that the principle of equality that is

[100] Monahan, *Politics and the Constitution*, 126.

[101] Frank Michelman, 'Welfare Rights in a Constitutional Democracy' [1979] Wash. ULQ 659. See also 'Constitutional Welfare Rights and a Theory of Justice', in N. Daniels, *Reading Rawls* (Stanford: University of Stanford Press, 1989).

[102] Ely, *Democracy and Distrust*, 164–70, Monahan, *Politics and the Constitution*, ch. 6.7; Sunstein, *Designing Democracy*, chs. 7, 8, 9.

[103] Monahan, *Politics and the Constitution*, 129.

[104] Sunstein, *Designing Democracy*, 177.

guaranteed in the American constitution is beyond the competence of the judiciary to apply he argues, like Ely, that the cause of women is better protected in the legislature than in the courts.[105]

The different opinions process theorists can offer on how actively courts should be involved on issues as basic as social and economic rights and sex discrimination confirms that, as a practical matter, a process model is incapable of defining neutral principles that will ensure that judges do not decide cases on their own personal (political) points of view. Judges, like the theorists, are free to invoke the model to justify whatever position they prefer. Like originalism, process theory can be used to defend just about any and every result.

The fact that process theorists have not been able to provide judges with a principled way of deciding hard cases did not, for many, come as a great surprise. For Ronald Dworkin, the failure of the process model parallels the inability of originalism to meet its own standards of neutrality.[106] Each aspires to a model of judging in which courts can avoid making decisions on substantive moral problems but both lack the resources, in history and procedure, to identify overarching first principles that can provide an objective framework in which arbitrary and illicit acts of government can be distinguished from those that are legitimate and benign. For Dworkin, and others, the lesson to be learned from the fact that neither originalism nor process theories can meet their own standards of legitimacy is the futility of trying to shield the courts from the highly charged and often painful moral dilemmas that are at the centre of all the really hard cases they are asked to resolve.

4. MORAL THEORY

Dworkin thinks that everyone who cannot see that moral reasoning is a necessary component of all constitutional adjudication has, like an ostrich, his or her head buried in the sand.[107] Because of the inevitability of its playing a crucial role in the resolution of every case, Dworkin's solution is to ensure it is carried out as sensitively and with as much sophistication as possible. He is convinced there is no other alternative.[108] It follows for Dworkin that moral neutrality is not the appropriate standard or status that judges should aspire to achieve. Rather, he says we need a more modest set of criteria to judge the integrity of constitutional theory; one that tests how thoughtfully judges have evaluated and reconciled the competing moral claims that are at the heart of every major constitutional case, rather than how skilfully they have pretended to avoid them. For him, the proper measure of a theory's integrity is how well it accords with the words of the constitution—as they have been understood by those for

---

[105] Ibid. 156, 175.   [106] Dworkin, *A Matter of Principle*, ch. 2.
[107] Ronald Dworkin, 'In Praise of Theory' (1997) 29 Arizona St. LJ 353, 376.
[108] Dworkin, *Freedom's Law*, 14.

whom they were written and by those who preceded them on the Bench (the criterion of fit), and how much good, how much justice it is able to achieve (the criterion of value). Fit and value, not some unattainable ideal of neutrality are, Dworkin thinks, all that can be asked of any theory.

Dworkin's call for relaxing the standards of constitutional theory cannot be dismissed as a crude attempt to manipulate the rules to suit his own purposes. Many would say that Dworkin is the pre-eminent legal philosopher in the world today. The breadth and depth of his writing is exceptional. In his capacity to speak to the big theoretical questions and to the practising judge simultaneously he has few, if any, peers. On the one hand, like Habermas, his ambition is nothing less than a general theory that can justify the coercive force of the law. His project, carried out in a series of books and essays, covers virtually every important dimension of legal theory.[109] His collective works purport to provide an account of law that overcomes the stalemate that has dominated debates in legal philosophy for hundreds of years between those ('positivists') who think its essence lies in the procedures and institutions through which it is enacted and proclaimed and those ('natural lawyers') who believe its true core consists in the justice and morality it secures.

Dworkin's concept of law, like Habermas's, grows out of a political philosophy that rejects the idea that democracy can be reduced to the simple formula of majority rule.[110] He shares, with process theorists, the belief that the judicial enforcement of constitutional rights is consistent with democratic principles and the sovereignty of the people to govern themselves. In his view, both democratic decision-making and the judicial enforcement of human rights give expression to and can be derived from a deeper moral principle, drawn from liberal political theory, that recognizes each person as someone entitled to being shown 'equal concern and respect' by the state. Indeed, as we have seen, Dworkin thinks the process of judicial review and the legal enforcement of individual rights is the most important contribution Americans have made to democratic theory.[111]

But unlike Habermas, Dworkin is not content to devote all his energy to exploring and explaining the theoretical foundations and connections between democracy and the law. As a common lawyer, Dworkin is just as interested in hard, practical cases and much of his writing is intended to provide guidance to judges on the nature of adjudication and, in the area of constitutional law, how they should exercise their powers of review. Much of what he has to say about courts is voiced through Hercules, a mythical jurist with superhuman powers of

---

[109] The books include: *Taking Rights Seriously* (Cambridge, Mass.: Harvard University Press, 1977); *A Matter of Principle* (Cambridge, Mass.: Harvard University Press, 1985); *Law's Empire* (Cambridge Mass.: Harvard University Press, 1986); *Life's Dominion* (New York: Knopf, 1993); *Freedom's Law* (Cambridge, Mass.: Harvard University Press, 1996); and *Sovereign Virtue* (Cambridge, Mass.: Harvard University Press, 2000).

[110] R. Dworkin, 'The Moral Reading and the Majoritarian Premise' in *Freedoms Law*, ch. 1.

[111] Dworkin, *Freedom's Law*, 6, 71. R. Dworkin 'The Arduous Virtue of Fidelity: Originalism, Scalia, Tribe and Nerve' (1997) 65 Ford L Rev. 1249, 1268.

reasoning, who is meant to represent the model of what everyone who sits on the Bench should aspire to be.[112]

A lot of Dworkin's advice to the judiciary is quite conventional. He agrees with originalists, for example, that when judges interpret large and sweeping phrases such as those that distinguish the American Bill of Rights, they must begin with what those who created the document actually said.[113] In that initial step, history is a crucial interpretative aid because, Dworkin says, 'we must know something about the circumstances in which a person spoke to have any good idea of what he meant to say in speaking as he did'.[114] Other sources of meaning to which judges should refer include 'the structural design of the Constitution as a whole' and 'the dominant lines of past constitutional interpretation by other judges'.[115] Dworkin encourages judges to think of themselves as joint authors writing separate chapters that fit in and make sense of a novel that never ends.[116] Their overarching ambition, he says, should be to develop 'the best conception of constitutional moral principles . . . that fits the broad story of [a country's] historical record'.[117]

Dworkin realizes that in many cases traditional legal sources will not be able to supply one single, dominant meaning. He admits 'very different, even contrary, conceptions of constitutional principle . . . will often fit language, precedent, and practice well enough to pass these tests'.[118] It is at this point in the review process, when no clear answer stands out, that Dworkin instructs judges to enter a 'postinterpretive or reforming stage',[119] in which they should look to the insights and analysis of moral and political philosophy, and it is here that he breaks new ground. Although he believes judges are instinctively inclined to this method of interpretation, he acknowledges that it is almost never openly endorsed in their decisions and that it would be 'revolutionary', even 'suicidal' if they did.[120] In mounting a sustained and passionate call for judges to do openly the moral and political philosophy that they cannot avoid, Dworkin, like Ely and the process theory he uncovered, was a pioneer. Although other scholars have since endorsed the method,[121] Hercules will always be recognized as law's original philosopher king.

In defending a moral reading of constitutional texts Dworkin makes no claim for its neutrality. The very idea strikes him as preposterous.[122] Like 'post Ely proceduralists', his position is that there are no morally neutral strategies for interpreting a constitution; no morally neutral answers to the controversial constitutional issues courts are called on to decide. The moral reading does not dictate that a constitution should be read from either a liberal or conservative

---

[112] See e.g. Dworkin, *Taking Rights Seriously*, 105 ff.; *Law's Empire*, chs. 7, 8, 9, 10.
[113] Dworkin, *Freedom's Law*, 10.   [114] Ibid. 8.   [115] Ibid. 10.
[116] Dworkin, *Law's Empire*, ch. 7.   [117] Dworkin, *Freedom's Law*, 11.   [118] Ibid.
[119] Dworkin, *Law's Empire*, 65–8.   [120] Dworkin, *Freedom's Law*, 3, 6.
[121] e.g. David Richards, *Toleration and the Constitution* (New York: Oxford University Press, 1986); Michael Perry, *The Constitution in the Courts: Law or Politics* (New York: Oxford University Press, 1994).
[122] Dworkin, *Freedom's Law*, 36–7, 313–20.

perspective. Rather, it is expected that liberal and conservative judges will each draw on their different legal and political philosophies to work out their particular conceptions of liberty, equality, and fraternity so that in every case competing theories of law and justice can confront each other and those with the best argument should carry the day.[123]

Dworkin himself favours a liberal conception of judicial review. He thinks the moral principles that can be derived from a constitution should be cast in the widest and most general terms possible. In the case of the US Bill of Rights, he believes these principles oblige government to 'treat all those subject to its dominion as having equal moral and political status . . . to treat them all with equal concern . . . and respect'.[124] For the judge that means 'if the constitutional rights acknowledged for one group presuppose more general principles that would support other constitutional rights for other groups, then the latter must be acknowledged and enforced as well'.[125] Even if it cannot meet a strict test of neutrality, Dworkin argues the liberal conception is superior to all its rivals because it fits the cases, particularly those decided in the era of the Warren Court, and shows them, and the political culture of which they are a part, in their best possible light.

As well as satisfying the twin (factual and normative) tests of 'fit' and 'value' better than any other method of interpretation, Dworkin argues moral readings of constitutional texts impose real constraints on judges deciding cases on the basis of their politics and personal preferences. Principled readings of text, history, and prior cases, he says, dictate the answers in most cases, 'and [leave] no room for the play of personal moral conviction'.[126] Most cases, he believes, are not hard cases and the criterion of fit 'sharply limit[s] the latitude the moral reading gives to individual judges'.[127]

The eloquence and erudition of Dworkin's writing has been acknowledged and applauded from the beginning and will no doubt continue to be for years to come. Colloquia are regularly convened to discuss different dimensions of his work and evaluations of his theory are a staple of the academic press. Much of the reaction is appropriately flattering and appreciative for his having raised new and challenging ways of thinking about the power of judicial review and in so doing substantially enhancing the quality of the debate. But, in the end, relatively few academics and as yet no judges have (openly at least) advocated that the limits of legitimate lawmaking ought to be marked out in the way he says they must. In fact, virtually no part of his theory has gone unscathed. Literary critics have challenged his ideas about interpretation and his claims for its objectivity and capacity to generate uniquely right answers in law.[128] Legal philosophers

[123] Dworkin, *Freedom's Law*, 2–3, 36–7, 82, 313–20.   [124] Ibid. 7–8, 10.
[125] Dworkin, *Sovereign's Virtue*, 455.   [126] Dworkin, *Freedom's Law*, 10–11.
[127] Ibid. 10.
[128] Stanley Fish, *Doing What Comes Naturally* (Durham, NC: Duke University Press, 1990), chs. 1, 2, 16.

questioned the coherence of his method of deriving individual rights.[129] Most critically, for our purposes, his theory of adjudication and especially his instruction to judges that in the hardest constitutional cases, when all else fails, they should reason as moral and political philosophers has been subjected to withering criticism from all sides.[130]

Originalists and proceduralists attack Dworkin's model of judicial review in exactly the same way and on the same basic grounds as he has trashed theirs. First, they reject his claim that a moral reading provides an effective check against judges practising politics rather than enforcing the law. Secondly, they say, the picture he paints of how judges should exercise their powers of review neither fits the way cases are actually decided by the courts nor shows the practice in its best possible light. Even on his own less demanding standards of fit and value, rival theorists argue that Dworkin comes up short.

From the judges' perspective, the biggest problem with Dworkin's model is that it effectively allows each of them to reach diametrically opposed conclusions about the constitutionality of whatever law they are asked to review. His theory provides them with little practical guidance about the method of reasoning they should use in any specific case. It doesn't, for example, show them a principled way of deciding when history and precedent should govern a case and when bedrock principles of moral and political philosophy should carry the day. In so many of the most controversial and contested cases about abortion, capital punishment, gay rights, or social and economic rights, fit and value pull in opposite directions.[131] On gay rights, for example, justice demands that they be given the same level of protection against discrimination as everyone else but the jurisprudence, at least in the United States, provides considerably less. American constitutional law has always taken the position that gays and lesbians are not as equal as women or blacks. They can only insist that governments act rationally, not that they also be fair. Precedent and principle hold out very different futures for lesbians and gays, and judges are, on Dworkin's theory, entirely unconstrained in deciding which tomorrow will see the dawn of another day.

Sometimes Dworkin thinks fit is controlling. He instructs American judges, for example, that it would be wrong and violate the integrity of the constitution for them to interpret the sweeping guarantees of liberty and equality in the Fifth and Fourteenth Amendments to include social and economic rights (such as housing and healthcare) for the displaced and the infirm. Even though he recognizes that people living in poverty are denied the equal concern and respect that is their

129 See e.g. H. L. A. Hart, 'Between Utility and Rights' (1979) 79 Colum. L Rev. 828.

130 See e.g. McConnell, 'The Importance of Humility in Judicial Review'; John Hart Ely, 'Professor Dworkin's External/Personal Preference Distinction' (1983) Duke LJ 959; Larry Alexander, 'Striking Back at the Empire . . . ' (1987) 6 Law & Philosophy 419; Bork, *Tempting of America*, 213; R. Posner, *The Problematics of Moral and Legal Theory* (Cambridge, Mass.: Harvard University Press, 1999); Monahan, *Politics and the Constitution*, ch. 5.

131 McConnell, 'The Importance of Humility in Judicial Review', 1270–8.

due, he thinks that American judges must defer to the fact that positive rights against the state are simply not part of 'the settled understandings . . . of the broad story of America's historical record'.[132]

In other cases, however, fit counts for almost nothing. The right answers to questions about the legitimacy of laws that mandate capital punishment or prohibit abortion and euthanasia are, in Dworkin's view, only to be found in the deepest and most profound insights of moral and political philosophy.[133] Even though there is little or nothing in the language or history or practice or settled understandings of the American constitution that suggests laws of this kind are unconstitutional, on the best moral reading, Dworkin insists they are.

What is missing in Dworkin's theory is a principled explanation for why judges must defer to settled practice and precedent in the case of social and economic rights but not when they tackle life and death issues such as capital punishment, abortion, and euthanasia. Fit and value may be necessary conditions for an adequate theory of judicial review but without an overarching principle that dictates how they should be reconciled they are plainly not enough. Whether fit or value, precedent or philosophy, is to be given priority in any case remains wholly within the discretion of each judge.

The ease with which history and precedent can be manipulated within Dworkin's theory has been widely seen as one of its major failings. On First Amendment issues and on the right to abort, for example, Cass Sunstein characterized his historical and doctrinal analysis as 'haphazard' at best.[134] Michael McConnell has been even more severe. He took Dworkin to task for his endorsement of the Supreme Court's declaration in *Romer* v. *Evans*, that gays have a right not to be subjected to laws that express the community's disapproval of their sexual morality, in spite of the fact that it was completely inconsistent with its earlier decision in *Bowers* v. *Hardwick* that it was perfectly proper for the state of Georgia to make sodomy a crime, and did not even mention *Bowers* by name. Dworkin's tolerance of such cavalier treatment of a ruling everyone considered a pivotal case shows, says McConnell, that the moral reading of a constitution 'collapses into self-contradiction'.[135]

Although much of his writing does attempt to respond to points made by his critics, Dworkin devotes relatively little time to this aspect of his theory of adjudication.[136] Indeed, even though he says his critics' charge that his model allows judges too much room to impose their own values on society is 'exaggerated', his method endorses practices and ways of reasoning that allow them to do

---

[132] Dworkin, *Freedom's Law*, 11, 36; *Law's Empire*, 404; 'The Arduous Virtue of Fidelity', 1254.

[133] Dworkin, *Life's Dominion*; McConnell, 'The Importance of Humility . . . ', 1277.

[134] Cass Sunstein, 'Earl Warren is Dead', *The New Republic*, 13 May 1996, 35–9.

[135] McConnell, 'The Importance of Humility', 1289.

[136] Although Dworkin has said that it would have been better for the Court to have explicitly overruled *Bowers* in *Romer*, he has never explained why the Court's opinion in *Bowers* wasn't binding on the judges who sat on *Romer*. See R. Dworkin, 'Reflections on Fidelity . . . ' (1997) 65 Ford L Rev. 1799, 1811 n. 67.

precisely that.[137] Each judge is expected to address every case from their different conceptions of justice and political morality. Dworkin not only concedes but thinks it is important to emphasize that every 'constitutional opinion is sensitive [to each judge's] political conviction'.[138] As a result, 'liberal' and 'conservative' judges who draw inspiration from different legal and political philosophers will read the same cases, even pivotal cases, quite differently.[139] So, for example, the reaction of liberals such as Dworkin and conservatives such as Scalia to landmark such cases as *Roe* v. *Wade* (recognizing a qualified right to an abortion) and *Bowers* v. *Hardwick* (upholding laws that make sodomy a crime) is exactly the opposite. Where Dworkin counsels respect for the former and reversal of the latter, Scalia encourages his fellow judges to do exactly the reverse.[140] In effect, because there are many political traditions from which a judge might proceed, outcomes could effectively be determined before a case even begins and judgments could be summarized, as John Hart Ely amusingly suggested, as 'We like Rawls, you like Nozick, we win 6–3. Statute invalidated.'[141]

Indeed, even among judges who share the same moral values and who can agree on the extent to which law and philosophy ought to figure in their deliberation, Dworkin's theory allows them to remain free to formulate whatever principles they find in the text, history, practice, and philosophical premises of the constitution at whatever level of generality they think best 'fits the broad story of America's constitutional record . . . and does most credit to the nation'.[142] Radically different principles can be drawn from precedents such as *Roe* v. *Wade* and *Bowers* v. *Hardwick* even among people who agree on whether either or both of them should be endorsed or overturned. Although he personally favours stating constitutional principles as broadly as possible, he considers it likely and legitimate for others, whose legal and philosophical orientations are different, to formulate them in a less expansive way.

Not only does Dworkin allow judges a huge discretion in deciding how broadly constitutional principles should be formulated, and what their 'gravitational force' should be, he also thinks it is within their prerogative to qualify and compromise their commitment to their principles whenever they think, on balance, that would be a good thing to do. Real judges, Dworkin acknowledges, who try to adhere to his method of constitutional interpretation will face the serious practical problem of having to decide when and how much they should sacrifice what their principles tell them is the right answer in order to gain the support of other justices whose moral reading leads them to a different

---

[137] Dworkin, *Freedom's Law*, 11; *Law's Empire*, 255 ('Different judges will set this threshold [of fit] differently').

[138] Dworkin, *Freedom's Law*, 2–3, 36–7, 319; 'Natural Law Revisited' (1982) 34 U Fla. L Rev. 165, 170.

[139] Dworkin, *Law's Empire*, 65–8, 240–50, 255–60.

[140] Compare Dworkin, *Freedom's Law*, ch. 3; *Sovereign's Virtue*, ch. 14; and Scalia, *A Matter of Interpretation*, 83, 144–9; *Lawrence* v. *Texas*.

[141] Ely, *Democracy and Distrust*, 58.

[142] Dworkin, *Freedom's Law*, 7–8, 11.

understanding of a case.[143] On courts in which each judge is encouraged to aspire to interpretations that 'do most credit to the nation' and in which decisions are made by majority rule, principled judgments must inevitably give way to rulings that are ultimately determined by how much each judge is prepared to wheel and deal. The only judge who never has to trade on his principles is 'Hercules', Dworkin's mythical jurist whose powers of reasoning are greater than any living judge and, being omnipotent, sits by himself.

The complaint that Dworkin's theory of judicial review provides no principled way for a court to distinguish laws that are legitimate from those that are not is a common refrain in the reviews of his work. Michael McConnell confesses to 'belabouring' the point.[144] For McConnell, the indeterminacy and subjectivity that plagues every attempt to reconcile the twin criteria of fit and value is made worse by the fact that the (moral) theory Dworkin says best meets their requirements has absolutely nothing to do with the way judges actually go about their work. It doesn't even satisfy his own criterion of fit. In McConnell's view, the disconnection between Dworkin's injunction to judges to draw on the resources of political and moral philosophy, and the way judges actually justify the decisions they make, is so extreme it amounts to trying to 'turn settled constitutional practice . . . on its head',[145] and it is hard to imagine anyone, including Dworkin, who would disagree. The image of the judge as a moral philosopher is certainly not one any originalist or proceduralist would embrace. They insist judges stick with the traditional sources of text, history, and precedent and say moral reasoning just doesn't fit the way the review process really works. The fact is—as Dworkin despairs—judges almost never openly engage in the kind of moral and philosophical reasoning that he recommends. Indeed, in the very hard cases, when 'very different, even contrary, conceptions of a constitutional principle . . . fit language, precedent and practice well enough',[146] typically they do just the opposite. In those cases in which the constitution is ambiguous and open to more than one interpretation, the standard practice is for judges not to interfere and to allow the people to do whatever they think is in the best interests of their state. 'Mainstream practice', McConnell reminds Dworkin, 'treats any decision of the representative branches that survives the filters of text, history, practice, and precedent *as constitutional.*'[147]

Because Dworkin's theory asks judges to reason in a way that does not fit their self-understanding of their craft, and which leaves them free to base their decisions on their own philosophies of politics and law, it can also be attacked as being riddled with inconsistency and self-contradiction at the level of ideal theory as well. Assigning final responsibility for the moral character of a com-

[143] Dworkin, *Law's Empire*, 380. See also 'In Praise of Theory', 369–72.

[144] McConnell, 'The Importance of Humility', 1278.

[145] Ibid. 1273; see also Sunstein, 'Earl Warren is Dead', 38.

[146] Dworkin, *Freedom's Law*, 11.

[147] McConnell, 'The Importance of Humility', 1272. See also Sunstein, 'Earl Warren is Dead', 37–8.

munity to judges who are unelected, and in no way accountable to the people, is impossible to square with democracy's most basic requirement of showing every person, including those who make up the majority, equal concern and respect. To insist, for example, that the judges rather than the elected representatives of the people must determine the moral status of a foetus, as Dworkin does,[148] constitutes a massive derogation from the authority of each person and the sovereignty of the people as a whole to decide the great questions of life and death for themselves. Especially in difficult cases, when different conceptions of a constitutional principle can be derived from the traditional methods of textual exegesis, the logic of showing everyone equal concern and respect entails allowing the people, through their elected representatives—not the courts—to decide which course of action does most credit to their nation.[149] On the model of constitutional adjudication Dworkin supports, the people lose control of the moral development of their communities to a professional elite.[150] His model of lawyers, robed with philosophical pretensions, working out the details of the moral character of their communities, is fundamentally at odds with the equal autonomy and sovereignty of each of its members. It is not easy to find fault with Michael McConnell's conclusion that on Dworkin's theory, 'democracy . . . [is] . . . just a charade'.[151]

That Dworkin's Herculean effort to fashion a new way to understand law, one that dissolves the tension and stands between legal positivism and natural law, failed to convince many theorists or jurists will be surprising to no one, not even, probably, to Dworkin himself. His critics have simply applied to him the same arguments he levelled against them. His theory does not meet its own standards of legitimacy (fit and value) and provides no assurance that judges will never decide cases on the basis of their politics rather than on the law.

5. JUDICIAL PRACTICE

The debate between Dworkin and his rivals has been passionate and unforgiving. At the end of the millennium constitutional theory is unquestionably richer and better for it. Our understanding of our legal order is more sophisticated than at any time in the past. Still, and notwithstanding our enlightenment, a state of impasse persists. Each new theoretical contribution has included an effective critique of everything that has gone before.[152] For all our cleverness, we remain

---

[148] Dworkin, *Life's Dominion*, 164–5; *Freedom's Law*, 102–10; *Sovereign Virtue*, ch. 12.

[149] McConnell, 'The Importance of Humility', 1273–5, 1290–1; Sunstein, 'Earl Warren is Dead', 37, 39.

[150] Although Dworkin recognizes that an argument can be made that the process of constitutional review ought to be carried out by institutions that are politically accountable, his belief is that the lesson of America's experience is that, all things considered, judges can do a better job. See *Freedom's Law*, 33–5.

[151] McConnell, 'The Importance of Humility', 1276.

[152] Cf. Dworkin, *A Matter of Principle*, ch. 2; Ely, *Democracy and Distrust*, chs. 1–3; Monahan, *Politics and the Constitution*, ch. 5; Bork, *Tempting of America*, chs. 9–12.

stalled in our search for a theory that can adequately explain and justify our choice of giving so much power to the courts.

To escape the stalemate that has plagued constitutional theory for so long it is time to think about coming at the issue from a different direction. We might do better, and we certainly could do no worse, if we didn't worry so much about the best way to read constitutional texts and focused instead on how the practice of judicial review actually works. We could take up Michael Ignatieff's suggestion and concentrate on what the entrenchment of constitutional and international human rights actually does for people.[153] One way to discover what the 'rights revolution' has meant in practice is to borrow the methods of the common law to study how courts actually exercise their powers of review. The great genius of this ancient legal tradition is its pursuit of theory and overarching principles from the bottom up. Common lawyers think inductively rather than moving down from premises by deduction. Reading a series of individual cases that address common problems leads one to larger principles of law. Instead of starting with a preconceived theory of law and democracy—of the right and the good—to which the jurisprudence is made to conform, the order is reversed and theory emerges out of the cases.

Using the approach of the common law to extend our understanding of constitutional theory, and in particular the practice of judicial review, would give us a new and fresh perspective on the problem. Studying cases, and how courts actually exercise their powers of review at the beginning of the inquiry, would give us for the first time a view from the ground floor. So far theorists of all persuasions—originalists, proceduralists, and moralists alike—have been inclined to reflect on the tension that exists between ideas of popular sovereignty and judicial review by looking down from the top. Each starts with a conception of what they think law and democracy should look like and what kind of government they imply and tries to construct a model of courts sitting in judgment of the people that is compatible with the model of democracy they prefer. Proceeding as common lawyers reverses the process by starting with the actual decisions of the courts and drawing out their implications for democracy at the end.

Trying to work out a theory of constitutional review as common lawyers might makes particular sense at this moment in time. For one thing, the approach has not been tried by any of the theorists who have dominated the debate so far and so would fill an obvious gap.[154] For another, there is now, for the first time, with so many different courts being entrusted with the powers of review, a rich jurisprudence to which the method of induction can be applied. Studying the courts' self-understanding of their role should also allow us to test whether

[153] Michael Ignatieff, *Human Rights as Politics and Idolatry* (Princeton: Princeton University Press, 2001), 54.

[154] See e.g. Dworkin, *Freedom's Law*, 35; Habermas, *Between Facts and Norms*, 229; see generally B. Markesinis, 'Comparative Law—A Subject in Search of an Audience' (1990) 53 Mod. L Rev. 1, and B. Schlink, 'The Dynamics of Constitutional Adjudication' (1996) 17 Cardozo L Rev. 1231.

Habermas's insistence that law is characterized by a unique and especially rational form of argumentation is justified or not. There is, it would seem, much to be gained and little to lose by initiating such a project and following where it leads. At worst it will save others the frustration of pursuing another dead end. At best it might finally explain why for the last fifty years ordinary people all over the world have chosen to put courts at the centre of their systems of government and whether, in the end, they were right.

2

Liberty

Anyone who is interested in discovering how judges have exercised their powers of review faces an initial problem of where to begin. The caselaw is large and there are numerous points of departure from which they might launch their inquiry. Cases that deal with the rights of people to live their lives according to their religious beliefs are one obvious possibility. People have been persecuted, tortured, even killed on account of their spiritual faith since the beginning of time.[1] For some, the essential idea of human rights is 'ineliminably religious'.[2] Freedom of religion, it could fairly be said, is *primus inter pares* of all the internationally recognized human rights. Claims for the right to choose one's own spiritual path were at the centre of the earliest struggles against oppression and arbitrary rule. In 1791 the authors of the American Bill of Rights thought religious freedom was so fundamental to the liberty of the individual and to justice in their communities that they picked it to be the first guarantee in the First Amendment they made to their constitution.

The American experiment was a bold and radical initiative. By making religious liberty a legally enforceable right, the Americans believed they could avoid the religious persecution and sectarian strife that has scarred all human history and, sad to say, has remained an open wound all over the world—witness Bosnia, India, Indonesia, Northern Ireland, Nigeria, Palestine, Pakistan, and the Sudan—to this day. The Americans hoped that by making courts responsible for resolving the most serious grievances of church/state relations, all the carnage and killing that has been carried out in the name of religion could be stopped. They thought reason and principle could strike a balance between the spiritual will of a community and the personal conscience of the individual that was just and fair to both.

Comparing the way different courts have treated people when issues of religious freedom are at stake provides a good test of whether those who wrote the American constitution were justified in believing that law is capable of providing an objective and impartial way of marking off the boundaries of church and

An earlier version of this chapter was published as 'The Forms and Limits of Constitutional Interpretation' in (2001) 49 Am. J Comp. Law 79 for which the author retains copyright.

[1] M. McDougal, H. Lasswell, and L. Chen, 'The Right to Religious Freedom and World Public Order: The Emerging Norm of Nondiscrimination' (1976) 74 Mich. L Rev. 865.

[2] Michael Perry, *The Idea of Human Rights: Four Inquiries* (New York: Oxford University Press, 1998), 11–41.

state. In the minds of many people, the idea that there are neutral principles that can reconcile the spiritual and secular dimensions of human life is an illusion. It is now conventional wisdom that there is no disinterested perspective that is not embedded in and contaminated by some personal or political point of view. In the words of Stanley Fish, even to search for such a vantage point is to embark on 'mission impossible'.[3]

So far none of the major theorists has been able to provide a satisfactory account of what rights and freedoms can be claimed in the name of some higher spiritual or moral force. Religious rights are, as we saw in the last chapter, an anomaly for those who say judicial review is all about process and democracy, and are either explained away or just ignored.[4] Dworkin has written surprisingly little on the subject of religious liberty[5] and even originalists such as Scalia, who have defended the cause of religious freedom, have not done so, as we shall see, in a consistent and principled way.

Over the course of the last fifty years, by contrast, a large jurisprudence has been written by courts around the world that can shed considerable light on this debate. Many courts have had to struggle with very basic questions about the extent to which a state may, or indeed must, accommodate the interests of its citizens who believe it is essential to live their lives according to the fundamentals of their faith. The place of religion (prayers, symbols, clothing) in public schools; the validity/necessity of religious exemptions to laws the general population is forced to obey; and the right of religious minorities to claim state support for their schools are controversies that courts have been asked to resolve all over the world. With the reflections of a lot of jurists on these and related questions it should be possible to say whether the early American idealists, or the postmodern sceptics, have it right.

1. INTERPRETIVISM

In choosing which cases to read first, there is an obvious logic starting with the Americans. The US Supreme Court was the first to grapple with questions about religious liberty and they have, over the course of almost a century and half, handed down more opinions on the subject than anyone else. Within this large and still expanding jurisprudence any number of judgments could be put at the top of the pile. There are lots of important landmark judgments that have been written by the Court. Every student of American constitutional law has his or her

---

[3] Stanley Fish, 'Mission Impossible: Settling the Just Bounds Between Church & State' (1997) 97 Colum. L Rev. 2255; *The Trouble with Principle*, ch. 9 (Cambridge, Mass.: Harvard University Press, 1999).

[4] See e.g. John Hart Ely, *Democracy and Distrust* (Cambridge, Mass.: Harvard University Press, 1980), 94, 100.

[5] Except, of course, in his discussion of life and death issues such as abortion and euthanasia which for him are matters of religious belief. See *Life's Dominion* (New York: Vintage Books, 1994); *Freedom's Law* (Cambridge, Mass.: Harvard University Press, 1996), Part 1; see also *Taking Rights Seriously* (Cambridge, Mass.: Harvard University Press, 1977), 106–7.

personal favourites. *Lee v. Weisman*[6] and *Oregon v. Smith*[7] are two that would rank very high with a lot of people. Both are relatively recent decisions of the Supreme Court that show off the most important features of how American judges think church/state relations should be structured. In the jargon of constitutional theorists, both qualify as 'pivotal' cases.[8] Each deals with an aspect of religion—prayers and ceremonies—that lies at its core, and both were regarded as precedent-setting/shattering decisions when they were handed down.[9] In *Lee v. Weisman*, the Court was asked whether allowing a non-denominational, ecumenical benediction and prayer to be said at the beginning of a high school graduation ceremony violated the First Amendment's injunction that Congress 'shall make no law respecting an establishment of religion'. In *Oregon v. Smith*, the Court's attention was focused on the words of the First Amendment that deny Congress the authority to pass laws that prohibit 'the free exercise of religion', and the issue was whether members of the Native American Church who ingested peyote during special spiritual ceremonies had a constitutional right to a religious exemption from a state law that made its possession a crime.

In both cases the Court was badly split. In *Lee v. Weisman*, five judges thought the prayer violated the First Amendment. Four disagreed. In explaining the reasons for their conclusion, three of the five in the majority felt compelled to write separate opinions. In *Oregon v. Smith* six judges voted to uphold the state's drug laws, three voted against. In this case, one of the judges in the majority— Sandra Day O'Connor—wrote a separate concurring judgment with which the three dissenting judges were in substantial agreement except in the conclusion she reached!

The division of opinion among the judges in both cases centred on how the critical phrases 'establishment' and 'free exercise of religion' should be read. In *Lee v. Weisman*, a majority of the Court said the meaning of the establishment clause should be drawn from its own precedents: from earlier readings of those who preceded them on the Bench. They said the Court's prior rulings were 'controlling' and 'compelled' the conclusion that prayers had no place in the life of public schools. Anthony Kennedy, who delivered the opinion of the Court, wrote that, 'by any reading of our cases, the conformity required of the [dissenting] student[s] in this case was too high . . . to withstand the test of the Estab-

---

[6] *Lee v. Weisman* (1992) 505 US 577. In *Santa Fe School Dist. v. Doe* (2000) 530 US 290, the Court reaffirmed the principles it developed in *Lee*.

[7] *Oregon v. Smith* (1990) 494 US 872.

[8] Ronald Dworkin, *Law's Empire* (Cambridge, Mass.: Harvard University Press, 1986), ch. 2, 45.

[9] *Oregon v. Smith*, in particular, attracted a lot of comment. See e.g. Michael McConnell, 'Free Exercise Revisionism . . . ' (1990) 57 U Chic. L Rev. 1109; D. Laycock, 'The Remnants of Free Exercise' [1990] Sup. Ct. Rev. 1. Not all the reviews were negative, see W. Marshall, 'The Case Against Constitutionally Compelled Free Exercise Exemption' (1990) 40 Case Western Res. L Rev. 357, M. Tushnet, 'The Rhetoric of Free Exercise Discourse' (1993) Brigham Young UL Rev. 117. For critiques of the Court's decision in *Smith* in conjunction with its ruling in *Lee*, see Suzanna Sherry, '*Lee v. Weisman*, Paradox Redux' (1992) Sup. Ct. Rev. 123; Tinsley E. Yarbrough, *The Rehnquist Court and the Constitution* (New York: Oxford University Press, 2000), ch. 6.

lishment Clause'. He thought the prayer and benediction were especially improper because, as a practical matter, 'the state . . . has compelled attendance and participation in an explicit religious exercise at an event [which] the objecting student had no real alternative to avoid'. Harry Blackmun and David Souter agreed with Kennedy that the case could be disposed of on a straightforward application of the Court's own precedents but they each wrote separate concurring opinions, which John Paul Stevens and Sandra Day O'Connor also signed, to emphasize that, on their understanding of the Court's past decisions, all school prayers violate the Establishment Clause because they constitute an illicit endorsement of religion whether or not anyone feels any pressure or coercion from the event.

Four justices—Scalia, Rehnquist, White, and Thomas—voted to sustain the validity of the graduation prayer and their disagreement with their colleagues was nasty and ill tempered. Writing for the group, Scalia condemned the majority's opinion as 'incoherent'; one that made 'interior decorating' look like a 'rock hard science'. Not only did they dispute the majority's reading of its earlier school prayer decisions, they even questioned the legitimacy of deciding the case on a jurisprudence which in their view had 'become bedevilled (so to speak) by reliance on formulaic abstractions that are not derived from but positively conflict with our long-accepted constitutional traditions'. Because its precedents were riddled with such inconsistency and incoherence, they argued that the meaning of the Establishment Clause should be determined 'by reference to historical practices and understandings'. They said the Court's interpretation should 'comport with what history reveals was the contemporaneous understanding of its guarantees'. On that test, because prayers and religious invocations were part of government ceremonies and proclamations at the time (1791) the First Amendment was adopted, they thought it was axiomatic that they should be permitted on this occasion as well.

The Court was also badly fractured in *Oregon* v. *Smith* but the division of opinion was not as deep or extensive as in *Lee* v. *Weisman*. In *Smith* the judges were agreed that precedent, not history, was where they should look for the answer to the question of whether the members of the Native American Church had a constitutional right to use peyote as part of their religious ceremonies. Where they differed was in the principles and tests they thought the prior caselaw supplied. Although Scalia's interpretation of the Establishment Clause fell one vote short in *Lee* v. *Weisman*, his reading of the caselaw on the Free Exercise Clause appealed to four of his colleagues in *Oregon* v. *Smith* and his judgment was delivered as the opinion of the Court. As he read its earlier pronouncements, the Court had never said people's religious beliefs could normally excuse them from obeying laws of general application that were binding on everyone else. Although he acknowledged there had been several occasions when the Court had required exceptions to be made to accommodate people's religious beliefs, he said they were different because they were not dealing with laws (like Oregon's), that made activities, such as the use of drugs, criminal offences for everyone in the state.

Sandra Day O'Connor and three justices who were widely regarded at the time as being the most liberal on the Court (William Brennan, Thurgood Marshall, and Harry Blackmun) thought Scalia's interpretation of the Court's earlier exemption cases to be way wide of the mark. O'Connor accused Scalia of 'dramatically depart[ing] from well-settled First Amendment jurisprudence'. Blackmun described the Court's opinion as 'a distorted view' that 'mischaracter-ized' the Court's precedents. As they read the Court's earlier interpretations of the Free Exercise Clause, religious exemptions had to be written into state laws unless it could be shown that it was essential to some compelling state interest that they be strictly enforced in a rigid and uniform way. At the end of her judgment, O'Connor took a different view than her three liberal colleagues on whether the state could satisfy this test on the facts of the case and ended up voting with the majority to reject Smith's appeal to be allowed to ingest peyote during the religious ceremonies of his church.

Lee v. *Weisman* and *Oregon* v. *Smith* are typical of the way freedom of religion cases are adjudicated in the United States. Together they reflect all the defining features of the large jurisprudence that has been written by the US Supreme Court on the subject of religious rights. Most fundamentally, both cases show that notwithstanding the diversity in their opinions, all American judges think that marking off the boundaries of church and state is essentially an interpret-ative task. When the US Supreme Court is asked a question about religious freedom, the assumption is always that the answers are embedded in and therefore can be drawn from the words of the text. Because, like most consti-tutional guarantees, the religion clauses in the First Amendment do not speak directly to such issues as school prayers or religious exemptions, judges who treat judicial review as an exercise in semantics must have resort to 'legal dictionaries', or sources of meaning, to point them to the rule or definition that will settle each case. When American judges are called on to explain how the words in the First Amendment speak to specific issues such as religious exemp-tions or school prayers, original understandings and the Court's earlier prece-dents are where they always go for help. In their earliest decisions, when precedents were few or non-existent, the judges relied mostly on historical sources. That was certainly true of its very first ruling on the religion clauses in *Reynolds* v. *US*,[10] handed down over 120 years ago, when it validated a federal law that made bigamy (which was an important part of the lives of adherents of the Church of Jesus Christ of Latter Day Saints) a crime. Over time, however, as more and more cases have been brought to the Court, its own prior rulings have come to play an increasingly dominant role as they did in both *Oregon* v. *Smith* and *Lee* v. *Weisman*.

In addition to showing how the judicial protection of religious liberty is understood to be mostly a matter of interpretation in the United States, *Lee* v. *Weisman* and *Oregon* v. *Smith* highlight at least three other characteristics that

---

[10] *Reynolds* v. *US* (1878) 98 US 145.

distinguish the American conception of the judicial role in the process of constitutional review. First is the categorical, rule-like quality of the decisions in the two cases. As in virtually all its pronouncements on the nature and extent of religious freedom that is guaranteed by the First Amendment, the judgments in *Lee v. Weisman* and *Oregon v. Smith* are marked by very sharp, categorical distinctions and by very rigid and unbending rules. Laws that make it difficult or unlawful to practise some part of a religion (*Smith*) are judged by one set of rules; laws that force people to defer to religious ideas and practices to which they object (*Weisman*) by another. The Free Exercise and Establishment Clauses are read as entirely discrete and separate parts of the constitution, that apply to different kinds of questions by means of very different rules. After *Lee v. Weisman*, the anti-establishment rule was the more rigorous of the two in protecting religious minorities against indirect as well as direct invasions of religious liberty and it superseded claims for accommodation under the Free Exercise Clause. The latter, according to the majority opinion in *Smith*, protected people only against direct and intentional limitations of religious activity and is vulnerable to virtually any public purpose a government might choose to pursue.

The second feature of how the US Supreme Court has approached the First Amendment's guarantee of religious freedom that is highlighted in these cases is the way in which religious rights in the United States can and have shifted and evolved over time. As both cases demonstrate, the historical record and the Court's own precedents are open to such radically different interpretations that settled meanings are never completely secure. Accusations in dissenting opinions that colleagues have 'broken faith' with the understanding that prevailed when the First Amendment was adopted (as in *Lee v. Weisman*), or 'distorted' the Court's own prior rulings (as in *Oregon v. Smith*), are common in the annals of American constitutional law. Competing interpretations and doctrines hold sway at different times and the scope of religious freedom ebbs and flows apace. Religious objections to having to salute the flag are rejected in one case and accepted in the next.[11] Funding educational programmes in parochial schools is proscribed on one occasion, endorsed on another.[12] A decision can become the leading precedent for a period of time and suffer a silent burial at a later date.[13] It is as if, to borrow Ronald Dworkin's provocative but revealing metaphor, in each era the Court writes a new chapter in a chain novel that never ends.[14]

The third, and for many the most striking feature of the way American judges think about religious freedom and the First Amendment that is prominent in both *Lee v. Weisman* and *Oregon v. Smith*, is its intensely personal character. Just as Justices Blackmun, Souter, O'Connor, and Scalia all felt compelled to

[11] *Minersville School District v. Gobitis* (1940) 310 US 586; *Board of Education v. Barnette* (1942) 319 US 624.

[12] *Aguilar v. Felton* (1985) 473 US 402; *Agostini v. Felton* (1997) 521 US 203.

[13] *Lemon v. Kurtzman* (1971) 403 US 602; *Lee v. Weisman*.

[14] Dworkin, *Law's Empire*, ch. 7.

write separate concurring or dissenting opinions in one or both of these cases, virtually every judge who has sat on the United States Supreme Court has assumed (and in the case of Antonin Scalia, Felix Frankfurter, and William Brennan explicitly defended)[15] the constitutional authority to decide for themselves which definitions, doctrines, rules, etc. to apply and, accordingly, what the parameters of religious freedom in America will be. Virtually every important ruling in the last fifty years is marked by the same multiplicity of opinions that were elicited in *Lee* v. *Weisman* and *Oregon* v. *Smith*. Together they confirm the empirical truth of Chief Justice Hughes's notorious confession that, in the United States, 'the constitution is what the judges say it is'![16]

Because there is more than one 'dictionary' from which they can choose, and because both history and precedent can be read in more than one way, each judge has an enormous discretion in defining which rights are protected in the First Amendment and what the practical meaning of state neutrality in matters of religion will be. From *Lee* v. *Weisman* and *Oregon* v. *Smith*, and even more from the full jurisprudence on religious freedom of which they are a part, it is quite easy to construct different profiles for each of the judges who have sat on the Court. Some take the view that the proper way to read the religion clauses is to define the principles of state neutrality so that the elected branches of government have as much room to manœuvre as possible. On this view, short of malevolent acts of coercion or discrimination, politicians and their officials are given free rein to enact whatever laws they please, regardless of what impact they have on the lives of religiously minded people and the communities in which they live. Only the ends or objectives of laws are assessed by the Court. No evaluation is made of the means—the particular programme or policy instrument—that governments choose to enact into law. This understanding of state neutrality has been favoured by a number of judges who have sat on the Court while William Rehnquist has been Chief Justice including Antonin Scalia, Clarence Thomas, Byron White, and Rehnquist himself. In fact this is the definition they invoked in the opinions they wrote upholding the Government's initiatives in both *Smith* and *Lee*.

This minimalist definition of state neutrality contrasts sharply with the more robust reading that the Court generally gave to both the Establishment and Free Exercise Clauses when it was under the stewardship of Earl Warren and Warren Burger. This earlier interpretation, which implies much more stringent limitations on the ways governments can act, has generally found favour with those justices who are inclined to a liberal conception of politics and the law. On this view, means as well as ends are scrutinized by the Court. William Brennan came to be one of the leading exponents of this more demanding understanding of

---

[15] See Frankfurter's judgment in *McGowan* v. *Maryland* (1960) 366 US 420, 459 and Brennan's and Scalia's extra judicial reflections in 'In Defense of Dissents' (1986) 37 Hastings LJ 427, and 'The Dissenting Opinion' (1994) J Sup. Ct. Hist. 133, respectively.

[16] Hughes's remarks are reprinted in R. I. Aldisert, *The Judicial Process* (St Paul, Minn.: West, 1976), 501, and parsed by H. L. A. Hart, in *The Concept of Law* (Oxford: Clarendon, 1961), 138–43.

state neutrality but others, including Thurgood Marshall, Harry Blackmun, and William Douglas as well as Warren and Burger, followed more or less the same analysis. Today, Sandra Day O'Connor and David Souter, who have said that most endorsements of religion by the state will constitute invalid establishments[17] and that sometimes states must make exceptions for people on account of their religious beliefs,[18] come closest to this approach.

For a judge such as Brennan, the religion clauses in the First Amendment impose two independent but complementary duties on governments and their officials. Like Jefferson, Brennan believed the prohibition against 'an establishment of religion' creates a wall of separation between churches and the state that is virtually insurmountable.[19] In addition, he thought that in order to respect each person's right to exercise his or her religious beliefs, the state is obliged to accommodate the choices and decisions of religiously minded people where it can do so without compromising its own interests and projects in any substantial way.[20] Thus, against the laissez-faire definition of state neutrality that the majority adopted in *Oregon* v. *Smith*, Brennan and his fellow liberals insisted that the state legislature should have granted the Native American Church an exemption from its law making any and all use of peyote a crime.

In between these two extreme positions it is possible to find judges who craft their visions of state neutrality in matters of religion by borrowing bits from both. Some judges, who have been accused of being insensitive, if not downright hostile, to religion have coupled the narrow, weak reading of the Free Exercise Clause that Scalia and the Court favoured in *Oregon* v. *Smith* with Brennan's strict interpretation of the Establishment Clause. On this approach, accommodating the religious beliefs of those adversely affected by some law or regulation is never required by the constitution and, coincidentally, state encouragement and support is almost never allowed. Felix Frankfurter[21] and Hugo Black[22] are two of the better-known justices in America's legal pantheon who have been attracted to such an understanding of state neutrality and John Paul Stevens[23] who voted with the majority in both *Lee* v. *Weisman* and *Oregon* v. *Smith* continues to rely on it to this day.

Standing opposite Stevens, Black, and Frankfurter was Potter Stewart who sat on the Court in the Warren–Burger years. His definition of state neutrality was based on a broad and expansive reading on the Free Exercise Clause[24] and a

[17] *Lynch* v. *Donnelly* (1984) 465 US 668 and *Lee* v. *Weisman*.

[18] *Church of the Lukumi Babalu Aye Inc.* v. *City of Hialeah* (1993) 508 US 520.

[19] *Aguilar* v. *Felton*.

[20] *Oregon* v. *Smith*; see also *Sherbert* v. *Verner* (1962) 374 US 398.

[21] *Minersville School District* v. *Gobitis*; *Everson* v. *Board of Education* (1946) 330 US 1; *Board of Education* v. *Barnette* 319 US (1943) 624; *McGowan* v. *Maryland* (1961) 366 US 420.

[22] *Everson* v. *Board of Education*; *Engel* v. *Vitale* (1962) 370 US 421; *Braunfeld* v. *Brown* (1961) 366 US 599; *Board of Education* v. *Allen* (1968) 392 US 236.

[23] *Lee* v. *Weisman*; *Oregon* v. *Smith*; see also *Santa Fe School Dist.* v. *Doe*; *US* v. *Lee* (1982) 455 US 263; and generally D. Laycock 'Formal, Substantive and Disaggregated Neutrality towards Religion' (1990) 39 DePaul L Rev. 993.

[24] *Sherbert* v. *Verner* (1963) 374 US 398; *Braunfeld* v. *Brown*.

correspondingly weak and relatively unconstraining interpretation of the anti-establishment rule[25]—just the reverse of theirs. As would be expected, this understanding tends to treat religious organizations and their members quite sympathetically and so receives their endorsement and applause.[26] On Stewart's interpretation, not only is the state required to grant exemptions to religiously minded people from laws that are especially burdensome for them when it can do so at little or no cost but, in addition, it must make public spaces and institutions as accessible to religious organizations and their members as they are to secular groups.

The broad picture of American constitutional law that can be drawn from a careful reading of the first two cases—*Lee* v. *Weisman* and *Oregon* v. *Smith*—that we have examined does not, of course, give anything close to a complete account of the legal rights of religiously minded people in the United States. To master all the detailed rules of First Amendment law that define the scope and substance of religious freedom in the United States, it would be necessary to read a lot more judgments of the Court. While undoubtedly of major importance to those whose lives its directly affects, such an effort would not add appreciably to what we now know about how the US Supreme Court goes about its work. For our purposes of learning as much as we can about how judges address issues of religious freedom and reconcile the competing authorities of church and state, our time would be better spent finding out about the patterns and practices of jurists in other parts of the world.

2. Pragmatism

Deciding to move beyond the frontier of American constitutional law leads immediately to the question of where to go next. Once again there is no single right answer as to the order in which the cases should be read. If experience counts, judgments from India, Japan, Germany, Italy, and Strasbourg (where the European Court of Human Rights sits) would be at the top of the list. Judges have been reviewing the decisions of politicians and their officials in these jurisdictions for roughly half a century. Within this group a case can be argued for the priority of any of them, but in the end a choice must be made. Recognizing that reasonable people can favour different points of departure and sites of exploration, the reasons why one might decide to compare the American model first with the experience of the judiciary in Germany seem particularly compelling.

Germany makes for a good comparison most importantly because the reputation of the Bundesverfassungsgericht—the Federal Constitutional Court—is very high. Except for the US Supreme Court, it is doubtful that any group of judges

---

[25] *Engel* v. *Vitale*; *School District of Abington* v. *Schempp* (1963) 374 US 203.

[26] M. A. Glendon and R. F. Yanes, 'Structural Free Exercise' (1991) 90 Mich. L Rev. 477.

has had more influence on the way judicial review and the legal protection of human rights is understood in other parts of the world than the judges who sit in Karlsruhe. The radiating effect of their decisions is especially felt in the courts of central and eastern Europe, whose legal traditions borrow heavily from German law, but its decisions are read and respected by jurists all over the world.

The jurisprudence of the Bundesverfassungsgericht also makes for an excellent first point of comparison for the way the US Supreme Court has come to defend religious liberty and draw the boundary between church and state because the two stand in such sharp counterpoint to each other. Their approaches are almost polar opposites. Even in their delivery, their opposition is striking. The idea that each and every member of a court has the authority to choose their preferred interpretative strategy and define for themselves the practical boundaries of religious freedom for their communities is not one that has found favour among those who have sat on the German Constitutional Court. Rather than each judge expressing his or her own personal opinion, more often than not the Bundesverfassungsgericht speaks unequivocally and in its institutional voice.

Not only do German judges favour a more collegial style of presenting their opinions than do the Americans, when they rule on issues of religious freedom they express themselves and reason in a quite different way. Compared to the Americans, the German judges devote much less time in their opinions talking about the meaning of their constitution, which is known as the Basic Law. The solutions to problems of religious freedom are not laid out as definitions and matters of interpretation the way they are for the Americans. Moreover, in those parts of their judgments that are given over to the textual exegesis, the German method of ascertaining meaning is to put more emphasis on the words and structure of the document, and on the purposes and values they express, than on the historical understandings or earlier decisions of the Court. Neither parsing cases nor probing founding moments is an important part of German constitutional law. Rather than looking to history and caselaw to give meaning to the text, the German Court proceeds in a more purposeful and logical way. In Germany, the meaning of religious liberty follows from recognizing 'human dignity . . . [as] . . . the highest value and . . . the free self-determination of the individual . . . as an important community value'.[27]

Interpretation serves quite different purposes for the Germans and the Americans. Instead of looking to the words of the document to provide precise definitions and rules that answer the hard, practical questions about school prayers and religious exemptions, the Federal Constitutional Court draws general principles from the text which it then uses to evaluate the facts of each case as impartially and objectively as it can. The German method is to apply the same principles to evaluate and reconcile the competing interests at stake regardless of

---

[27] *Blood Transfusion* (1971) 32 BverfGE 98, translated and reproduced in part in D. Kommers, *The Constitutional Jurisprudence of the Federal Republic of Germany* (2nd edn. Durham, NC: Duke University Press, 1997). See generally W. Brugger, 'Legal Interpretation, Schools of Jurisprudence and Anthropology: Some Remarks From a German Perspective' (1994) 42 Am. J Comp. Law 395.

whether the claim is cast in positive or negative terms and whether the state defends its action on the well-being of the community at large or on the rights of some of its members. Practical, fact-specific reasoning, rather than interpretative insight, is how the Germans decide whether someone's religious freedom has been violated or not.

In giving its opinion on the place of prayers and religious symbols in public schools, for example, the Constitutional Court starts from the position that both the positive freedom to publicly acknowledge one's religious beliefs and the negative freedom from being forced to defer to someone else's faith are at stake. The Court sees these cases as involving a conflict of competing rights and conceives its task as having to strike a balance between the two. To guide its judgment, the Court relies on a principle it calls 'practical concordance', according to which conflicting values must be harmonized in a way that will preserve as much of each of them as possible.[28] The principle is understood to be implicit in the logic of the Basic Law and provides a metric around which the different rights and freedoms that are guaranteed can be reconciled. To satisfy the principle, the Court has said the state must show it has reached an 'optimization of the conflicting interests' that are affected by the relevant law and has avoided policies that are 'excessive'.

Within this framework of analysis the judges in Karlsruhe have ruled that the state does no wrong if it allows voluntary prayers to be spoken in its schools but it does if it affixes crucifixes to classroom walls. In a judgment that echoes many of the sentiments that were expressed by Antonin Scalia and the other three judges who dissented in *Lee* v. *Weisman*, the Court concluded that the harm that would be suffered by anyone who opted out of the prayers would not be very great. Forcing dissenting pupils to abstain from school prayers, it said, would rarely put them 'into an unbearable position as an outsider'. Allowing the objection of a single student to automatically trump the rights of religious students to express their beliefs would be out of all proportion to the injury or harm involved. In the words of the Court: 'An assessment of the conditions under which the prayer is to occur, the function that the teacher has in connection with this exercise, and the actual conditions in the school leads us to conclude that we need not fear discrimination against a pupil who does not participate in the prayer . . . '[29]

In the opinion of the Court, the same could not be said about the state of Bavaria's decision to nail crosses all over its schools and so the case called for a different conclusion. From the perspective of non-Christian students, the Court said, the cross is a 'symbol of missionary zeal' and its embrace by the state 'constitutes a deeply moving appeal [and] underscores the faith commitment it symbolizes, thus making that faith exemplary and worthy of being followed'.[30]

[28] *Classroom Crucifix II* (1995) 93 BverfGE 1; translated and reproduced in part in Kommers, *Constitutional Jurisprudence*.

[29] *School Prayer* (1979) 52 BverfGE, trans. and reproduced in part in Kommers, ibid.

[30] *Classroom Crucifix II* case.

For non-Christian students, the sectarian nature of the cross and the fact that they could never escape its glare made its force much more powerful than voluntary prayers. As well, in the context of the Court's earlier validation of voluntary prayers, the principle of practical concordance 'that no one of the conflicting legal positions be preferred and maximally asserted, but all given as protective as possible an arrangement', meant that the limits of the state's authority to support the interests of its religiously motivated citizens had been reached.

Even though the Court came down on opposite sides of the case in its rulings on the place of prayers and sectarian symbols in state schools, the analysis in both was the same. Each case was determined by the Court making a pragmatic and impartial assessment of the facts as they were perceived by those for whom the issue mattered the most. Facts, rather than the words of the text, have also controlled the Court's thinking on the question of whether laws of general application should have to make exceptions for religious minorities or whether they should be treated the same as everyone else. In its *Blood Transfusion* decision, for example, the Court was asked whether a person who was acting out of a serious religious conviction could be convicted of a criminal offence for allowing his wife to die when, following her instructions, he did not transfer her to a hospital when she was in need of a blood transfusion. A unanimous Court concluded that he couldn't. On the facts of the case, the Court ruled that labelling and treating the husband as a criminal would represent an 'excessive social reaction'. Condemning his behaviour in society's harshest terms, the Court said, did not respect his human dignity, the constitution's highest value, because it denied him 'the right . . . to orient his conduct on the teachings of his religion and to act according to his internal convictions'. In the Court's mind: 'Criminal punishment, no matter what the sentence, [was] an inappropriate sanction for this constellation of facts under any goal of the criminal justice system . . . '[31]

The different methodologies that have been employed by the German and American courts have led them to quite different understandings of what it means for the state to remain neutral in matters of religion. In American constitutional law, neutrality is defined, for the most part, by the aims and objectives of the state. The Establishment Clause rules out of order every religious purpose no matter how benign. By contrast, the only protection that is provided by the Free Exercise Clause, as it was interpreted by the majority in *Smith*, is against laws and other state action that are deliberately aimed at restricting the practice of some act of religious faith.[32] After *Smith*, the rule of law in the United States is that in limiting the religious freedom of the American people, the (secular) ends of government justify virtually any means.

In Germany, the rules are completely different. As a practical matter, state neutrality can be defined by a single principle of proportionality or mutual toleration. Whether the Court is considering a claim to be free to follow the

---

[31] *Blood Transfusion.*   [32] See e.g. *Church of the Lukumi Babalu Aye Inc.*

dictates of one's faith or to be free from orthodoxy and pressure to conform, the test is the same. Neutrality insists that whatever limitations or restrictions state authorities impose on the religious liberty of its people, whether intentional or inadvertent, the burdens must not be 'excessive' or 'unbearable'. Whereas the two rules of neutrality that currently define the meaning of First Amendment law focus primarily on the purposes that underlie the state action being reviewed, the German conception of neutrality is aimed much more at the efficacy of its means and the significance of its effects.[33] On the question of how much religion should be allowed in public schools, the German conception of neutrality requires the state to compare the affirmative freedom of worship with the negative freedom of those who are opposed to such public professions of faith. It must strive to 'preserve to the extent possible',[34] all the constitutional values and rights and try 'to reach an optimisation of the conflicting interests'[35] that are involved in each case. Applied to the criminal justice system, neutrality precludes the state prosecuting people who commit punishable acts on the basis of their religious beliefs in those cases where 'the use of society's harshest weapon' would represent 'an excessive social reaction'.[36]

Like *Lee* v. *Weisman* and *Oregon* v. *Smith*, the *School Prayer*, and *Blood Transfusion* cases provide a fair depiction of a larger jurisprudence that has been written by the German Constitutional Court on the question of religious liberty. Where the approach of the Americans is almost exclusively interpretative and focused on the words of the constitution (as they have been elaborated in the historical record and in the Court's earlier opinions), the Germans are much more pragmatic and focused on facts. There are, of course, exceptions and variations in the jurisprudence of both courts. Historical inquiries and textual exegesis can play a role in the analysis of the Bundesverfassungsgericht[37] and dissenting opinions appear with increasing frequency over the years. In ruling that state authorities could not hang crucifixes and crosses on its classroom walls, for example, the Court split 5 : 3.

Equally, even though historical interpretation and doctrinal analysis are the methodologies favoured by the US Supreme Court, in a number of its leading religion cases, including its seminal decision in *Reynolds* v. *US* and its landmark ruling in *Lemon* v. *Kurtzman*,[38] the Americans have endeavoured to evaluate the relative importance of the competing rights and freedoms that are at stake by

---

[33] The instrumental, means-oriented character of the Court's approach is one of the defining features of the pragmatic method. See J. Habermas, *Between Facts and Norms* (Cambridge, Mass.: MIT Press, 1996). See also T. Dewey, 'My Philosophy On Law', in *John Dewey, The Later Works*, (Carbondale, Ill.: Southern Illinois University Press, 1985), xiv. 115–22. R. Posner, *Law, Pragmatism and Democracy* (Cambridge, Mass.: Harvard University Press, 2003).

[34] *Classroom Crucifix II*.

[35] *School Prayer*.

[36] *Blood Transfusion*.

[37] See W. Brugger, 'Legal Interpretation'. For an introduction to the evolutionary character of historical jurisprudence and its place in German constitutional law, see Ernst-Wolfgang Böckenförde, *State, Society and Liberty* (New York: St Martins Press, 1991), ch. 1.

[38] *Lemon* v. *Kurtzman*.

doing a kind of balancing or cost/benefit analysis. Its rulings on whether religious symbols have a place in any public space are notorious for their meticulous attention to the facts.[39] Indeed, in *Lee* v. *Weisman*, part of the disagreement between the majority and the minority was the latter's assessment of how significant the profession of public prayers was to the students who wanted to include them in their graduation ceremonies and how coercive they were to those, like Deborah Weisman, who objected to their being said. Similarly, the critical division of opinion between O'Connor and her dissenting colleagues in *Oregon* v. *Smith* centred on the differing assessments each of them made of the harm that would be suffered by the public at large if the state's drug laws were required to make exceptions for those who used them in the celebration of their religious beliefs.

3. RELIGIOUS LIBERTY AND POPULAR SOVEREIGNTY

It is important to be conscious of the fact that the Americans and Germans do know something of each other's methods. Neither relies exclusively on one approach. Interpretation and pragmatic reasoning figure in the analysis of both. However, it would be just as wrong to exaggerate the similarities and overlap between the two courts, as it would be to ignore them altogether. The fact is American and German jurists address issues such as school prayers and religious exemptions in radically different ways. They contemplate judges engaged in quite different tasks and, as we have seen, ultimately they lead to opposing results.

Some, like Stanley Fish, will be inclined to see the conflicting decisions of the Germans and Americans as hard evidence that should explode the myth that there are neutral principles of law that can reconcile the competing claims of church and state in a way that is impartial to both. From a sceptical perspective, these cases support their position that law, like politics, is indelibly coloured by the culture to which it applies. They seem to show each court giving expression to different conceptions of neutrality that prevail in their corners of the world. Where the Americans give priority to the private space of spiritual peace and reflection over the public profession of faith, the ordering in Germany is just the reverse. Choosing between these competing conceptions of neutrality is just a matter of political culture and personal preference, not a question of right or wrong, not even of better or worse.

As plausible as the sceptical explanation of the American and German decisions on school prayers and religious exemptions first appears, it is not a good read of the cases. It focuses too much on the results and not enough on the processes of reasoning that led the courts to positions that are diametrically

[39] *Lynch* v. *Donnelly* (1984) 465 US 668; *Allegheny County* v. *Greater Pittsburgh ACLU* (1989) 492 US 573.

opposed. For the sceptical account to be credible, it must make a connection
between the methods of analysis used by the two courts and the constitutions
they oversee. To make the case that law is as subjective and culturally specific as
politics, the sceptic must show that the two different styles of reasoning are
themselves embedded in, and give expression to, the different constitutional
values and foundations of each country.

The cases certainly establish that it is the interpretivism of the Americans and
the pragmatism of the Germans that puts them on opposite sides of questions
such as school prayers and religious exemptions. What is missing is an argument
linking them to the constitutional cultures of their countries. Even to meet
Dworkin's standards, sceptics need to demonstrate that the interpretivism of
the Americans and the pragmatism of the Germans are the best expressions of
their countries' constitutional traditions, and that is not an easy thing to do.
There is nothing in the words of either constitution that speaks to the methods of
legal analysis their courts should employ. The sixteen words that make up the
religion clauses of the First Amendment say only that 'Congress shall make no
law respecting an establishment of religion or prohibiting the free exercise
thereof.' The German Basic Law speaks at much greater length about relations
between church and state. At the same time that it outlaws a state church, the
Basic Law guarantees, among other things, the undisturbed practice of religion,
religious instruction in public schools, conscientious objection to military service, Sunday as a day of rest, as well as freedom from discrimination on the basis
of one's personal beliefs. But, in the end, it too is silent on the analytical
framework the Court should use in addressing issues such as school prayers
and religious exemptions. Without anything in the texts to assist them, sceptics
will not find it easy to sustain the claim that interpretivism and pragmatism are
indigenous to American and German legal cultures. Neither court gives reasons
for their choosing the analytical frameworks they favour and, the fact is, it is very
hard to think of any aspect of interpretivism that serves America's constitutional
tradition as well as the pragmatic approach. Even in terms of its own foundational ideals of popular sovereignty and religious liberty, pragmatism does a
better job.

The interpretive approach has certainly not worked to the advantage of
religiously minded people in the United States. As we have seen, together *Lee
v. Weisman* and *Oregon v. Smith* allow governments to act in ways that radically
restrict the freedom of people to practise their religion. On the one hand,
religious minorities, like the members of the Native American Church, have
been told they have no cause to complain about laws that, it turns out, gratuitously interfere with the practice of their religion. On the other hand, the freedom
of spiritually minded people to express their beliefs publicly and collectively and
in all aspects of their lives has been radically restricted by the Court. In Antonin
Scalia's evocative turn of phrase, the Court treats religion as 'some purely
personal avocation that can be indulged entirely in secret, like pornography, in

the privacy of one's room'.[40] As a practical matter, two hundred years after its entrenchment, the First Amendment really only guarantees Americans that they will not be subject to rules and regulations that deliberately burden or discriminate against them because of their religious beliefs.[41]

In *Oregon* v. *Smith*, the Court adopted the weakest possible definition of state neutrality. For a majority of the judges, the reference in the First Amendment to 'the free exercise' of religion guarantees protection only against laws that are enacted with the purpose of penalizing people on account of their religious beliefs. On this reading of the Free Exercise Clause, only state action that gives expression to some hostile and malevolent intent fails the test. Laws passed for the general welfare of the community can override any free exercise claim even when it can be shown that the law is more restrictive and burdensome on the affected religious activities than it needs to be. In *Oregon* v. *Smith*, even though the members of the Native American Church were able to show that the federal government and twenty-three states had provided exemptions in their drug laws, that allowed for the use of peyote in religious ceremonies, without any apparent adverse effect on the health and well-being of their communities, and that even in Oregon the law was never enforced, that was not enough to prove a violation of their First Amendment rights. Even though Oregon's law constituted a gratuitous and arbitrary restriction of their religious freedom, it was allowed to remain on the books.

Compounding its evisceration of the Free Exercise Clause, the Court's reading of the prohibition against 'an establishment of religion' has radically restricted the spaces in which people can organize their lives by their religious beliefs. For more than half a century, the First Amendment has been read to favour Jefferson's belief that the best way to guarantee religious liberty is to ensure the wall of separation between the church and the state is as 'high and impregnable' as it can be.[42] The prohibition against 'an establishment of religion' has been read by the Court to mean not only that governments cannot exert the slightest degree of coercion on their citizens to recognize or defer to any spiritual practice or belief but, in addition, they must also be very careful not to act in ways that could be seen as an endorsement by the state.[43] Any law that is enacted to support a religious interest or organization is at risk of being invalidated by the Court. The lesson of *Lee* v. *Weisman* is that even the most attenuated forms of pressure exerted by the state can flunk the test.

Together, the logic of *Lee* v. *Weisman* and *Oregon* v. *Smith* leaves religiously minded people and their communities isolated and exposed. Rather than

---

[40] *Lee* v. *Weisman*.

[41] See e.g. *Church of the Lukumi Babalu Aye Inc.* v. *City of Hialeah*; *McDaniel* v. *Platy* (1978) 435 US 618.

[42] *McCollum* v. *Board of Education* (1947) 333 US 203, 212; and see generally L. Tribe, *American Constitutional Law*, 2nd edn. (New York: Foundation Press, 1988), 14:7–11.

[43] *Lynch* v. *Donnelly*, *Allegheny County* v. *Greater Pittsburgh ACLU*.

providing a definition of state neutrality that fosters the expression of religious practices and ideas, the Court has read the First Amendment to shrink the space in which a person's religious beliefs can govern how they conduct their lives.[44] In the Court's mind, neutrality not only requires religious organizations to be banished from almost all public places and causes that are connected to the state, but also recognizes governments having a broad authority to interfere in how these religious communities organize their affairs in private and at the margins of society.

Just how little protection religious liberty gets from the constitution in the United States is brought into sharp focus by comparing what the Constitutional Court has done for religiously minded people in Germany. German students can say prayers publicly and collectively in the regular course of a school day so long as they are ecumenical and non-sectarian and entail no legal coercion to participate. As well, people who run afoul of the criminal law on account of their adherence to some religious belief cannot be punished if labelling them as criminals would represent 'an excessive social reaction' and deny their human dignity as 'responsible personalit[ies], developing freely within the social community'.

The German cases show that people enjoy a greater measure of religious freedom when courts apply a principle such as practical concordance to test the constitutional validity of whatever laws they are asked to review than when they do not. If the US Supreme Court had ever adopted such an approach, spiritually minded Americans would be unambiguously better off. Had Oregon's law been tested against this principle, it is difficult to imagine how it could have survived. The fact that Oregon never thought it was necessary to prosecute anyone for using peyote in their religious services and that the federal government and twenty-three states were able to provide an exemption in their drug laws to accommodate the religious use of peyote, without compromising the welfare of their communities, proves Oregon's law was excessive and so impossible to defend.

In *Lee* v. *Weisman*, none of the judges in the majority undertook a careful evaluation of the factual circumstances of either those who wanted to include a prayer in the graduation ceremonies, or those who were opposed, and religious liberty suffered as a consequence. Although all the judges recognized the significance of the prayer to its supporters, only Antonin Scalia tried to get a real fix on exactly how serious a burden Deborah Weisman had to bear in being forced to witness the invocation. Both Anthony Kennedy and David Souter (in his concurring opinion) said the ecumenical, non-sectarian nature of the prayer had no bearing on their decision. In his judgment, Kennedy simply assumed that the offensiveness of the prayer to such students as Deborah Weisman was equal to its

---

[44] Stephen L. Carter, *The Culture of Disbelief* (New York: Basic Books, 1993); Michael W. McConnell, 'God is Dead and We Have Killed Him: Freedom of Religion in the Post Modern Age' (1993) Brigham Young UL Rev. 163.

significance for the Rabbi who offered it and those who wanted to publicly acknowledge their recognition of divine authority.

Although there are not a lot of factual details reported in the case, what evidence is cited provides no support in equating the significance of the prayer to its supporters and the dissenters in this way. As Scalia pointed out, the only coercion the dissenting students were made to endure was being forced to be tolerant and civil, sensitive to their fellow students whose understanding of life differed from their own. They were forced to stand, coerced into abstaining from conduct that would disrupt the proceedings. In the context of an auditorium in which everyone would, as a practical matter, show the same measure of respect, the possibility of suffering the additional harm of alienation or discrimination, let alone conversion, was virtually non-existent. Moreover if, as the facts suggested, Deborah Weisman did not object to the reference to a Supreme Being in the Pledge of Allegiance that immediately preceded the prayer, then whatever harm she suffered from being caught up in the event was virtually nil. Her own tolerance of the Pledge of Allegiance would provide the best evidence of how little she was affected by the two fleeting, ecumenical references to God. Her own behaviour puts the lie to Kennedy's equating the significance of the graduation prayers in the lives of the dissenting students and those who regarded them as 'an essential and profound recognition of divine authority'.

If Deborah Weisman's toleration of the reference to God in the Pledge of Allegiance was a fair measure of how deeply her objection to the prayer was felt, religious freedom was not well served by the Court's ruling. School authorities were instructed not to allow one group of students to engage in an activity that was, for them, of profound religious significance in order to spare others a measure of embarrassment and offence which, on the facts of the case, could only be characterized as marginal at most. Moreover, as students of American constitutional law will know, *Lee* v. *Weisman* is not an exceptional case. Among those who study the Court's First Amendment jurisprudence there is a widespread feeling that, for the most part, the judges have trivialized the idea of religion. In Stephen Carter's poignant turn of phrase, the Court has treated religion 'like a hobby'.[45] For some it is a jurisprudence that is marked by hostility and even bigotry.[46]

The failure of the interpretative approach to provide as much protection for religious liberty as a more pragmatic, fact-specific analysis can guarantee is compounded by the very undemocratic character of its methodology and its rules. The way it has been practised by the Americans, interpretivism suffers a double disadvantage. It imposes very serious constraints on the scope of democratic politics without securing the same measure of religious freedom that courts which address issues of church/state relations pragmatically have been able to provide.

[45] Stephen L. Carter, *The Culture of Disbelief* (New York: Basic Books, 1993).
[46] Michael M. Connell, 'Religious Freedom at a Crossroads' (1992) 59 U. Chic. L Rev. 115.

Undoubtedly the single most sweeping restriction that the interpretative method has imposed on the sovereignty of the American people to legislate their priorities and preferences into law is the rule (in the Establishment Clause) that makes practically all state support of religious institutions and events unconstitutional. All religious objectives, such as those that motivated the graduation prayer, are absolutely proscribed. No matter how fundamental a community's spiritual beliefs are to its own self-understanding, it is an inviolate rule that they can play no part in the enactment of any law. The whole of their morality that is religiously inspired is put beyond the power of the people in defining the public character of the communities in which they live.

In its focus on which purposes governments can lawfully pursue, the American rule on school prayers (and religious exemptions) contrasts sharply with Germany's pragmatic approach where more attention is paid to the means by which politicians and their officials put the policies that got them elected into law. In its explicit recognition of religious education being part of the normal curriculum in state schools, Germany's Basic Law rejects the idea that there is something intrinsically wrong with church and state sharing public space. In Germany, the question is not whether the state can show its support for religiously minded people and their institutions and ideas but how: what means are used and with what effects. The basic idea is that it is perfectly legitimate for governments and churches to establish co-operative relationships so long as it is done in a way that shows equal respect for all religions as well as for those who believe the jurisdiction of church and state extend to different spheres of authority and should be kept separate and apart.[47]

Compared to the German rule, the American definition of state neutrality cuts deeply into the lawmaking powers of the people. In fact, the incompatibility between interpretivism and the sovereignty of the people extends much further than the rule that puts virtually all support for anything religious beyond the powers of the state. The most serious threat interpretivism poses for democratic forms of government actually lies in the method of reasoning on which it is based. Because each judge is able to pick and choose the dictionaries and sources of meaning from which their analysis proceeds, their personal philosophy concerning church/state relations, much more than the imperatives of the constitution, determines which conception of neutrality will prevail in any case. Judges such as Rehnquist, Scalia, Thomas, and Bork, whose political philosophy is populist and conservative, are naturally inclined to look to historical sources and original understandings, whereas more progressive judges such as Brennan and Marshall look to underlying values and the Court's own earlier decisions that allow them to give larger and more liberal readings to the text.

Interpretivism sanctions a process of reasoning that puts each judge at the centre of the case and gives him or her unfettered discretion to chose which

---

[47] The same idea has been endorsed by India's Supreme Court in upholding the right of the state to introduce instruction in religious philosophy in its schools, see *Aruna Roy v. Union of India*, AIR 2002 SC 3176.

approach to take. Competing sources of meaning are considered equally legitimate and no one strategy has priority or takes precedence over the others.[48] Often, as in *Lee* v. *Weisman*, two conflicting techniques that lead to opposite results are invoked simultaneously. The possibility that nine judges will find more than one principle of neutrality buried beneath the words of the text becomes a near certainty when the sources themselves, like history and precedent, are fraught with ambiguity and uncertainty. In *Lee* v. *Weisman*, it will be recalled, the Court was divided not only on whether a historical or doctrinal analysis should be applied in the case, but also on what each of those sources said.

History could not answer the question of whether school prayers violated the First Amendment because there was no hard evidence that established a common understanding of the issue. Although prayers and invocations of faith were part of political life in the United States in the late eighteenth century, it is impossible to know what they thought of such activities in public schools because in those days few people considered education to be a responsibility of the state.[49] Precedent was indeterminate because it too was open to a number of equally plausible interpretations. The five judges in the majority wrote three different opinions on the meaning of the Court's prior decisions and Scalia offered a fourth that was just as credible.

The division of opinion on the Court in *Oregon* v. *Smith* shows very clearly that one very serious problem with precedents is that they can be read at very different levels of generality. No one formulation—in this case, of how broadly the principle of religious exemptions should be extended—dominates the alternatives. It is impossible to say that either the majority, or those who ended up writing in dissent, read the relevant cases in a way that was mistaken or wrong. Neither the majority, who said the Court had never insisted in any of its prior rulings that a religious exemption must be included in a criminal statute, nor the minority, who declared no precedent had ever drawn a distinction between laws that confer benefits and those that punish conduct, could be contradicted in their description of the Court's past decisions. As a matter of interpretation both were accurate statements of what the Court had and had not done in its previous consideration of the issue. All the doctrinal analysis that dominates both opinions creates a veneer of legality and an impression of legitimacy but it cannot cover up the fact that the split on the Court was all about politics and had nothing to do with the law.

As a practical matter, interpretivism makes it easy for judges to rely on their own political and moral ideas in deciding whether any law or initiative proposed by the state is constitutional or not. It allows each judge to pick and choose

---

[48] See Philip Bobbitt, *Constitutional Fate: Theory of the Constitution* (New York: Oxford University Press, 1982); *Constitutional Interpretation* (Oxford: Blackwell, 1991); Richard Fallon, 'A Constructivist Coherence Theory of Constitutional Interpretation' (1987) 100 Harv. L Rev. 1189.

[49] See *Wallace* v. *Jaffree* (1985) 472 US 3880: 'the simple truth is that free public education was virtually non-existent in the late 18th century' (O'Connor); see also Rehnquist's dissenting opinion challenging the 'wall of separation' understanding of the Establishment Clause.

which interpretative strategy to employ and, as we have seen, it also encourages playing fast and loose with the facts. In *Lee* v. *Weisman*, the majority was able to claim the significance of the prayer was roughly equal for the two groups of students by ignoring the factual details of the prayer and ceremony that strongly suggested otherwise. In *Oregon* v. *Smith*, all the judges expressed the opinion that courts should never even try to figure out how important a particular interest or activity that the law proscribes is to a religion and its adherents in deciding whether what a state has done is constitutional or not.

In both cases, the Court defended its decision by hypothesizing potentially calamitous consequences that might transpire if it ruled the other way. In *Oregon* v. *Smith*, Scalia argued that the Court 'would be courting anarchy' if it ruled in favour of Smith's claim for a religious exemption because it 'would open the prospect of constitutionally required religious exemptions from civic obligations of almost every conceivable kind'. In *Lee* v. *Weisman*, Anthony Kennedy invoked the 'lesson of history' that any breach in the wall that separates church and state 'may end in a policy to indoctrinate and coerce'. Harry Blackmun warned that the mixing of government and religion could be a threat to both. However, neither judgment refers to any hard evidence that would suggest such hypothetical horribles were even remote possibilities. Scalia never explained how the twenty-three states and areas under federal jurisdiction were able to avoid collapsing into anarchy and neither Kennedy nor Blackmun made any mention of the experience of countries such as Germany that have allowed the spheres of church and state to overlap without suffering the calamities they prophesy.

Interpretivism then, at least as it has been practised by the Americans, imposes virtually no constraints—no disciplining rules—on the discretion of judges to rely on their own political/moral theories to solve the hard, practical problems of church/state relations, such as school prayers and religious exemptions, that come before the courts. Each judge is able to develop the law to suit his or her own purpose. This profoundly undemocratic characteristic of the interpretative approach, together with its failure to protect religious liberty in a meaningful way, makes it an entirely unsatisfactory method of judicial review. Compared to reasoning pragmatically, both in terms of respecting the sovereignty of the people and protecting basic human rights, it is decidedly second best.

The fact that the American understanding of judicial review does not compare favourably with alternative approaches will come as a surprise to many people. In legal circles, no less than in music halls, 'Made in America' and 'Born in USA' still have a glamour all their own. Whatever their flaws, decisions of the US Supreme Court are often referred to by judges in other countries as a way of enhancing the credibility of their own opinions.[50] From a global perspective, it would be fair to say interpretative methods of analysis are as popular with the

---

[50] See e.g. Aharon Barak, 'A Judge on Judging: The Role of a Supreme Court in a Democracy' (2002) 116 Harv. L Rev. 19 ('United States Supreme Court decisions . . . have always been, to me and many other judges in modern democracies, shining examples of constitutional thought and constitutional action.')

judges in other parts of the world as the pragmatic, fact-specific evaluations of the Germans.

It is the case, in fact, that the jurisprudence that has been written on the issue of religious freedom in other parts of the world is largely a mirror image of the German and American. When one looks beyond the rulings from Washington and Karlsruhe, one finds judges thinking along one or both of these lines no matter where they sit. Interpretivism and pragmatism dominate the analysis of religious rights wherever they arise. Sometimes judges openly debate the strengths and weaknesses of each.[51] In some cases, the answer is clear-cut and it does not matter which method is used. For example, regardless of whether an interpretative or pragmatic strategy is employed, judges are unanimous that states can force children to undergo blood transfusions against their will and the wishes of their parents even when it is deeply offensive to their religious beliefs.[52] More often than not, however, it is of critical importance which approach is followed. Time and again, when judges differ on whether a semantic or pragmatic analysis is the best way to resolve a question of religious liberty, the cases show that everyone's interests are better served when the courts base their decisions on a close and careful evaluation of the facts than when they spend most of their energy trying to divine answers from the words of the text. There is, it turns out, no getting around the hard jurisprudential fact that interpretivists have never been able to match the results that pragmatists have been able to achieve anywhere in the world. Familiarity with the comparative jurisprudence dispels any doubt about that.

4. RELIGIOUS LIBERTY ON THE SABBATH

An illuminating set of cases that highlight the comparative advantages of the pragmatic approach involve challenges to sabbatarian laws that restrict ordinary, everyday activities—such as shopping or driving—on days that for some are reserved for reflection and prayer. The sabbatarian cases provide an especially interesting jurisprudence to study because they raise the same two issues that were at the centre of the American and German decisions we have been considering. On the one hand, legislative initiatives that seek to protect the sabbath and other religious days (such as those permitting prayers to be said in state schools) force consideration of the extent to which states can use their powers to facilitate the expression of religious beliefs in their communities. At the same time, they also pose the problem of granting exemptions to laws of general application, in these cases to members of minority religious faiths whose most important days of prayer and reflection fall on different days of the week.

[51] See e.g. *B. (R.) v. Children's Aid Society of Metropolitan Toronto* (1995) 122 DLR (4th) 1; *Re J. (An Infant): B and B v. Director Social Welfare* [1996] 2 NZLR 134.

[52] *B. (R.) v. Children's Aid Society*; *Re J. (An Infant)*; *Jehovah's Witnesses v. King County Hospital* (1967) 390 US 598.

Studying cases that evaluate the legitimacy of sabbatarian laws also provides an introduction to a very diverse and interesting group of jurists. Laws of this kind have been tested all over the world, in Canada, Ireland, Israel, Hungary, and South Africa as well as in the United States. To varying degrees, the Supreme Courts in the first three countries have used a pragmatic approach to test the legitimacy of such laws and, as a result, they have been able to provide more protection for religious liberty in their countries than the courts in the United States and South Africa where interpretative methods have been dominant. Indeed, by using standards such as the German principle of practical concordance that try to maximize all the interests at stake in a case, Canadian, Irish, and Israeli jurists have been able to come to the defence of religious minorities in their communities without restricting the sovereignty of the people to express its collective identity in the laws they enact to any significant degree.

The judgment of Aharon Barak, the President of Israel's Supreme Court, in *Lior Horev* v. *Minister of Communication/Transportation*,[53] provides an especially powerful image of the great jurist, Solomon-like, reasoning pragmatically to resolve a highly charged, politically volatile issue of church/state relations in a way that is equally sensitive to both. At issue was a government regulation that would have closed a major artery running through the heart of Jerusalem—Bar Ilan Street—during the hours of prayer on the Jewish sabbath. The street cut across a number of orthodox neighbourhoods and the Government's hope was that a partial closing would be accepted as a compromise between the orthodox community who argued for a complete ban on all traffic for the duration of the sabbath and secular Israelis who insisted their mobility rights guaranteed them unimpeded access to the street seven days a week, twenty-four hours a day. The dispute was a 'deep and bitter' one that divided the country and even spilled over into violence on the street. Neither side was satisfied with the Government's solution and the issue was referred to the seven judges who sat on Israel's Supreme Court.

Barak was acutely aware of the political dimension of the dispute, but he insisted the Court could not concern itself with the general state of relations between the orthodox and secular communities. The issue in law was the authority of the relevant state official to invoke the force of the Israeli state to bring about a partial closing of Bar Ilan Street. For Barak, the case was about reconciling the mobility rights of secular Israelis with the religious way of life of orthodox Jews on Bar Ilan Street, 'plain and simple'. In contrast with the Americans, Barak refused to be drawn into a hypothetical discussion about how the Court's ruling in this case might affect future decisions by the Government to close other roads. He disagreed with three of his colleagues who voted to strike down the regulation because they thought it would act as a precedent for other closings. He thought 'slippery-slope' arguments of this kind were 'danger-

---

[53] Supreme Court of Israel, April 1997, translated and reproduced in part in P. Gewirtz (ed.), *Global Constitutionalism: Religion* (New Haven: Yale Law School, 1997).

ous' because they were based on fears and speculation that had no basis in fact.[54] As a pragmatist, he took the view that each road closing had to be judged on its own set of facts. The way he understands constitutional law, the legality of one road closing does not logically entail the closing of any others and, by a bare 4 : 3 majority, his views carried the day.

Barak began his judgment by looking at Israeli's Basic Law on Human Dignity and Freedom to identify principles and a framework of analysis that would allow him to evaluate the conflicting claims of the two communities over the use of Bar Ilan Street in a way that would be fair and even-handed to both. He read its declaration that Israel was a 'democratic state' to mean that governments could pass laws for the purpose of protecting the religious sentiments of their people so long as they did not entail any religious coercion and they respected a basic principle of proportionality or 'toleration'. 'Toleration', he wrote, 'is a basic value in every democratic conception. . . . It is crucial to a democracy based on pluralism.' It was this principle, rather than anything actually written in the Basic Law, that Barak used to evaluate the closing of Bar Ilan Street. First, he endorsed the idea of a partial closing. Stopping traffic during the hours of prayer was much more in keeping with the principle of toleration than either of the all-or-nothing (open or closed for the entire day) positions put forward by the parties. During those periods of the day when prayers were being said Barak accepted the claim of the orthodox community that the harm they would suffer from an unrestricted flow of traffic would be 'harsh and bitter'. It would, he said, constitute 'a powerful contradiction to the peace and serenity' the orthodox communities sought for their neighbourhoods to allow cars and other vehicles to drive past their places of worship when they were conducting their religious services. By comparison, the inconvenience most Israelis would suffer from being denied access to the street during such times would be trivial. Commuters who used the street as a thoroughfare would be obliged to take an alternative route which, Barak calculated, would add an additional two minutes to their trip. At least during the times when prayers were being said, the proportionalities—in the significance of the closing for the two communities—were clear.

Barak's ruling that a partial closing of the street was consistent with the Basic Law on Human Dignity and Freedom works to the clear advantage of religious freedom. It recognizes the right of the state to pass laws that protect and support religious communities and their way of life even to the point of overriding what the Court regarded as important human rights of others. It did not, however, ignore the interests of secular Israelis. Toleration required orthodox Jews to show the same measure of respect for the life choices of their secular countrymen that the partial closing guaranteed for them. Thus, according to Barak, not only did motorists have the right to use the street when prayers were not being said, but those who lived in the orthodox communities had a right to drive to their

---

[54] On the shaky empirical foundations of slippery-slope arguments generally, see F. Schauer, 'Slippery Slopes' (1985) 99 Harv. L Rev. 361.

homes at any time of the day. Because even a partial closing would constitute more significant interference in the lives of secular residents (and especially those who were handicapped in some way), than for those for whom the street was simply a preferred route of travel, Barak instructed the Government to consider ways (such as permits) that would exempt them from the ban.

Barak's judgment provides a very clear example of how a principle of proportionality ('toleration') tests the aims and objectives governments pursue when they pass laws—such as the traffic regulation in Jerusalem—in a way that allows religious liberty and popular sovereignty to flourish simultaneously. The Israeli state can pass laws for the purpose of protecting the spiritual freedom of religiously minded people so long as it shows an equal respect for those whose lives they burden the most. Except for its proscription of laws that are deliberately aimed at restricting people's freedom to live their lives by their religious beliefs, proportionality leaves it to politics and the elected branches of government to decide what values and goals their communities will collectively embrace.

Barak's judgment shows, in a concrete case, what a principle of proportionality requires of sabbatarian laws in both the objectives they pursue and the methods they employ to realize their ambitions. Two other judgments, one rendered by the Supreme Court of Ireland, in *Quinn's Supermarket,*[55] the other by Canada's highest court, in *Edwards Books,*[56] provide additional examples of the way the principle constrains the policy choices governments can make when they are drafting regulations that will organize life on the sabbath and turning them into law. In both cases, the critical question was whether laws that restrict shopping on certain hours or days of the week, have to make exceptions for people whose religion demands they close their shops at times when everyone else is open for business. Both courts said they did, but the Canadians were badly split on the issue and almost half the judges would have upheld the law whether it contained an exemption or not.

In Ireland, no one doubted that some accommodation for retailers of kosher meat, who remained closed during normal trading hours on Saturdays, was required. Everyone was agreed that, for as long as its dietary rules remained 'a strict commandment in the code of Jewish law', some exemption, allowing them to remain open after hours, was a must. Without some relief, the law would interfere with the freedom of the Jewish community to practise its religion by making it impossible to purchase kosher meat any time on Saturday or Sunday without violating either the rules of their religion or the laws of the state. None of the judges thought complaints by non-Jewish butchers against allowing kosher shops to open after regular hours on Saturday evening could be sustained. To the contrary, they said such an exemption promoted equality between the two groups by relieving the Jewish retailers of the extra burden that the law's restriction on business hours imposed on them.

[55] *Quinn's Supermarket* v. *Attorney General* [1972] IR 1.
[56] *Edwards Books & Art* v. *The Queen* (1986) 35 DLR (4th) 1.

The only difference among the judges was how extensive the exemption should be. Four of the five judges who sat on the case thought the exemption that was contained in the law—which allowed Jewish butchers to remain open extra hours every day of the week—was broader than it needed to be. They said that if the purpose of the law was to alleviate the burden it (indirectly) imposed on the religious freedom of the Jewish community, a dispensation that was limited to Saturday evening would do the trick. On their view of the facts, there was no evidence to suggest 'the free practice of the Jewish religion' would be hampered in any way by requiring kosher shops to keep the same trading hours as everyone else every other day of the week.

The ruling by Ireland's Supreme Court that sabbatarian laws must make appropriate exemptions for those for whom their impact is especially severe illustrates again how judges who reason pragmatically test both the means and the ends of the laws they are asked to review. Like their counterparts in Germany and Israel, the Irish judges simply required their government to ensure everyone's interests were accommodated as best it could. Granting religious minorities carefully tailored exemptions from laws that restrict their activities on days that have no religious significance for them was an easy case. Other courts, however, including the American and Canadian Supreme Courts, have not found it so straightforward. The Americans in fact have taken the position that sabbatarian laws in the United States do not have to contain any exemptions for people whose religion requires them to observe a day of rest on some other day of the week.[57] In *Edwards Books*, the Canadians openly debated and ultimately rejected the position of the Americans, but the Court was badly split and almost half the judges who sat on the case would have upheld the Government of Ontario's *Retail Business Holidays Act* whether it contained an exemption or not.

In fact, the judges who have sat on Canada's highest court have shown themselves to be quite ambivalent about whether a principle of proportionality should be used to test the constitutionality of the country's Sunday shopping laws and, if so, how rigorously it should be enforced. In *R. v. Big M Drug Mart Ltd.*,[58] in which it reviewed the Federal Government's *Lord's Day Act*, the Court showed a strong preference for the American approach of definitional solutions and the categorical rule against states showing any encouragement or support for religion. In striking down the law because its objectives were overtly religious, the Court never even entertained the idea that laws that are passed for religious purposes might be constitutional if they can meet a proportionality test. Moreover, in its subsequent review of Ontario's *Retail Business Holidays Act*, that was passed for the purpose of providing retail workers with a common day of rest and recreation with their families, almost no one on the Court was inclined to follow the example of the Irish and subject the particular exemption

[57] *Braunfeld v. Brown* (1961) 366 US 599; *McGowan v. Maryland* (1961) 366 US 420.
[58] *R. v. Big M Drug Mart* (1985) 18 DLR (4th) 321.

that was chosen by the Government to a strict and searching review. Except for one judge—Bertha Wilson—everyone on the Court thought judges should not substitute their opinions for those of the legislators as to where the line should be drawn. They said that to insist that Sunday shopping laws be drafted to minimize the burdens they impose on people who celebrate their sabbath on some other day of the week was an 'excessively high standard' for governments to have to meet.

In the end, however, by a slim 4 : 3 majority, the Court decided not to go all the way with the Americans and it held that, even though judges should generally defer to the legislature's policy choices in its design of such laws, some minimum exemption for religious minorities who were especially burdened by restrictions on Sunday shopping was required. They pointed out that if the purpose of the law was to ensure retail workers had time with their families, it would be punitive, if not perverse, to force family-run businesses, that operated without any outside help and that remained closed on some other day of the week, to stay shut on Sundays as well. No purpose of the law would be served by such an insensitive, heavy-handed approach. The failure to provide an exemption for such enterprises would interfere with their religious liberty in ways that were gratuitous and unnecessary. The only way retailers who closed on some other day of the week could enjoy a level playing field with their competitors would be to defy the laws of their religious faith and remain open on the day that was supposed to be set aside for reflection and prayer.

The difference between the Canadian and American Supreme Courts on the issue of religious exemptions in sabbatarian laws is not huge. There is more in common in how the two courts approach questions of church/state relations than there are values and ideas that set them apart. Still, in insisting on the necessity of some exemption in sabbatarian laws of this kind, the Canadians were able to guarantee a measure of protection for religious liberty that in the United States is still vulnerable to the vagaries and vicissitudes of politics. The comparison between the two courts shows that even when it is embraced only tentatively and cautiously, pragmatism is able to remedy the most blatant forms of arbitrary treatment by a state in a way that a semantic and deferential analysis of the issues does not.

Canadian judges are not alone in falling under the influence of the Americans when it comes to decide whether a piece of sabbatarian legislation is constitutional or not. The South Africans also relied heavily on the jurisprudence of the US Supreme Court in the case of *Lawrence, Negal and Solberg v. The State*[59] when they were asked to review the validity of a liquor law that restricted the retail sale of beer and wine on Sundays, Good Friday, and Christmas Day. Indeed, the interpretative approach of the Americans proved to be decisive in the South African Constitutional Court's disposition of the case. All nine judges who heard the case recognized that, in limiting the restriction on the sale of beer

[59] *Lawrence, Negal and Solberg v. The State* [1997] 4 SALR 1176.

and wine to days that are religiously significant only to Christians, adherents of other religions could reasonably feel that the state was treating their beliefs as second class. Four of the nine, however, said there was nothing they could do. Led by Arthur Chaskalson, the President of the Court, these four took an avowedly interpretative approach. They read Article 14 of the South African Constitution the same way Anthony Kennedy understood the establishment clause in *Lee* v. *Weisman*, as protecting people's religious beliefs only against intentionally coercive acts of the state. Thus, even though they recognized its symbolic discrimination, because the law did not force anyone to embrace or forgo any religious belief, they refused to intervene.

Chaskalson's definition of Article 14 was ultimately rejected by a majority of his colleagues, but his views still carried the day because two other judges (Albie Sachs and Yvonne Mokgoro), who thought the constitution protected people against laws that were discriminatory as well as those that were overtly coercive, were also of the view that the state's objectives in reducing opportunities for alcohol abuse were so important to the welfare of the country that whatever discriminatory messages were latent in the law would just have to be endured. They thought the case came down to weighing the 'symbolic effect of religious favouritism . . . against the very palpable and quite terrible consequences of alcohol abuse'. Adopting the perspective of the 'reasonable South African . . . who is neither hypersensitive nor overly insensitive' to the beliefs of non-Christians, Sachs and Mokgoro had no doubt that, in a contest of this kind, 'the state's interest in encouraging temperance on these particular days [was] a powerful and legitimate one' that ought to prevail.

Kate O'Regan disagreed with both Chaskalson and Sachs and she wrote a dissenting opinion for herself and two of her colleagues. O'Regan took a very close look at the facts of the case and came to the conclusion that singling out Christian holy days for special treatment was inequitable and unfair. For O'Regan, the decisive fact in the case was the glaring inconsistency in the way the Government pursued its objectives. Although she was prepared to accept that the purpose of the law—regulating alcohol consumption—was a valid one, she would not 'weigh [it] heavily for the purposes of proportionality' because the Government made no effort to extend the law to Saturdays or other secular holidays when the risks of alcohol abuse were just as high. Even though she recognized the infringement of religious liberty that was effected by the law was not 'severe or egregious', the Government's behaviour was arbitrary and discriminatory none the less.

The fact that no serious issue of religious freedom was at stake in *Lawrence, Negal & Solberg* v. *The State* does not affect its significance jurisprudentially. The division of opinion within the South African Court is actually a replay of everything we have seen so far. The contrast between the judgments of O'Regan and Chaskalson proves, once again, that judges can guarantee a greater measure of neutrality in relations between church and state when they organize their analysis around the principle of proportionality and play close attention to the facts of a case than when they try to solve such issues with semantic solutions, categorical injunctions and absolute, inviolate rules. Even if the discriminatory character of the liquor law were purely symbolic, O'Regan was able to deal with it in a way that, on his interpretative understanding of judicial review, Chaskalson was powerless to redress.

When O'Regan's judgment is read alongside Albie Sachs's concurring opinion, it also shows how analyses that are focused on the facts of a case have an empirical integrity that is lacking when judges base their opinions on their own sense of priorities. The difference in their two judgments lies in their assessment of the government's interest in minimizing the occasions on which people might be inclined to drink excessively. Where Sachs thought the consequences of alcohol abuse were 'grave' and could amount to a 'serious menace', O'Regan argued that the Government's own action in failing to extend the restriction on retail sales to Saturdays and other secular holidays, demonstrated that the state did not regard the public interest in controlling drinking on such occasions to be so significant. O'Regan's judgment can claim to be based on an objective assessment of the facts of the case in a way that Sachs's cannot. Where she insisted the state must be held to its own evaluation of its interests, Sachs would substitute his personal concerns about drinking on holidays and weekends for the Government's very tolerant, almost cavalier attitude towards people who drink too much.

The debate between Chaskalson, O'Regan, and Sachs shows judges in South Africa are just as divided on how one should analyse questions of church/state relations as their counterparts in Canada and the United States.[60] Indeed, one can find similar divisions of opinion within almost every court that has ever been asked to protect someone's religious liberty from what they allege is arbitrary and discriminatory treatment by the state. As one moves beyond cases dealing with laws that limit people's activities on the sabbath, it is common to find judges on the same court drawing the line between church and state in different places essentially because of the opposing methodologies and processes of reasoning they employ. Some courts show a tendency to favour one approach, other courts the other, but in almost all cases, there is a vocal minority expressing its dissent. It is, in fact, quite exceptional to find decisions like those of the German Constitutional Court, in which a single opinion is able to attract the unqualified support of everyone on the Bench.

5. RELIGIOUS LIBERTY AND STATE MORALITY

The conflicting opinions that exist within and between courts as to the best method of resolving questions about religious freedom cut across a wide range of

---

[60] On other issues, including the right of religious minorities to be exempted from laws that made important parts of their religious faith—such as the use of cannabis or corporal punishment—a crime,

issues and provide more hard data that lends itself to comparative analysis. The rights of people to proselytize, for example,[61] or refuse medical treatment for themselves and their families,[62] or claim public support for religious schools that have been accredited by the state,[63] have all been tested in a number of courts and judges have displayed the same diversity of opinion on these issues as they have to laws that restrict people's liberty on the sabbath. On each of these questions, judges have started a global conversation about the scope and limits of religious freedom with colleagues on their own courts and beyond. Within this large and growing body of caselaw, the European Court of Human Rights and the Supreme Court of Japan have each handed down rulings, on the question of when people can legitimately complain about governments that support or promote particular moral or religious points of view, that are especially revealing.

The European Court of Human Rights and the Supreme Court of Japan are both mature, well-established courts. Each has exercised the powers of judicial review for almost half a century. However, even though both of them have written several opinions that have addressed this issue, neither has been able to get everyone to agree on what the right answer is or even how best to proceed. Although the judges on the European Court of Human Rights have shown a preference for the interpretative approach and definitional solutions of the Americans, in each case there is always someone who dissents.[64] In Japan,

the judges in South Africa have been much more sympathetic to the pragmatic approach. See *Prince* v. *President Cape Law Society* [2002] 2 SA 794; *Christian Education South Africa* v. *Minister of Education* [2000] 4 SA 757; (2000) 9 BHRC 53.

[61] *Cantwell* v. *Connecticut* (1940) 310 US 296; *Murdock* v. *Pennsylvania* (1943) 319 US 105; *Prince* v. *Massachusetts* (1943) 321 US 158; *Heffron* v. *Iskon* (1981) 452 US 640; *Watchtower Bible and Tract Society* v. *Village of Stratton* (2002) 536 US 150; *Rev. Staninslaus* v. *State* (Madhya Pradesh) AIR 1977 SC 908; *Chan Hiang Leng Colin et al.* v. *Minister for Information* (1997) 2 BHRC 129; *Kokkinakis* v. *Greece* (1993) 17 EHRR 397; *Young* v. *Young* (1993) 108 DLR (4th) 193; *Roy Murphy* v. *Independent Radio and Television Commission* [1998] 2 ILRM 360 (Ireland). For an illuminating treatment of the issue in post-communist Russia, see Harold J. Berman, 'Freedom of Religion in Russia' (1998) 12 Emory Int. L Rev. 313.

[62] *B. (R.)* v. *Children's Aid Society*; *Re. J. (An Infant)*; *Jehovah's Witnesses* v. *King County Hospital*; *Hoffman* v. *Austria* (1993) 17 EHRR 292; *Nishida* v. *Japan* (1963) 17 Keisha 4 p. 303, translated and reproduced in part in L. Beer and H. Itoh, *The Constitutional Caselaw of Japan 1961–70* (Seattle: University of Washington Press, 1978).

[63] *Agostini* v. *Felton* (1997) 521 US 203; *A. G. (Victoria) Ex rel. Black* v. *CTH* (1981) 55 ALJR 154; In *Re Gauteng School Education Bill* (1996) 3 SA 165; *Campaign to Separate Church and State* v. *Minister of Education* [1998] 3 IR 321; (1998) 2 ILRM 81; *Resettlement of Church Property (Hungary)* [1994] 1 EERR 57; *Interdenominational School* (1975) 41 BverfGE 29, translated and reproduced in part in Kommers, *Constitutional Jurisprudence of Germany*; *Adler* v. *Ontario* (1996) 140 DLR (4th) 385; *St. Stephen's College* v. *University of New Delhi* AIR 1992 SC 1630; (1991) Supp. 3 SCR 121.

[64] As well, on other issues, including the obligation of the state to accommodate people's religious practices and beliefs, the Court has been more sympathetic to the pragmatic approach and the principle of proportionality plays a more prominent role in its analysis. In *Thlimmenos* v. *Greece* [2000] 31 EHHR 411 for example, the Court's Grand Chamber of seventeen judges unanimously concluded, like Germany's Constitutional Court, that a state cannot treat a person who commits a crime out of a deep religious conviction as an ordinary felon. See also *Jewish Liturgical Ass'n* v. *France* [2000] 9 BHRC 27; *Kokkinakis* v. *Greece*.

both the semantic and pragmatic modes of reasoning have their supporters among the judges and each has played an important part in the Court's thinking on the extent to which the state could support events such as a Shinto ground-breaking ceremony, or the enshrinement of a serviceman, that have a clear religious dimension to them.

Once again, the opposing inclinations within these two courts confirms that people are better protected from conformism and orthodoxy when judges reason pragmatically, and pay close attention to the facts of a case, than when they concentrate on the words of the text and impose solutions as matters of definition. They show that judges who reason pragmatically get the better of the debate even when their opinions fail to carry the day. Indeed, even when the two approaches come to the same conclusion, pragmatic judges are able to offer an explanation that shows religiously minded people more respect than the reasons that are given by their colleagues who favour interpretative justifications for the decisions they make.

The arbitrariness and injustice of the interpretative approach is especially evident in the way the European Court of Human Rights spoke to parents in Denmark and Greece who objected to their children having to take part in activities and be exposed to ideas that were antithetical to their religious beliefs. In the first case, *Kjeldsen, Busk and Madsen* v. *Denmark*,[65] objection was taken to a compulsory course in sex education, and in the second, *Valsamis* v. *Greece*,[66] to a regulation that required all students to take part in a national parade, honouring the country's past, that included the military. In both cases, the Court's response was based entirely on the way it read the relevant articles and protocols of the European Convention of Human Rights. In *Kjeldsen*, and again in *Valsamis*, the Court interpreted the requirement in Article 2 of Protocol 1—that states must respect the rights of parents to ensure the education of their children conforms to their own 'religious and philosophical convictions'—to mean only that governments are forbidden from trying to 'indoctrinate' people. 'That', said the Court, 'is the limit that must not be exceeded.' The way it understood the Convention, once a member state points to a non-indoctrinating purpose that is served by the law, that is the end of the case. Because there was no evidence that the objective of either the Danish or Greek Governments was to indoctrinate students about sexual practices or with patriotic fervour, both cases were thrown out of court. Like the conservative wing of the US Supreme Court, the European Court of Human Right's conception of neutrality was extremely deferential and partial to the state.

Not all the judges who sat on these cases, however, were averse to holding the governments involved to a more demanding standard. Like their counterparts in Karlsruhe, Dublin, and Jerusalem, these judges were interested not only in the

---

[65] *Kjeldsen, Busk and Madsen* v. *Denmark* (1976) 1 EHRR 711. See also the decision of the German Constitutional Court in *Sex Education Case* (1977) translated and reproduced in part in Kommers, *Constitutional Jurisprudence of Germany*, 500.

[66] *Valsamis* v. *Greece* (1996) 24 EHRR 294.

ends of the laws they were asked to review but in their methods and effects as well. In *Kjeldsen*, Judge Verdross disputed the narrow reading the majority gave to the Convention. He said the regulation did violate the complainants' right to their religious liberty because, unlike their children, students who attended private schools were only required to study the biology of sex and were excused from having to learn about its psychological and sociological dimensions. Like O'Regan in *Solberg*, Verdross held the state to its own standards and ruled that if the Government could carve out an exemption for religiously minded students in private schools without compromising its educational goals, there was no reason for it not to show the same measure of respect for students in the public system.

In *Valsamis*, two members of the Court, Justices Vilhjalmsson and Jambrek, took issue with the majority's finding that there was nothing in the purposes or arrangements of the parade that could offend the Valsamis family's pacifist convictions and religious beliefs. They said the Court had a duty to accept the Valsamis's perception of the parade unless it could be shown to be 'unfounded and unreasonable'.[67] They rejected the argument that the state could justify its position on the basis of its authority to educate its citizens about the collective memory and historical accomplishments of their country because they said the school authorities could have achieved these objectives within the regular curriculum and in a way that would not have offended the Valsamis's religious beliefs.

In both cases, religious liberty was sacrificed and the court's neutrality compromised because most of the judges paid no attention to, and in *Valsamis* actually distorted, the facts. In *Valsamis*, the Court took the unprecedented step of not accepting the factual basis of Victoria Valsamis's claim that, as a Jehovah's Witness, participation in the parade would offend her pacifist beliefs. Without any suggestion that her beliefs were 'unfounded and unreasonable', it simply substituted its own perception of the significance of the parade and disclaimed any authority to consider whether the school authorities could have taught the students everything they needed to know about their country's past in regular courses in the classroom.[68]

In *Kjeldsen*, because of the very narrow reading it gave to the words of the Convention, the Court ignored the most pertinent fact of the case and the religious liberty of a small group of fundamentalist Christians was needlessly compromised as a result. The Court never called on the Danish Government to explain why it was necessary that all public school students receive instruction in every aspect of sex education when, simultaneously, it exempted religiously observant students who attended private schools from those parts of

---

[67] The same complaint underlined a dissenting opinion signed by seven of the seventeen judges who participated in the Court's decision in *Jewish Liturgical Ass'n v. France*.

[68] An unwillingness to accept an individual's self-assessment of the religious significance of a case is a characteristic of the Court's decisions that has been noted by other commentators. See Carolyn Evans, *Freedom of Religion under the European Convention of Human Rights* (Oxford: Oxford University Press, 2001), 120–2.

the curriculum that offended them most. Except for Verdross, none of the judges pressed the Government to explain how extending the same accommodation to public school students that it recognized for those who attended private schools could compromise its educational objectives in any way. Having satisfied themselves that no attempt at indoctrination was involved, they were prepared to validate the glaring inconsistency in the Government's treatment of the two groups.

In contrast with the judges in Strasbourg, when Japan's Supreme Court has been asked to mark off the limits of legitimate state support for particular moral or religious events and ideas, it has not shown as strong an attachment for the interpretative approach. In its seminal ruling on the propriety of a municipal government making a small ($60) financial contribution to help defray the costs of a Shinto groundbreaking ceremony (celebrated to mark the beginning of construction of a public gymnasium) that had a clear religious element, the Court's approach was very practical and down to earth.[69] Even though the words of Article 20 of the constitution were absolute and unconditional and required the state to 'refrain from . . . any . . . religious activity', and the historical understanding seemed to call for the strictest separation of church and state, a large majority ruled that reality and common sense argued otherwise. For them, some connection between the spiritual and secular was unavoidable. Like their Irish brethren, the majority pointed out that it would be discriminatory and inconsistent with the guarantee of religious liberty in Article 20 if the state did not permit religious activities in public institutions (such as prisons), or help support artistic treasures owned by religious groups. In the result, the Court read the prohibition against the state having 'any' contact with religion to mean only linkages that 'exceeded reasonable limits'.

In determining whether the Government's support for the Shinto groundbreaking ceremony met the constitutional principle of reasonableness or not, the Court demonstrated the same concern for the facts and details of the event that the German Court showed in its *School Prayer*, *Classroom Crucifix*, and *Blood Transfusion* decisions. 'The place of the conduct, the average person's reaction to it, the actor's purpose in holding the ceremony, the existence and extent of religious significance, and the effect on the average person,' the Court said, 'are all circumstances that should be considered to reach an objective judgment . . . ' In the circumstances of the case, the majority was of the opinion that even though the ceremony 'was undoubtedly . . . of a religious nature', it was not prohibited by the constitution because most people, including those on the city council who voted for the expenditure, regarded it primarily as a secular ritual dedicated to the safe construction of the gymnasium that lacked a religious meaning of any significance.

---

[69] *Kakunaga* v. *Sekiguchi* (*TSU Groundbreaking*) (1977) 31 Minshū 4 533, trans. and reproduced in part in L. Beer and H. Itoh, *Constitutional Caselaw of Japan 1970–90* (Seattle: University of Washington Press, 1996).

Several of the judges who sat on the *TSU Groundbreaking* case favoured a more categorical rule of strict separation between church and state. They doubted that a standard of reasonableness could be applied in an objective and neutral way. Like the Americans, these justices were more inclined to read the words in Article 20 with an eye to history than with a concern for the practical realities of the case. For them, the disastrous consequences that followed the elevation of Shintoism as the established religion of Japan in the first half of the last century meant no entanglement, however innocent, could be allowed. Even though they recognized that the ceremony had as much or more secular significance as religious, they thought that the only way of not sliding down the slippery slope connecting the relatively innocuous support of the groundbreaking ceremony and the creation of a quasi-religious state, was by drawing a very bright line in the jurisprudence and defining the principle of neutrality in absolutely rigid, categorical terms.

Chief Justice Fujibayashi issued a separate dissenting opinion in the *TSU Groundbreaking* case in which he stressed the sense of alienation and isolation non-adherents feel whenever the state shows a preference for one particular religion, no matter how fleeting or small. In his mind, the fact that those who opposed the groundbreaking ceremony were being 'hypersensitive' did not affect the result. Like Anthony Kennedy, he thought the right of non-adherents to be free from such state-imposed anxiety and stress was absolute, paramount, and immune to any compromise or qualification.

Fujibayashi's categorical ruling against any state support of anything religious lacks the impartiality and neutrality of the majority's judgment because of its very selective treatment of the facts. Like the US Supreme Court's analysis of school prayers, Fujibayashi ignored the interests of everyone connected with the event except those who objected to it. The majority, on the other hand, took account of all of the relevant interests involved and religious liberty gained a little ground. Instead of a rule outlawing all governmental support of religion, the Court was open to church and state joining in a project such as a ground-breaking ceremony, which served both of their interests, so long as it did not impinge too deeply on the lives of those who were offended by any linkage between the two.

Twenty years later, when the Court was asked to rule on whether offerings that were made by municipal officials to support important religious ceremonies at two national Shinto Shrines (*Yasukuni* and *Gokoku*) were constitutional or not, twelve of the fifteen justices who sat on the case reaffirmed their commitment to the pragmatic approach that had been laid out in the *TSU Groundbreaking* case.[70] However, on the facts of this case, all but two of the judges were of the opinion that the ceremonies that were being supported did not have the same significant secular dimension that the groundbreaking ceremony had for the average Japanese. They thought that the religious character of these ceremonies

---

[70] *Yasukuni Shrine* case 156 of 1997, <http/www.courts.go.jp>.

was so prominent that the average person would have regarded their subvention as an act of official endorsement and special recognition by the state. Because the municipality had never made offerings to other religious groups to support similar events, the singling out of national Shinto ceremonies was seen to have had a discriminatory effect and so was incapable of meeting the standard of reasonableness that had been established in the *TSU Groundbreaking* case.

In between its decisions in the *TSU Groundbreaking* and *Yasukuni Shrine* cases, the Supreme Court of Japan was asked whether the state went too far when officials in the Ministry of Self-Defence Forces helped to facilitate a religious service in which the soul of a serviceman who died while on duty was enshrined and in this case a majority of the judges favoured an interpretative analysis to settle the case.[71] They said that having one's religious peace of mind disturbed by the religious activities of others was not a legal interest that was protected by the constitution and so the serviceman's widow who had objected to the ceremony had no cause to complain. Several concurring opinions were written by other members of the Court including two by Atsushi Nagashima and Toshio Sakaue. They thought that the widow's peace of mind did fall within the constitutional guarantee of religious freedom but that it had to be set alongside and evaluated against the wishes of the deceased's father and siblings whose religious beliefs inclined them to favour the ceremony. Only one judge, Masami Ito, was of the opinion that the Government's involvement in the enshrinement was improper and, like Fujibayashi in the *TSU Groundbreaking* case, he read the words of the constitution as requiring 'a perfect separation of religion from the state'.

The diversity of opinion among the judges who sat on the *Serviceman En-shrinement* case provides a particularly striking contrast between the semantic and pragmatic models of judicial review. Both the majority and Justice Ito in dissent based their decisions on very narrow and conflicting interpretations of Article 20 of the Japanese Constitution and on very partial and incomplete evaluations of the facts. Like the European Court of Human Rights in *Valsamis*, the majority simply rejected the factual basis of the widow's claim and asserted that the general public would not have regarded the Government's actions as encouraging or discouraging religious freedom in any way. Justice Ito came to exactly the opposite conclusion because not only did he accept the widow's evidence that she was offended by the state's support of a religious ceremony that was antithetical to her own beliefs, he effectively ruled that hers was the only relevant interest in the case. Neither judgment provides a satisfactory resolution of the issue because both fail to take seriously the views of everyone who was affected by the ceremony. Like Fujibayashi's dissent in the *TSU Groundbreaking* case, Justice Ito's reading of the constitution took no account of the religious liberty of the serviceman's father and siblings. On his interpret-

---

[71] *Japan v. Nakaya (The Serviceman Enshrinement Case II)* (1988) 42 Minshū 5 277, trans. and reproduced in part in Beer and Itoh, *Constitutional Caselaw of Japan.*

ation, their religious choices were not deserving of any respect and were simply ignored.

The majority's ruling was equally arbitrary because it refused to accept the undisputed evidence of the widow that the state's endorsement of the enshrine-ment of her dead husband's soul was offensive to people such as she who held different religious beliefs. Even if its decision could be shown to be a fair resolution of the case, there was nothing in their judgment which would make the widow feel that her religious beliefs were taken seriously by the Court. By contrast, Justices Nagashima and Sakaue, who came to the same conclusion as the majority, explained to the widow that even though they recognized that her religious peace of mind was worthy of constitutional protection, the beliefs of the deceased's father and siblings had to be considered as well. Rather than telling her that the discomfort and disturbance to her peace of mind were not significant enough to be protected by the constitution, they said she must recognize that the religious beliefs of her in-laws were entitled to the same measure of respect as she claimed for herself.

The *Serviceman Enshrinement* case shows that even when interpretative and pragmatic approaches to questions of church/state relations lead to the same result, judges who stick to the facts of the case are able to show more respect for the religious liberty of those who seek their protection than their colleagues who try to draw answers directly from the words of the text.[72] The case provides another powerful example of the superiority of the pragmatic approach. It continues and extends the pattern that has run through all the cases we have considered so far and more cases could be added to the list. On issues such as the right of religiously inspired people to seek converts to their faith,[73] or refuse medical treatment for themselves and their family,[74] or claim public support for the non-religious education they provide in their schools,[75] the same story is repeated again and again. Judges who base their decision on an evaluation of all the relevant interests in a case are consistently better able to protect religious liberty in the aggregate and in a way that respects the sovereignty of the people to express itself democratically than their colleagues who devote most of their energies divining final answers from a text.[76]

---

[72] Another case in which judges who reasoned pragmatically were able to show more respect for the beliefs of a religious minority than their colleagues who followed an interpretative approach, even though they reached the same result, is the decision of the Supreme Court of Canada in *Re B. (R.) v. Children's Aid Society*. All seven judges thought the state acted constitutionally when it authorized the medical authorities to give a child a blood transfusion over the objections of the parents. In explaining the reason for their decision, four judges said the religious freedom that was protected by the Charter did not include the right of parents to make medical decisions for their children according to their religious beliefs if it threatened their well-being. Three other judges spoke more directly to the parents and explained that, even though their religious liberty must include their right to choose medical treatments for their children, in the circumstances of this particular case, that right had to be weighed against and ultimately give way to the independent right (to life) of their child.

[73] *Supra* n. 61.   [74] *Supra* n. 62.   [75] *Supra* n. 63.

[76] It bears repeating that even though religious liberty is better protected when courts use the principle of proportionality to evaluate the facts of the case, the pragmatic approach does not

Anyone who is interested in acquiring a comparative understanding of constitutional law will want to study these cases carefully. All of them make for interesting reading. The US Supreme Court, for example, has analysed people's right to proselytize as a matter of free speech rather than religious liberty and, as a consequence, has been much more pragmatic in its analysis of the limits of legitimate state regulation than other courts who have had occasion to address the issue.[77] At the other end of the spectrum, Singapore's Court of Appeal has denied that proportionality even exists as an independent principle of judicial review and, as a result, has upheld a ban on the distribution of religious material, including the Bible, by an International Student's Association, on the ground that the refusal of its members to do any national service was a threat to the security of the country.[78] Other cases, on school funding,[79] as well as a ruling by Spain's Constitutional Court on whether the state has an obligation to provide medical treatment that is consistent with a person's religious beliefs or pay its financial equivalent,[80] offer an insight into the way the two different models of review address claims for positive social and economic rights. The school funding cases provide a window on claims for group rights as well. In all these cases, however, the comparative advantages of the pragmatic approach reassert themselves. No matter how many judgments one analyses, pragmatism dominates interpretative strategies on every relevant criterion. When judges 'think things not words', as Oliver Wendell Holmes famously put it more than a hundred years ago,[81] religious liberty and popular sovereignty flourish simultaneously.

6. REVELATIONS

No matter where courts have been made responsible for safeguarding religious liberty against the excesses and arbitrariness that is, shamefully, still part of political life all over the world, pragmatic judges outperform those who believe solutions are to be found in the meaning of words and there is no reason to think that will ever change. Rolling up one's sleeves and grappling with the intense flesh and blood stories of people who feel aggrieved by the state is a more honest, effective, and straightforward way of resolving conflict than indulging in arid word games. There is an objectivity and neutrality about facts that words rarely

---

guarantee that religious liberty will always prevail. On a proportionality analysis neither refusing a blood transfusion for (*supra* n. 52) nor beating a child (*Christian Education South Africa* v. *Minister of Education*) receive protection from the courts.

[77] *Watchtower Bible and Tract Society* v. *Stratton*; see also *Good News Club* v. *Milford Central School* (2001) 533 US 98. For an introduction into the place of pragmatic 'balancing' in the Court's free speech jurisprudence, see Posner, *Law, Pragmatism and Democracy*, ch. 10.

[78] *Chan Hiang Leng Colin et al.* v. *Minister for Information*.

[79] *Supra* n. 63.

[80] *Amezqueta* v. *Health Service of Navarre*, Judgment 166/96, 28 October, translated and reproduced in part in Gewirtz, *Global Constitutionalism*.

[81] O. W. Holmes, 'Law in Science and Science in Law' (1899) 12 Harv. L Rev. 443, 460.

if ever can match. Where words can only represent and describe, facts can claim to be the real thing. Facts have a certainty, predictability, and reality about them that allows for more precise measurement and analysis. Factual claims can be tested for how accurately they conform to an independent empirical world, as it actually exists. Definitions cannot. So, as we have seen, it is possible to determine, as a matter of fact, whether Deborah Weisman's religious freedom or the mobility rights of motorists in Jerusalem were as serious as they claimed by looking at how the state's proposed course of action actually affected their larger life stories. Similarly, the assertions by Denmark and the state of Oregon that their general welfare would be compromised if they were required to make exceptions to important public policies for religious minorities can be evaluated against their own (lack of) enforcement and the experience of neighbouring states. When errors and omissions and misstatements of fact are made—such as Kennedy's equating the significance of the benediction for Deborah Weisman and the students who wanted to profess their faith publicly, or Albie Sachs's making more of the state's interest in curbing alcohol abuse than the Government's own record showed to be true—they are easy to spot. Unlike disagreements about the meaning of words or the proper way to describe the principle to be extracted from a long line of precedents, a dispute about the truth of a factual claim can be settled on the basis that one side is right and the other is wrong.

In the cases we have encountered so far, the most important facts have typically not been in dispute and so judgments as to whose interests are most seriously affected by the Government's proposed course of action are not difficult to make. Judges who let the facts—and the parties—speak for themselves usually have no problem identifying whose interests are paramount in any individual case. Judges know just by looking, just by sight, as Potter Stewart once famously said,[82] even when precise calibrations are hard to provide. Very few people are blind to the fact that the significance of their most sacred prayers is infinitely more important for orthodox Jews than a two-minute detour is in the life of the passing motorist. Similarly, when twenty-three states and the federal Government have permitted peyote to be used in religious ceremonies without suffering any adverse consequences, Oregon's arguments to the contrary can be rejected as having no basis in fact. The inconsistency in Denmark's treatment of students attending public and private schools is incontestable and equally impossible to defend. In each of these cases sticking to the facts means judges are naturally predisposed to rule in ways that will maximize the rights of those who ask for their protection without either threatening the sovereignty of the people to define the moral character of their communities or jeopardizing their own neutrality.

Even though the pragmatists' domination of interpretivists can be proven as a jurisprudential fact, it will be hard for many to accept. Until now, interpretivist

---

[82] *Jacobellis* v. *Ohio* (1964) 378 US 184; cf. Clarence Thomas in *Grutter* v. *Bollinger* (2003) 123 S.Ct. 2325.

theories, as we saw in the last chapter, have been the only game in town. Today, calls for courts to concentrate on the facts of each case are not non-existent, but they are comparatively rare.[83] It is to be expected that challenging what is generally accepted as conventional wisdom will be met with a healthy measure of scepticism and even resistance. That is particularly true with respect to the traditional understanding of judicial review as an interpretative enterprise, where the reluctance to abandon the old paradigm will be especially acute for those who worry that the alternative, reasoning pragmatically, allows judges to balance the competing interests at play in each case according to their own personal preferences and priorities. For many constitutionalists, balancing is an unprincipled, and therefore illicit method of legal reasoning because, they say, there are no objective or neutral criteria judges can use to evaluate the validity of whatever law or act of state they are asked to review.[84] If pragmatism is just freewheeling balancing by another name, it lacks legitimacy and violates the principle of separation of powers, precisely because it permits an elite group of legal professionals to substitute their values and ideas for those of the elected representatives of the people.

In the cases we have encountered so far there was not much balancing going on because, in most of them, the courts could rely on the parties' own evaluations of how significant the law was to them. The closing of Bar Ilan Street was typical. There was no need for Barak to second-guess what a two-minute detour meant for the average Israeli compared to the significance of a tranquil environment for orthodox Jews during their prayers on the sabbath. So too Antonin Scalia and Kate O'Regan could take Deborah Weisman and the South African state, respectively, at their word. But what happens if they can't? What should judges do when, as in the *Serviceman Enshrinement* case, someone's perspective is thought to be 'hypersensitive' and unreasonable? What then? How can judges claim their decisions are objective and neutral in cases of that kind?

Others will want to ask questions about how much deference judges should show to the decisions of the political branches of government in virtue of their being directly elected by the people. As we have seen, pragmatic judges tend to concentrate on the means and the effects rather than the ends of the laws they are asked to review. Except for laws that deliberately aim at coercing people in their spiritual beliefs, legislatures are given free rein to pursue whatever objectives got them elected, including supporting religious interests and groups, so long as it is done in the appropriate way. But how far does this deference extend? On complex issues of social policy—such as whether religious groups are bound to comply with a state's rules against sex discrimination, for example—does pragmatism instruct the judge to defer to the Government's choice of means as well?

[83] But see Cass Sunstein, *One Case at a Time: Judicial Minimalism on the Supreme Court* (Cambridge, Mass.: Harvard University Press, 1999); and Richard Posner, 'Against Constitutional Theory' (1998) 73 NYU L Rev. 1; *Law, Pragmatism and Democracy*, ch. 2.

[84] See Dworkin, *Law's Empire*, ch. 5; T. A. Aleinikoff, 'Constitutional Law in an Age of Balancing', (1987) 96 Yale LJ 943.

Do claims for public funding of private religious schools, that may have implications for the public treasury if they were successful, also warrant a deferential standard of review?

The very uneven record of the courts in their protection of religious liberty tells us such questions are not idle concerns. We need to learn more about the pragmatic approach, about its methods, and the values on which it is based. Even for judges who are inclined to exercise their powers of review pragmatically 'weighing considerations of faith against those of reason' is anything but an easy task.[85] To get a better understanding of what it means to think about judicial review as a principled evaluation of how laws reconcile the conflicting interests they affect, rather than an exercise of textual exegesis, we need to focus on cases where judges are naturally inclined to reason pragmatically and where interpretative questions generally will not come into play. Cases on gender equality are one obvious possibility. Discrimination against women has been one of the hot points of global politics for more than a century and all constitutions, either explicitly or by judicial implication, now proscribe laws that discriminate on the basis of sex. Cases alleging sex discrimination are almost never treated as matters of interpretation any more.

Studying how the courts have responded when women and others, including gays and lesbians, complain of being disadvantaged on the basis of their sex will give us a clearer picture of how the pragmatic method works in practice and whether the neutrality of its method holds true beyond the domain of religious rights. The possibilities for doing creative comparative research on these and related issues have never been better. Like all areas of constitutional law, this is a jurisprudence that is large and growing rapidly. Reading the many opinions that have reflected on the question of when it is legitimate for governments to treat people differently because of their sex should move our project forward significantly. These cases can tell us a lot about the virtues and vices of pragmatic reasoning and in so doing they should help us discover whether a coherent theory of judicial review can be drawn from law's understanding of itself.

---

[85] *Christian Education South Africa* v. *Minister of Education*, para. 33 (Sachs).

3

Equality

1. SEX DISCRIMINATION

The ideal of equality was a vital part of the politics of the twentieth century from beginning to end. In the early years, women agitated for the right to vote and an equal status as citizens and in law all over the world. At the same time, communists and social democrats justified revolutions in its name. In mid-century black Americans marched for freedom and went to court to bring the discrimination that was practised against them to an end. After the Second World War, and especially when the Berlin Wall came down, dozens of countries guaranteed a right to equality in their constitutions and then lots of other ethnic, linguistic, and religious minorities, people with disabilities, and gays and lesbians, were able to press parallel claims that they be shown the same respect as everyone else.

Although the century also witnessed some of the most horrible acts of depravity known to human history, and tolerated egregious injustices to its end, on some fronts huge strides were made.[1] Women who lived in the mature and established democracies of the world were especially successful in their attacks on laws that treated them as inferior to men. It is hard to think of another group of people whose position in the political and economic organizations of their societies improved more dramatically. In 1900 very few women had the right to vote. By the year 2000, many had achieved the highest offices of government and ordinary women all over the world could claim a constitutional right to be treated as equals and be free from discrimination at least in their dealings with government and officials of the state.[2]

To secure their emancipation, women relied almost entirely on the traditional methods of politics and community organization. Governments were pressured in one manner or another, sooner or (more often) later, to remove laws that disadvantaged women from the books. Voting, property, and matrimonial laws that treated women less well than men became relics of the past. An international Convention condemning discrimination against women was made part of international law.[3] For the most part, women were able to make the powers that be

---

[1] E. J. Hobsbawm, *The Age of Extremes* (New York: Vintage, 1996).

[2] Though not all women everywhere in the world, as the women of Kuwait discovered when their Supreme Court ruled against their claim for the right to vote. *The Economist*, 22 January 2001.

[3] *Convention on the Elimination of All Forms of Discrimination Against Women*, GA Res. 34/180; UN Doc. A/34/46, 1979.

take notice of their numbers and over time gained recognition of their equal standing in law if not in all aspects of their personal and professional lives.[4]

One of the few areas where politicians were not persuaded to stop drawing distinctions between men and women on the basis of their sex was in their regulation of various employment opportunities and training programmes that were regarded as being too arduous or dangerous for the 'fair sex'. Laws that decreed that only men can fill certain positions in the military, for example, showed up in regulations and statute books all over the world and were surprisingly resistant to amendment or repeal. In many countries, parallel restrictions on the freedom of women to work in difficult and demanding jobs on the civilian side of life were enacted by paternalistic governments who defended their position on the basis that their purposes were benign. These were protective measures, it was said, and were not discriminatory in an invidious or pejorative sense.[5]

Even in these circumstances, when politicians were reluctant to give up traditional, stereotypical images of women, progress could be made. Women who lived in countries with entrenched bills of rights did not have to lie down in the face of such discriminatory treatment by the state. In Europe and the United States, in Israel, India, and Japan women could and did ask their judges to strike down these last vestiges of the traditional female stereotype and in virtually every case they were successful in their pleas. The highest courts in all these countries handed down judgments in which they ruled that gender-biased laws that denied women training and vocational opportunities on the basis of their sex violated their constitutional right to the equal benefit and protection of the law.

Women who could claim the protection of a written bill of rights could, of course, attack any law that disadvantaged them because of their sex, and that is exactly what they did. Citizenship laws that treated men and women differently, for example, were taken before the Supreme Court of Canada, the Court of Appeal of Botswana, and the European Court of Human Rights and suffered the same fate as laws that limited women's employment opportunities.[6] American women have challenged all kinds of laws that denied them the same status as males and, although initially they did not have a lot of success,[7] over the last thirty years of the century their Supreme Court has generally been very sympathetic to their complaints.[8]

---

[4] See e.g. K. Offen, *European Feminisms 1700–1950* (Stanford, Calif.: Stanford University Press, 2000); D. Anderson, *The Unfinished Revolution: The Status of Women in Twelve Countries* (Toronto: Doubleday Canada, 1991).

[5] K. Offen, *European Feminisms*, 227 ff.

[6] *Benner* v. *Canada* (1997) 143 DLR (4th) 577; *Dow* v. *Attorney General* (Botswana) (1992) LRC (Constit.) 623; (1994) 6 BHRC 1; *Abdulaziz* v. *U.K.* (1984) 7 EHRR 471.

[7] See e.g. *Bradwell* v. *Illinois* (1873) 16 Wall 130, upholding a state law limiting the practice of law to men, *Goesaert* v. *Cleary* (1948) 335 US 464, upholding a law prohibiting women from becoming bartenders. Cf. *Murtagh Properties* v. *Cleary* [1972] IR 330.

[8] L. Tribe, *American Constitutional Law*, 2nd edn. (New York: Foundation Press, 1988), ch. 16: 25–30.

It is true that in those parts of the world where governments were not constrained by constitutional bills of rights, there was little women could do if the political leadership remained intransigent in its views. They simply had to endure the fact they had fewer vocational opportunities than men and hope that not too many of them would have to give up on their chosen careers. Also, other groups did not fare as well as women in attacking discriminatory treatment by the state. The experience of gays and lesbians, for example, was and remains decidedly more mixed. The ordinary processes and institutions of politics have not been nearly as responsive to their claims of discriminatory treatment as they have to the petitions of women. Gays and lesbians are discrete and insular minorities who have lost as many or more battles in the trenches of politics as they have won. At the end of the millennium, laws were still being enforced that blatantly discriminated against them because of their sex. Sodomy, for example, is still a crime in many places (including until very recently many parts of the United States), and only in Belgium and the Netherlands are same-sex couples able to get married the same way as everyone else.

Nor have gays and lesbians done as well as women in the courts. Judges have been much more divided in their views about discrimination when gays and lesbians complain that a law offends their equality rights than when parallel claims are pressed by heterosexual women. In contrast with their near-unanimous condemnation of gender-biased employment and citizenship laws, courts have been much more tolerant of rules and regulations that discriminate against gays and lesbians on the basis of their sex. Although landmark rulings invalidating clear cases of discrimination have been handed down by some courts, just as frequently laws that imposed special burdens or denied general benefits to gay and lesbian people have been certified as constitutional. The Supreme Courts of Ireland,[9] the United States,[10] and Zimbabwe,[11] and the Constitutional Court of Germany,[12] for example, all have validated sodomy laws that differentiated offenders on the basis of their sex. As well, the Supreme Court of Canada,[13] the Constitutional Court of Hungary,[14] and the Court of Appeal of New Zealand[15] have each said that states can deny gays and lesbians various of the benefits associated with the status of being married that they provide for couples of the opposite sex. For its part, the European Court of

[9] *Norris v. A. G.* (Ireland) [1984] IR 36.

[10] *Bowers v. Hardwick* (1986) 478 US 186. Conforming to the pattern of huge swings in the jurisprudence, which we noticed in the previous chapter, seventeen years later in *Lawrence v. Texas* (2003) 123 S.Ct. 2472, *Bowers* was overruled.

[11] *Banana v. State* (2000) 8 BHRC 345.

[12] *Homosexuality* case (1957) 6 BVerf GE 389, trans. and reproduced in part in W. F. Murphy and J. Tannenhaus, *Comparative Constitutional Law, Cases and Materials* (New York: St Martins Press, 1977).

[13] *Egan v. Canada* [1995] 2 SCR 513; 124 DLR (4th) 609.

[14] *On the Legal Equality of Same Sex Partnerships*, Decision 14, 1995; trans. and reproduced in L. Sólyom and G. Brunner, *Constitutional Judiciary in a New Democracy, The Hungarian Constitutional Court* (Ann Arbor: University of Michigan Press, 2000).

[15] *Quilter v. Attorney-General* (New Zealand) [1998] 1 NZLR 523; [1997] 3 BHRC 461.

Human Rights has categorically rejected the idea that gays and lesbians have the same right to adopt children as everyone else.[16]

The fact that gays and lesbians have had limited success persuading politicians to respond to their allegations of discrimination is not difficult to understand. In democratic societies in which majorities rule, women have a natural authority in their numbers that gays and lesbians will rarely, if ever, enjoy. Without the votes, cries of discrimination by gays and lesbians stand less chance of being heard, especially in communities where large majorities regard conjugal relationships between people of the same sex to be morally depraved and deeply offensive to their most strongly felt religious beliefs. The different treatment the two groups have received from the courts, however, is more difficult to explain. Selectively protecting people from being discriminated against on the basis of their sex seems completely at odds with the most basic understanding of equality and the rule of law. If employment and citizenship laws that are gender-biased cannot pass the test, it seems arbitrary and unprincipled that marriage, family, and criminal laws that treat people differently because of their sex are not struck down as well. For anyone who is instinctively sceptical about the neutrality of the law, the different treatment of the two groups will suggest that judicial politics are at work. The integrity of law is put in question when it allows the validity of rules and regulations that overtly discriminate on the basis of sex to turn on who seeks the favour of the court.

Suspicions of judicial bias and partiality in the enforcement of equality rights cannot be dismissed as groundless and/or delusional acts of paranoia. The fact is that laws that punish people for having sexual relations with others of the same sex, and deny the status and benefits of being married to lesbians and gays, do discriminate on the basis of people's sex just as much as laws that limit job and training opportunities for women. In the case of the latter, the discrimination is stark and plain for everyone to see. The law says explicitly 'no women allowed'. The gender bias of traditional marriage and family laws is not expressed so blatantly but that doesn't mean it isn't there. It is true that both sexes are treated the same. Neither exclusively male nor female relationships are recognized. There is no wholesale discrimination between the sexes but its existence, at the retail level, cannot be denied. Laws that benefit and burden people on the basis of whether their sexual preferences are straight or gay do make sex the determining condition of who is included within their terms. Sodomy laws that punish people for having sexual relations with someone of the same sex, and marriage laws that refuse to recognize same-sex conjugal relationships, do so explicitly because of the sex of the people involved. It is legal for David to have sexual relations with and marry Ninette, because she is a woman, but not Michael, because he is a man.

That courts have generally been more sympathetic to complaints of gender bias when they are made by women than when equivalent claims are pressed by

---

[16] *Fretté* v. *France*, ECHR 36515/97, 26.02.02, <http://hudoc.echr.coe.int/>.

lesbians and gays is a jurisprudential fact that is a matter of public record. However, what conclusions we should draw from this disparate treatment is more difficult to say. In order to know what we should make of this jurisprudence it is necessary to study the judgments first-hand. Most courts do not openly acknowledge that they harbour different feelings about gender-biased laws depending on whether the rights of women or gays and lesbians are at stake. The major exception is the Supreme Court of the United States which has developed an elaborate system of tiers or levels of review that applies different standards of equality depending upon who is the victim of the discrimination. It is a long-standing rule of American constitutional law that women get more protection against discrimination from the Fourteenth Amendment than lesbians and gays; although it is also the case that they get significantly less than blacks.[17]

To find out what is going on in this collection of conflicting judicial opinions on sex discrimination it makes sense to begin with those cases in which the courts have struck down laws that open more career opportunities to men than women. Although the Americans initially struggled with this issue, by the end of the century there were very few judges anywhere who thought laws of this kind could survive. Even though the laws in many of these cases did not affect large numbers of women, this is a significant body of caselaw that can teach us a lot. Precisely because the differential treatment accorded the sexes is so deliberate and overt, the courts' strong condemnation of them reveals clearly what the concept of equality (and its opposite, discrimination) means in law, and what constraints it imposes on governments when they exercise the lawmaking powers of the state. Understanding the way courts have analysed laws that limit employment opportunities for women can also provide a template for assessing the claims of gays and lesbians who say they were just as much victims of gender discrimination at the end of the century as women were at the start. By allowing us to see why easy cases are not difficult to decide,[18] these decisions can help us when we think about more controversial questions such as the claims of gays and lesbians to equal sexual freedom and an equal right to marry.

2. EQUAL OPPORTUNITIES FOR WOMEN

One of the most striking features of the cases in which courts have invalidated laws that discriminate between men and women in the career opportunities that are open to each is the uniformity of their approach. The judgments are as similar in their reasoning as they are in their results. Even though constitutional and international bills of rights vary enormously in the way they guarantee equality rights and proscribe acts of discrimination by the state, the method of

---

[17] For a description of the American approach, see Tribe, *American Constitutional Law*, ch. 16.

[18] F. Schauer, *Easy Cases* (1985) 58 So. Cal. L Rev. 399; cf. Allan C. Hutchinson, *It's All in the Game* (Durham, NC: Duke University Press, 2000), 81–4, 121–6.

analysis judges use is basically the same all over the world. To distinguish laws with sex-based classifications that are consistent with a constitutional guarantee of equality from those that are unjustified and unfair, judges think pragmatically and pay close attention to the facts. They focus most of their attention on the purposes, methods, and consequences of the laws whose legitimacy has been questioned and they pay comparatively little attention to the words of the constitution.

This common methodology holds true no matter what structure or style of expression the drafters happened to favour. Some constitutions can be very wordy when it comes to detailing what the right to equality and freedom from discrimination require of the state. Others are succinct and to the point. India's constitution is characteristically profuse in its commitment to equality and has five separate articles dedicated in its name.[19] The Fourteenth Amendment to the US constitution, by comparison, speaks of guaranteeing every person the 'equal protection of the laws' in five simple words. Israel's Basic Law on Human Dignity and Liberty is unique in deliberately making no explicit reference to equality or discrimination at all. Some texts, such as the European Convention of Human Rights, use the language of discrimination.[20] Others, including the US Bill of Rights and Germany's Basic Law[21] favour the rhetoric of equality. Modern constitutions typically make reference to both and often they also identify specific circumstances in which it is legitimate for the state to make special arrangements for individuals and groups, including women.[22]

None of this rich variation in constitutional texts, however, has had any effect on the way judges think about laws that intentionally provide more training and employment opportunities for men than women. All the details and adornments that are so important to those who negotiate and draft constitutions and international human rights treaties have absolutely no bearing on how these cases are resolved. What is decisive for the judges is the formal idea or analytical structure that is generic to all conceptions of equality, however they are expressed. Courts rely on first principles to tell them when laws that classify and draw distinctions between people on the basis of their sex are compatible with the idea of equality and when they constitute illicit discrimination by the state. These principles organize the courts' evaluation of the ends and the means and the effects of whatever classification is under review and insist that there be an appropriate connection, or measure of proportionality, between all three. Classifying people

---

[19] Constitution of India, Articles 14–18. In addition the constitution specifically outlaws discrimination in educational institutions in Article 30 and directs the state to strive to eliminate economic and material inequality in Article 38. The constitutions of all national states, including India's, can be found in A. P. Blaustein and G. H. Flanz, *Constitutions of the Countries of the World* (loose-leaf) (Dobbs Ferry, NY: Oceana).

[20] European Convention for the Protection of Human Rights and Fundamental Freedom, 04/11/50, 213 UNTS 221, Article 14.

[21] German Basic Law, Article 3, in Blaustein and Flanz, *Constitutions*.

[22] Canadian Charter of Rights and Freedoms s 15(2); Constitution of the Republic of South Africa s 9(2) in Blaustein and Flanz, *Constitutions*.

on the basis of their sex is tested for (1) how well it promotes the aims and objectives of the legislative regime of which it is a part, and (2) how prejudicial it is to those who are denied membership in the privileged class.

Typically, employment laws that open more career opportunities for men than women have no difficulty establishing that their purposes are benign. Courts everywhere recognize that not every distinction that is drawn on the basis of a person's sex is arbitrary and unjust. No one questions the integrity of the purposes that single-sex schools (educational diversity) or washrooms (personal privacy)[23] are designed to serve. It is also widely accepted that gender classifications can be passed for the purpose of removing a disadvantage or alleviating a condition (such as pregnancy) that only women experience. While the different natural capacities of men and women cannot be used to the prejudice of either, there is nothing wrong with singling out one or the other for special treatment when it is done to promote greater equality between the two.[24] All that is required is that in defending laws that discriminate between people on the basis of their sex, governments be able to prove that they were in fact their real objectives and not some convenient afterthought.[25]

The only purpose that courts have said gender classifications cannot promote is the inequality of the sexes. Their motivation cannot be malevolent, hostile, or deliberately prejudicial.[26] Laws can't be passed for the purpose of degrading women or branding them as inferior or second-class or to entrench a traditional, stereotyping role that imposes extra burdens and disadvantages on them that men do not have to endure. Although citizenship laws that differentiate the legal status of men and women have sometimes been seen to evince such illicit intentions,[27] it is rare to find laws that limit women's career opportunities being tainted in this way. When courts invalidate laws that deny women the same vocational opportunities as men, it is either because they find classifying by gender to be an arbitrary way of accomplishing whatever the (benign) objectives of the state may be or because its impact on the lives of those it adversely affects is too severe compared to how much (or how little) it improves the well-being of the community at large.

---

[23] See e.g. A. Scalia, *A Matter of Interpretation* (Princeton, NJ: Princeton University Press, 1997), 149; R. Bork, *The Tempting of America* (New York: Free Press, 1990), 329; *Cleburne v. Cleburne Living Center* (1985) 473 US 432, 468–9, 'A sign that says "men only" looks very different on a bathroom door than on a courthouse door' (per Marshall); *Granovsky v. Canada (Min. of Employment and Immigration)* [2000] ISCR 703, Pr. 59 (per Binnie). See also A. Koppelman, *The Gay Rights Question in Contemporary American Law* (Chicago: University of Chicago Press, 2002), 57–9.

[24] See e.g. *President of the Republic of South Africa v. Hugo* (1997) 4 SA 1; *Miller v. Minister of Defence* [1998] 32 Is. L Rev. 157; *Nocturnal Employment Case*, 85 BVerfGE 191 (1992) trans. and reproduced in part in David Currie, 'Comparative Constitutional Law', Univ. of Chicago Law School (unpublished, n.d.); as well as in D. Kommers, *The Constitutional Jurisprudence of the Federal Republic of Germany* (Durham, NC: Duke University Press, 2nd edn. 1997).

[25] See e.g. *United States v. Virginia* (1996) 518 US 515; *Kriel v. Germany*, C-285/98, [2000] ECRI 69, para. 25; *Miller v. Minister of Defence*.

[26] See e.g. *Air India v. Nergesh Meerza* AIR 1981 SC 1829, para. 26.

[27] See e.g. *Benner v. Canada*; *Dow v. Attorney General* (Botswana).

Gender classifications are seen to be arbitrary when they pursue their objectives by means that are under- and/or over-inclusive. For example, the German
Constitutional Court struck down a law restricting the employment of women in
industrial jobs at night because it disqualified them even if they would not suffer
any of the harms (to their health and safety) that the law was meant to prevent
(over-inclusive) and because it left out other workers—males with primary
childcare responsibilities and females in non-industrial jobs—who were in need
of its protection (under-inclusive). On the evidence before the Court, the most
serious harm of working at night fell on those who were burdened with
parenting and housekeeping responsibilities which would include many single
fathers as well as mothers who worked in non-industrial jobs. To redress this
problem the Court advised that the law should focus directly on those circumstances. For example, rather than disadvantaging all women workers, the Court
suggested particular dangers could be addressed by less draconian strategies such
as providing transportation to and from work in company vehicles.[28]

Both the Supreme Court of Japan[29] and the European Court of Justice in
Luxembourg[30] have also found fault with laws that limited women's employment opportunities because they were more exclusionary than they needed to be.
The judges in Tokyo invalidated an employment regulation that established a
lower age of retirement for women than men because it was based on the
unwarranted assumption that the productivity of all female workers fell off at
an earlier age than that of their male colleagues. They said that if productivity
was the purpose of the rule, individual testing was a more appropriate policy
instrument than a categorical gender classification because the latter would
invariably result in the termination of women who were perfectly capable of
meeting all the requirements of the job.

The European Court of Justice invalidated a section of Germany's Law on
Soldiers that barred women from serving in any military position involving the
use of arms even though such an exclusion seemed to be expressly contemplated
by an amendment to the country's constitution.[31] In the view of all nine judges
who heard the case, such a sweeping exclusion was much broader than it needed
to be. In the result, the Court ruled that if the purpose of the law was safeguarding the country's national security, the exclusion should be limited to those
particular activities or units in the military where it could be established the

---

[28] *Nocturnal Employment* case; cf. *Muller* v. *Oregon* (1908) 208 US 412 upholding a law restricting the hours of employment of women working in laundries to 10 hours a day.

[29] *Nissan Motors Inc.* v. *Nakamoto* (1981) in L. Beer and H. Itoh (eds.), *The Constitutional Case
Law of Japan 1970–1990* (Seattle: University of Washington Press, 1996). The US Supreme Court has
also insisted that the rules governing the retirement of women be calibrated on an individual rather
than group basis. See *City of Los Angeles* v. *Manhart* (1978) 435 US 702; *Arizona Governing
Committee* v. *Norris* (1983) 463 US 1073; cf. *Air India* v. *Nergesh Meerza.*

[30] *Kriel* v. *Germany.*

[31] Article 12A of the Basic Law for the Federal Republic of Germany provides 'Men who have
attained the age of eighteen may be required to serve in the Armed Forces', in Blaustein and Flanz,
Constitutions.

engagement of women would present a real threat.[32] According to the Court, the mere fact a woman might be called on to use weapons could not justify her exclusion because the evidence showed women who had received basic training in the use of arms were fully capable of defending themselves and those with whom they served.

Even if a woman's sex may affect how she will perform in a job or a training programme, laws that systematically exclude all females from career opportunities that are open to men may still be struck down where it can be demonstrated that they do more harm than good. To establish their legitimacy, gender classifications must show they can also meet the metric of proportionality in reconciling their purposes and effects. When any woman is not allowed to do with her life those things that are central to her self-identity, and indeed to the liberation of women more generally,[33] in order to enhance the public interest in ways that are superficial and cosmetic, she is virtually certain of receiving a sympathetic hearing from a court.

Both the Supreme Courts of the United States and Israel have invalidated regulations that limited training and career opportunities of women in the military on the basis of the gross disparity in their purposes and effects. In *US v. Virginia*,[34] seven of eight judges voted to strike down a state law that did not permit females to attend the Virginia Military Institute (VMI) essentially because even women who were capable of meeting all aspects of the school's unique bullying ('adversative') method of training were excluded and because the evidence strongly suggested that their admission would not compromise its standards and the qualifications of its graduates in any significant way. As William Rehnquist recognized, in a concurring opinion he wrote, even if some aspects of the adversative system would have to be changed to accommodate the admission of women (for example the communal living arrangements), there was no evidence that substitutes could not be devised that would be just as effective in producing the desired character traits (loyalty, solidarity) in their graduates. Indeed, the experience of the integration that had already taken place in the most prestigious federal military academies, such as West Point and Annapolis, provided the Court with strong evidence to the contrary.

The Supreme Court of Israel evaluated an administrative regime that denied women the opportunity to prove they had the requisite qualifications to serve as pilots in the country's Air Force along exactly the same lines and found it wanting for the same set of reasons.[35] On one side of the case were the interests of women for whom a career as pilots in their country's armed forces was at the

---

[32] See e.g. *Sirdar v. Army Board* [1999] All ER (EC) 928. For a discussion of how the principle of proportionality figures in the ECJ in thinking about occupational discrimination against women, see N. Emilou, *The Principle of Proportionality in European Law* (Dordrecht: Kluwer, 1996) 161–6.

[33] On the importance of work in the emancipation of women in the twentieth century, see Mary Ann Glendon, *The New Family and the New Property* (Toronto: Butterworth, 1981).

[34] *US v. Virginia*; but see *Rostker v. Goldberg* (1981) 453 US 57.

[35] *Miller v. Ministry of Defence.*

core of who they were and wanted to become. On the other, the Government could defend the exclusion of women only for organizational and practical considerations about their availability for reserve duty when they were pregnant or raising a family. After reviewing the factual details of the case, and in particular the experience of women becoming military pilots in other countries and entering other branches of Israel's own armed forces, a majority of judges concluded that the Government's concerns were based 'entirely on speculations and hypothetical evaluations' and had no solid foundation in fact.

Other examples of courts invalidating laws that discriminated against women because they lacked the requisite measure of proportionality between their purposes and effects can be added to the list. In one high-profile ruling, India's Supreme Court struck down a government regulation that provided for the termination of 'hostesses' employed by Air India if they became pregnant.[36] A panel of three judges led by S. Murtaza Fazal Ali were indignant at the gross imbalance in the law, calling it 'callous and cruel . . . [and] an open insult to Indian womanhood'. From their perspective, the regulation amounted 'to compelling the poor [air hostesses] not to have any children and thus interfere with and divert the ordinary course of human nature' in order to save the company what, on the evidence, would be the relatively minor cost and inconvenience of arranging replacements for hostesses who became pregnant. For all three judges, there was no comparison between the two. Evaluated in this way, the regulation 'smack[ed] of a deep rooted sense of utter selfishness at the cost of all human values' and so violated the constitutional right of these women to the equal protection of the law.

The European Court of Human Rights has always put the principle of proportionality at the centre of its understanding of equality. Indeed, the judges in Strasbourg have explicitly defined the right to be free from discrimination in Article 14 of the European Convention of Human Rights to entail a 'reasonable relationship of proportionality between the means employed and the aim sought be realised'[37] and it has used that principle to strike down a British immigration rule that made it easier for men than women to settle their non-national spouses in the United Kingdom.[38] Although the Court accepted that the Government's objectives in protecting its labour market and preserving public tranquillity were legitimate, it was unanimous that neither would be sufficiently advanced by categorically differentiating between men and women in this way. On the evidence before the Court, the threat immigrant male spouses posed to the local labour market was not different enough from the impact of female spouses to justify their being treated so unequally.

Because it is a judgment of an international court, with members drawn from different legal traditions and political cultures, the ruling of the European Court

---

[36] *Air India* v. *Meerza*, para. 80

[37] *Belgian Linguistic* case (1968) 1 EHRR 252, 284, para. 10. See also *Marckx* v. *Belgium* (1979) 2 EHRR 330, para. 33, and *Rasmussen* v. *Denmark* (1985) 7 EHRR 371, para. 38.

[38] *Abdulaziz et al.* v. *UK*, para. 72.

of Human Rights in *Abdulaziz* shows just how pervasively judges think about laws that disadvantage women through the lens of proportionality. *Abdulaziz* is another unanimous opinion that laws that treat men better than women are discriminatory essentially because the benefits they promise are either not supported by the evidence or, in any event, are not sufficiently vital to the well-being of the community to justify designating some central aspect of a woman's personhood, such as her citizenship rights or career ambitions, as inferior or second class. Putting it alongside the judgments of the other courts that have struck down gender-biased laws that discriminate against women creates a very significant body of judicial opinion that is distinguished by its commitment to a common framework of analysis that has, by and large, been applied in an objective and impartial way.

As impressive as the courts' performance has been in protecting women against laws that discriminate against them because of their sex it is, however, not perfect and wholly unblemished. Even though the American and Indian Supreme Courts and the European Court of Justice can all claim to have handed down important judgments in the cause of women's liberation, it is also the case that each of them has validated laws that categorically restricted the career opportunities of women because of their sex.[39] In addition, even when courts have invalidated laws that are biased against women, dissenting opinions, that argue that sex-based classifications do not violate constitutional guarantees of equality, are often written. Also, when judges have been asked to review laws that treat women better than men, rather than the other way round, their commitment to the equality of the sexes appears more tentative and ambivalent.[40]

The number of judgments that have been written that would validate laws that disadvantage men or women because of their sex is not large but they are, jurisprudentially, critical to establishing the impartiality and the integrity of principles of equality and proportionality and the rule of law. The mere fact of their having been written poses a challenge to those who would defend the practice of allowing courts to sit in judgment on the other two, elected branches of government. If these opinions must be accepted as legitimate expressions of judicial authority, they suggest that even on an issue as basic as the equality of the sexes there are no right answers; that reasonable people can disagree about what equality means and what it requires governments to do. However, if that were true, if it were the case that it was just a matter of each judge's personal opinion whether laws that treat men and women differently are constitutional or not, then the practice of judicial review wouldn't make any sense. Giving courts the final say on the most controversial issues of the day would be impossible to

[39] Cf. *United States* v. *Virginia* and *Bradwell* v. *Illinois*; *Kriel* v. *Germany* and *Sirdar* v. *Army Board*; *Air India* v. *Meerza*.

[40] See e.g. *Petrovic* v. *Austria*, European Court of Human Rights, judgment of 28 February 1998, Reports of Judgments and Decisions 1998, no. 67, B579; *Rasmussen* v. *Denmark*; *R* v. *Hess* [1990] 2 SCR 906; *Hugo* v. *South Africa*; *Rostker* v. *Goldberg*; *Parham* v. *Hughes* (1979) 441 US 347.

defend. If sex discrimination is not a matter of right or wrong, it would be profoundly undemocratic to privilege the views of a tiny group of people, who are accountable to no one but themselves and who are drawn from a professional elite, over those of the people and their elected representatives. Only if law is made up of principles that tell judges when gender-biased classifications are discriminatory and when they are not, can judicial review be reconciled with democracy and the sovereignty of people to establish the rules of social order for themselves and the communities in which they live.

As threatening as judicial opinions that validate gender-biased rules and regulations first appear, it turns out that they actually provide more evidence that confirms the objectivity and impartiality of the pragmatic understanding of law and judicial review. In fact, when they are read carefully, these judgments show that it is precisely when judges fail to apply the principles of proportionality even-handedly that rules and regulations that disadvantage some people because of their sex are certified to be constitutional. Sometimes judges say that allegations of gender discrimination should not be tested against a standard of proportionality and they substitute a weaker test. Typically, when judges openly declare their intention to abandon the principle of proportionality in favour of a softer, more deferential standard of review, they do so out of respect for prior rulings of their courts and/or out of a concern about their own abilities to do the job. In other cases, although there is no categorical repudiation of the proportionality principle, the analysis of the factual details of the case is partial and incomplete. In either case, what is evident is that validation of gender-biased laws has nothing to do with the principle of proportionality or the pragmatic method more generally and everything to do with the personality and the politics of the judge.

Of all of the explanations judges have offered when they have said that there is nothing wrong with states treating people differently because of their sex, the most familiar to lawyers is the appeal to the rulings of those who preceded them on the Bench. Reasoning from precedents is the way judges decide most cases in common law jurisdictions and in constitutional cases it is used by courts all over the world. Even the European Court of Human Rights, which does not adhere to a strict rule of *stare decisis*, followed its method in justifying two decisions to exempt laws that treated mothers better than fathers in the provision of parental allowances,[41] and in establishing their parental status with their children,[42] from having to reflect a measure of proportionality in their means and effects. The Court's own precedents, the judges ruled, gave member states a wide 'margin of appreciation' in designing policies to deal with issues of public morality on which there is a lot of diversity of opinion.[43] Because there was no consensus among member states on policies such as paid parental leave, that concerned

---

[41] *Petrovic* v. *Austria.*   [42] *Rasmussen* v. *Denmark.*

[43] *Belgian Linguistic* Case; *Handyside* v. *UK* [1976] 1 EHRR 737, para. 48; *Sunday Times* v. *UK* [1979] 2 EHRR 245, para. 59.

basic family values, the Court did not insist everyone had to conform to a common standard.[44]

Antonin Scalia's dissenting opinion in *VMI* is a particularly forceful example of a judge openly rejecting a comprehensive and rigorous review of a gender-biased law on the basis of a long line of prior cases in which the US Supreme Court had scrutinized laws that discriminated between men and women on the basis of their sex against a more relaxed, 'intermediate' test. Even though he condemned the different levels of review as 'made up tests' that allowed judges to promote the values of 'a law trained elite', he scolded his colleagues for not being faithful to the analytical framework the Court had followed for the previous thirty years. On the more deferential, less demanding standard, he pointed out, both the fact the some women were capable of meeting all the requirements of VMI's distinctive method of training and the fact that VMI would not have to change very much if they were admitted, were not pertinent to the resolution of the case. His concern was entirely with those aspects of the adversative system—such as the communal living arrangements and some of the physical exercises—that would have to be altered if qualified women were admitted. Even on these questions, however, he never responded to William Rehnquist's observation that there was no evidence that the adversative system was the only or even the best way of guaranteeing the qualifications and characters of the 'citizen-soldiers' who graduated from VMI. Instead, employing the same technique (of inventing horrible hypotheticals) that he used to reject the pleas of the Native American Church in *Oregon* v. *Smith*, he speculated that the admission of women would not only destroy a historic military institute, it would presage the death of all single-sex educational institutions in the whole of the United States.

Legal arguments, based on precedents, are not the only reason judges have given for relaxing the requirements of proportionality in cases of gender discrimination. Sometimes it is a concern for their own lack of qualifications and competence to review complex issues of government policy, such as national security, that has disinclined judges from probing the facts of a case very deeply. For example, when Yaakov Kedmi and Tsvi Tal of Israel's Supreme Court dissented from their colleague's ruling that the Air Force Command had to entertain applications from qualified women, they were open and candid about their doubts of their capacity to make decisions in which the security of the country could be at stake. Prudential concerns about their own institutional and personal competence were the reasons they gave for their decision not to test whether categorically denying all women even the opportunity to prove their qualifications as pilots was justifiable or not.[45]

---

[44] See e.g. S. Greer, *The Margin of Appreciation: Interpretation and Discretion Under the European Convention on Human Rights* (Strasbourg: Conseil de l'Europe, 2000); R. St. J. Macdonald, 'The Margin of Appreciation', in R. St. J. Macdonald, F. Matscher, and H. Petzold (eds.), *The European System for the Protection of Human Rights* (Dordrecht: Martinus Nijhoff 1993); P. Mahoney, 'Marvellous Richness of Diversity or Invidious Cultural Relativism' (1998) 19 HRLJ 1.

[45] *Miller* v. *Minister of Defence*. The US Supreme Court relied on the same argument in refusing to question their country's male-only draft, see *Rostker* v. *Goldberg*.

Respect for the decisions of those who preceded them on the Bench and sensitivity to the limits of their own qualifications are important virtues for judges to possess, but neither can justify their refusing to investigate fully every plea for protection against what are claimed to be official acts of discrimination by the state. In fact, arguments based on precedent are inconsistent with the status of constitutions being supreme laws in legal systems and arguments based on institutional modesty sacrifice the most important comparative advantage that judges, alone among government actors, possess. Each argument is wanting on what it purports to care about most—legality and prudence.

For many people who are not trained in the law the idea that a court should follow its own earlier rulings, even when it believes them to be wrong, seems absurd. If a panel of judges fails to remedy a case of gender discrimination because an earlier generation of their 'brethren' refused to provide such protection in the past, it seems to compound the injustice not to confront and rectify the error of their ways. Down on the farm one would say two wrongs can't make a right; they can only make things worse.

Lawyers are not unaware of the paradoxical nature of precedent. It is generally accepted in the legal community that no one has yet written a fully satisfactory account that justifies the practice of making decisions on the basis of earlier rulings that are thought to be wrong and mistaken in some way. As one American legal scholar has put it, 'our theoretical understanding of [following precedent] is still at a very primitive stage'.[46] Moreover, the status of arguments based on prior cases is widely understood to be especially tenuous in constitutional cases when they come before a court of final appeal.[47] As early as 1849 Roger Taney, then Chief Justice of the US Supreme Court, wrote that every judicial 'opinion upon the construction of the Constitution is always open to discussion when it is supposed to have been founded in error, and that its judicial authority should hereafter depend altogether on the force of the reasoning by which it is supported'.[48] Even though it is recognized that reasoning from prior cases can further values of equality, continuity, stability, etc., there comes a point at which decisions that are understood to be serious mistakes must be reversed.[49] The decision of the US Supreme Court in *Brown v. Board of Education*[50] overturning

[46] Larry Alexander, 'Constrained by Precedent' (1989), 63 So. Cal. L Rev. 3.

[47] H. P. Monaghan, 'Stare Decisis and Constitutional Adjudication' (1988) 88 Colum. L Rev. 740; Gary Lawson, 'The Constitutional Case Against Precedent' (1994) 17 Harv. JL and Pub. Pol'y 23; Bork, *Tempting of America*, 157–9; M. J. Gerhardt, 'The Role of Precedent in Constitutional Decision Making . . . ' (1991) 60 Geo. Wash. L Rev. 68; Edward Levi, *An Introduction to Legal Reasoning* (Chicago: University of Chicago Press, 1949) 41. See also Stone and Cardozo JJ. in *St. Joseph Stock Yard v. US* (1936) 298 US 38, 94: 'The doctrine of stare decisis, however appropriate and even necessary at times, has only a limited application in the field of constitutional law'; and Felix Frankfurter in *Graves v. NY* (1939) 306 US 466, 491–2: 'the ultimate touchstone of constitutionality is the Constitution itself and not what we have said about it.'

[48] *Passenger Cases* (1849) 48 US (7 How.) 283, 470.

[49] Even the House of Lords eventually recognized than an absolute rule of *stare decisis* would produce intolerable results in individual cases and so abandoned it for a more flexible approach. See [1966] 1 WLR 1234.

[50] *Brown v. Board of Education* (1954) 347 US 483.

its earlier ruling in *Plessy* v. *Ferguson*[51] and bringing segregated education to an end, marks a historic boundary beyond which it is universally recognized that the writ of precedent doesn't run.[52]

Even though the status of precedents—or what is sometimes referred to as doctrinal reasoning[53]—is still marked by uncertainty and ambiguity, that has not been enough for most judges and lawyers to abandon them completely. It is rare (but not unheard of[54]) to find someone arguing that precedent should play no role in how judges reach their decisions when they exercise their powers of constitutional review. The instinct of most lawyers is to hang on to the belief that looking back to the ideas and experience of those who preceded them on the Bench is a proper way for courts to distinguish acts and assertions of state authority that are legitimate from those that are not. The importance of precedents in the review process is one of the few points of law on which originalists, proceduralists, and moralists are all agreed.[55]

Psychologically the loyalty and commitment of common lawyers to the practice of reasoning from prior cases is easy to understand but intellectually it is incoherent and unprincipled and so impossible to defend. Logically, arguments based on precedent should never be used by judges who sit on their country's highest courts, if the constitutional validity of any rule, regulation, or act of a government official is at stake.[56] In constitutional cases, precedents are at best superfluous and at worst they purport to defy the supremacy of the constitution. Among those who have reflected on the status of precedents in constitutional

[51] *Plessy* v. *Ferguson* (1896) 163 US 537.

[52] Monaghan, 'Stare Decisis and Constitutional Adjudication'; F. Easterbrook, 'Stability and Reliability in Judicial Decisions' (1988) 73 Cornell L Rev. 422; L. Alexander, 'Constrained by Precedent' (1989) 63 S. Cal. L Rev. 1; 'Bad Beginnings' (1996) 145 U Penn. L Rev. 57; R. Bork, 'Neutral Principles . . . ' (1971) 47 Indiana LJ 1, 15; R. Dworkin, *Law's Empire* (Cambridge, Mass.: Harvard University Press, 1986), 389. (So if *Plessy* is really a precedent against integration, it must be overruled now.)

[53] P. Bobbitt, *Constitutional Fate: Theory of the Constitution* (New York: Oxford University Press, 1982), ch. 4; C. Fried, 'Reply to Lawson' (1994) 17 Harv. JL and Pub. Pol'y 35.

[54] But see Lawson, 'The Constitutional Case Against Precedent'.

[55] See e.g. Dworkin, *Law's Empire*, 240–50, 387–99; *Freedom's Law* (Cambridge, Mass.: Harvard University Press, 1996), ch. 1; C. Sunstein, *Legal Reasoning and Political Conflict* (New York: Oxford University Press, 1996), 71–2, 76–7; Bork, *Tempting of America*, 155–9; Antonin Scalia, *A Matter of Interpretation* (Princeton: Princeton University Press, 1997), 138–40.

[56] It is only when a constitutional case is being decided by a country's highest court that arguments based on precedent carry no weight. The argument does not apply in non-constitutional cases because, except for the constitution, no other part of the legal system can always claim to be trump. Nor are precedents without significance when they are invoked in lower courts and administrative tribunals. 'Inferior' judges and administrators are bound by the hierarchical structure of the legal system to follow the decision of those who sit above them. All subordinate institutions must faithfully apply whatever rules of constitutional validity are fixed by the 'apex' court. Even if they believe it is wrong, they have no constitutional authority to question, let alone overturn, an opinion of 'higher-ups'. They can and should explain to the parties why a precedent they must follow is defective, but that is all they can do. Allowing every judge and public official to act on their own personal interpretation of the constitution would constitute legal anarchy. It would be a repudiation of the rule of law. It is only because no one stands above those who sit on final appellate courts that they never face such a systemic constraint. Cf. Evan M. Caminker, 'Why Must Inferior Courts Obey Superior Court Precedents?' (1994) 46 Stan. L Rev. 817.

cases it is widely understood that this method of reasoning has a critical edge, or independent force, only when the court that is faced with the earlier rulings believes them to be flawed or mistaken in some way.[57] If a judge thinks that a ruling in a previous case is correct, the precedent itself is redundant. It contributes nothing to the integrity and legitimacy of the subsequent decision. The fact two groups of judges have applied the correct legal principle cannot add to or enhance its truth or authority in law. The second judge could follow the same (legally correct) analysis that the precedent court used directly, without referring to the earlier ruling, and nothing would be lost. If every judge only applied the correct legal principles properly in each case, none of the virtues of equality, consistency, fairness, predictability, efficiency, etc.—that are said to be promoted by doctrinal reasoning—would be compromised in any way.

Precedents are problematic in constitutional cases precisely because they insist judges base their rulings on cases that they regard as having been decided incorrectly. In effect, they instruct judges to apply principles and rules from prior cases that are inconsistent with the constitution and so would have them act in ways that were themselves unconstitutional. Because constitutions rank above all other laws in all legal systems, a prior ruling that is assumed to have interpreted or applied the constitution incorrectly would itself be unconstitutional and so of no legal force or effect. Like any part of the legal system, if a judicial opinion is in conflict with the requirements of the constitution, it must give way. John Marshall saw that logic more than 150 years ago[58] and the meaning of the supremacy of the constitution remains the same today. Because of its subordinate status, no precedent that is thought to be in conflict with a constitution can have any standing or authority in law. When, like Scalia, a judge on a court of final appeal believes that a rule or principle that is laid down in a prior case is a 'made up test' that promotes the political values of judges from times gone by, she or he is under a constitutional obligation to explain why it is wrong and not to be used in the future.

If it is constitutional for a state to disadvantage women because of their sex, it can't be because that is what another group of judges held sometime in the past. Judgments such as Scalia's, based on bad precedents, have no connection to any part of the constitution. They are purely the product of the legal imagination and the personal preference of the judge. Judges who believe a constitution tolerates some kinds of gender discrimination need some other argument to defend that position. The opinion of Yaakov Kedmi and Tsvi Tal, that there may be occasions when it is prudent for judges to validate laws that discriminate against women, strikes many people as offering a promising possibility. Unlike arguments grounded in precedent, invocations of institutional modesty initially look quite attractive to lots of people, including people who are not trained in the law. They seem to provide wise counsel to the judge who is asked for his or her

[57] See e.g. Fred Schauer, 'Precedent' (1987) 39 Stanford L Rev. 571, 576.
[58] *Marbury* v. *Madison* (1803) 5 US 137, 1 Cranch 137, 177–8; and see Ch. 5.2.1 *infra*.

opinion on what are often the most complex and controversial issues of the day. Intuitively it seems right to say that difficult and divisive issues such as the place of women in the military should not be decided by judges, who lack the training and experience of the experts, in a process that was designed to settle private disputes between ordinary people, not disagreements about how a country's armed forces should be organized.

Prudential arguments,[59] calling for courts to defer to the decisions of the executive branch and the expertise of its officials, have more credibility than doctrinal arguments for at least two reasons. First, they don't openly challenge the supremacy of the constitution, and second, they seem to give expression to the principle of separation of powers which contemplates each branch of government having its own distinctive powers and special role to play. On closer inspection, however, it can be seen that, like reasoning from prior cases, arguments based on institutional competence cannot succeed even on their own terms.

The idea that there are cases in which it would be prudent for courts simply to defer to the decisions of the elected branches of government misconceives how judges reason when they evaluate the conflicting interests in a case against the principle of proportionality. The perception of those who believe courts should relax their standards of review when particularly weighty matters of state are at stake seems to be that judges are being called on to balance and do a quantitative cost/benefit analysis of fundamental human rights and life-threatening interests of the state that are impossible to compare. The assumption is that some issues, like the place of women in the military, must be the exclusive responsibility of the executive branch because there is no independent and objective standard against which the competing values and claims can be measured. They are simply incommensurable and so not amenable to categorical rulings of rank ordering let alone of right and wrong. In fact, however, as a reading of the cases in which claims of gender discrimination have prevailed has shown, when judges measure laws and acts of state officials against the principle of proportionality, they focus on the means and the effects of the specific rule or regulation they have been asked to review. There is no balancing, in the sense of totting up a list of pluses and minuses and/or ranking the intrinsic value or importance of each.

When courts test whether laws that exclude women from night work or compel them to retire early are under- and/or over-inclusive, they examine whether there are any less drastic/restrictive policies (means) available to the governments that would allow them to accomplish all their objectives in a way that does not impinge on people's constitutional rights so severely. The purposes behind the law are taken as a given and the only inquiry is an empirical one of establishing whether there are better policy alternatives than the law the government chose to enact. Similarly, when judges assess how seriously a law adversely affects the constitutional rights of those who fall within its terms, they do not try

---

[59] Bobbitt, *Constitutional Fate*, ch. 5.

to calibrate the relative importance of the affected rights and interests against a common yardstick or measure of value of their own making. The job of the judge testing for this dimension of proportionality is to assess whatever hard empirical evidence throws light on the question of how significant the law under review is to those it affects the most. Rather than evaluate the competing interests at stake against some external, objective standard or principle, judges try to assess the affected parties' own understanding of how significant the law being tested is for them.

In *VMI*, there was no comparison in the significance of the classification for the state and for the women involved. The uncontradicted evidence before the Court showed that some women were qualified to handle the aggressive training methods at VMI and that other elite military institutions had admitted women cadets without suffering any adverse effects on the quality of their programmes or the qualification of their graduates. The Court's ruling to strike down the discriminatory regulation was based on a straightforward finding of fact that its impact on the lives of women who could qualify for admission on every criterion but their sex was out of all proportion to its contribution to the state of Virginia's educational and military objectives and no balancing of factors or ranking of values was involved. Nor, in passing judgment on the regulations that banned women from all military posts in the German Armed Forces that involved the use of arms, did any of the justices of the European Court of Justice have to add up all the costs and benefits of such a gender classification and pronounce a mathematical or quantifiable result. Their condemnation of the total ban on women was based on the fact that some women had already been successfully trained in the use of arms in positions that were open to them. The fact some women had received basic training with weapons was seen by the Court as providing conclusive proof that the total ban adopted by the Government was wider than it needed to be.

In *Miller*, the task facing the judges of Israel's Supreme Court, including Justices Kedmi and Tal, was exactly the same. To decide the place of women in the Air Force, the Court did not have to 'balance' their right to be free from discrimination against the right of the rest of society to its collective security. Nor was it necessary to declare one or the other to be the more important of the two. Rather, as with every allegation of gender discrimination, the judges had to gauge the significance of the exclusion both from the perspectives of women and from those responsible for the defence of the country on the basis of the evidence that was before the court. And once again, the evidence was clear and compelling in showing that allowing women to prove they could satisfy all the qualifications that Israel's Air Force Command required of its pilots would not threaten the security of the country to any measurable degree. The fact women had been successfully integrated into other branches of Israel's military service, and could be enlisted into the Air Force gradually and under controlled conditions as they had in Canada and the United States, provided the Court with solid evidence that the fears of the military authorities were exaggerated.

When it is understood that the job of the judge is to evaluate the significance of the laws she or he is asked to review from the perspective of those they most directly affect, an opinion such as Kedmi's and Tal's, that those sitting on the Bench are not qualified to decide such questions as the place of women in the military, is impossible to defend. The record of the judiciary in eliminating gender discrimination in the military and other male enclaves suggests courts are actually better suited than either of the other two branches of government to settle disputes of this kind. Because of their independence from the two elected branches of government, judges have a unique capacity for impartiality and objectivity that is often difficult for politicians (and their officials), who have a natural bias towards their own rules and regulations, to attain. Their vantage point allows them to evaluate the evidence and the concerns of both those who defend and those who oppose limiting people's opportunities on the basis of their sex, in a detached and impartial way. Indeed, it is precisely because judges have generally appreciated that their disinterested perspective is an institutional advantage, and have been prepared to exercise their powers of review in a principled way, that they have been able to advance the career opportunities of women in the military by ensuring that their exclusion from any part of the service is proved to be necessary and drawn as precisely and narrowly as possible.

Prudential arguments, then, are no better than those based on doctrine and precedent. Neither can provide a good reason why laws that disadvantage people because of their sex should be allowed to remain on the books. Even if prudential arguments do not suffer the same logical failings that make reasoning from prior cases incoherent and ultimately unconstitutional, they recommend that the members of the third branch of government should abdicate their powers precisely in those cases in which, because of their unique capacity for neutrality and impartiality, they are especially well positioned to act.

When judges vote to uphold a law that discriminates between people on the basis of their sex, it is not always because they choose not to apply the principle of proportionality and analyse the case pragmatically. In some cases, judges do focus on the facts of the case but they just do it badly. Typically they make one of two mistakes; either their assessment is partial or it is incomplete. Sometimes judges mistakenly focus all their attention on the particular features of the impugned classification without ever asking what purposes they serve. In others, they base their decision on their own views about the significance of the discriminatory treatment to the persons it affects rather than being guided by what these people say—in their own words and deeds—the classification means to them. In either case, the reason that the law is allowed to pass the test is because of the court's failure to apply the proportionality principle in a neutral and impartial way.

Two landmark rulings, one from India's Supreme Court and the other from South Africa's Constitutional Court, illustrate how easily such mistakes can occur. In *Air India*,[60] at the same time that it invalidated the rule that required air hostesses to resign if they became pregnant, the Supreme Court of India upheld two other regulations that called for their termination if they got married within four years of being hired and forced them to retire earlier than members of the flight crew who were male. In reaching this conclusion the Court made the very basic, yet remarkably common mistake of judging the classification in terms of itself rather than against the larger purposes it was supposed to serve.[61] The Court devoted much of its opinion highlighting the different qualifications, pay scales, seniority lists, and number of positions open to males and females, rather than probing how this segregation of the sexes served the interests of the airline in any significant way.

The Court recognized that there was not a lot of difference in the tasks that were performed by members of the flight crews, but it did not see that their common functions meant that the separate classifications into which men and women were slotted were entirely gratuitous. When it was pointed out that Air India's hostesses, working in the United Kingdom, could not be retired early under British law, and that Air India's rules for its female employees did not compare favourably with those of other major international carriers, the Court was still unwilling to make a finding of discrimination. At one point, the Court defended the company's rules on termination and early retirement as furthering the cause of family planning and saving 'huge expenditures' that would have to be incurred in finding replacements for hostesses who married early and had children, but it never asked why family planning wouldn't be better served by a rule that applied equally to men and women, nor did it provide any evidence of what it would cost if females had the same freedom to marry as the male members of the crew.

The flaw in the Court's judgment in *Air India* is its very uneven and selective treatment of the facts. At no point did the Court examine the significance of the rules against marriage and mandating early retirement from the perspective of the hostesses. Those (remunerative, promotional, etc.) features of the sexually segregated classifications, that were entirely of the company's own creation and were the central issues in dispute, were taken as givens while the most pertinent questions about their necessity, utility, and adverse effects were effectively ignored. The error is a common one and is not unique to the judges in New Delhi. The US Supreme Court did the same thing when it ruled it was not discriminatory for Congress to draft men but not women into the armed forces because military regulations excluded women from all combat roles without ever questioning the legitimacy of the latter.[62] Antonin Scalia also made the same mistake of conflating ends (the educational goals) and means (the gender classification) when he voted to uphold the state's male-only admission policy in *VMI*. Like the Indian Supreme Court, he focused most of his attention on the different

---

[60] *Air India.*
[61] J. Tusman and J. tenBroek, 'The Equal Protection of the Laws' (1949) 37 Calif. L Rev. 341.
[62] *Rostker v. Goldberg.*

attributes of the classification (in particular on the 'adversative' (bullying) method of training) without ever asking himself how essential they were to the state's goal of graduating the most qualified 'citizen-soldiers'. The Supreme Court of Canada committed the error of collapsing ends and means, when it said that the Parliament of Canada had not acted in a discriminatory fashion when it passed a law against sexual assault that protected only young girls.[63] According to Bertha Wilson, because the physical nature of an assault against girls is different than when the victim is male, it was not improper for the Government to limit the protection of the law in this way even though she recognized that young boys who were sexually abused would suffer serious physical and psychological harm.

When judges focus all of their attention on the classification itself, the analysis becomes tautological. In effect one dimension of the facts that are in dispute is privileged over all others and what are arguably the most salient facts—of what interests are served by treating the sexes differently—are all but ignored. For the principle of proportionality to provide an objective framework of analysis, courts must evaluate the significance of the rule or classification for the parties whom it most directly affects and for the public at large as well. Judges must take the measure of both sides of the scale.

Indeed, not only must they consider both sides of a question, they must do so, as the image of justice blindfolded is meant to convey, from the perspective of those whom the law most directly affects. Just as in giving their opinion on questions of religious liberty, judges must resist the temptation of imposing their own opinion of whether a classification does more harm than good. They must base their decision on the evidence that is before them and not speculate on or substitute their own perception of the significance of a law for those it most directly concerns. Antonin Scalia failed to maintain a detached and disinterested perspective in his dissenting opinion in *VMI* when he prophesied the demise not only of Virginia's most celebrated military academy, but of all single-sex educational programmes in the country. In venting his fears, Scalia substituted his own values and preferences for the empirical realities of the case which showed that the integration of women into the most prestigious military academies, including West Point and Annapolis, had been accomplished without precipitating such calamitous results.

South Africa's Constitutional Court made the same mistake when, with only Johann Kriegler dissenting, it upheld a general pardon that Nelson Mandela had granted, on the day of his inauguration as the country's first democratically elected President, to mothers but not fathers of young children who had been imprisoned for non-violent crimes.[64] In reaching its conclusion, the Court made no serious effort to evaluate the significance of the discriminatory character of

---

[63] R. v. *Hess*; see also *Michael M.* v. *Superior Court* (1981) 450 US 464.
[64] *Hugo* v. *South Africa*.

the pardon from the perspective of either of the parties to the dispute. First the Court downplayed the seriousness of the discrimination that fathers, such as John Hugo, were made to endure. Richard Goldstone, who wrote the majority opinion, said that fathers did not suffer any great harm because the pardon 'merely deprived them of an early release to which they had no legal entitlement'. It did not, in his opinion, 'fundamentally impair their dignity and self-worth'. Kate O'Regan echoed the same sentiment when she wrote that 'the harmful impact of the discrimination in this case was far from severe'. Even worse, although helping young children was Mandela's primary goal in granting the pardon, the interests of those whose only parent was a father who was incarcerated in jail were given no weight at all.

Goldstone dismissed the possibility that Mandela could have granted fathers who were primary childcare providers pardons on an individual basis as 'well nigh impossible', even though he conceded that such a procedure would have been viable had Mandela enacted general legislation and put in place some kind of regulatory regime. Yvonne Mokgoro wrote a concurring opinion in which she also refused to find fault with Mandela for not insisting on a case-by-case assessment of each inmate's childcare responsibilities because of the 'great administrative inconvenience' she thought it would entail.

In none of their separate opinions could Goldstone, O'Regan, or Mokgoro be said to have exercised their powers of review in a detached and impartial way. In different ways all three based their decisions on their own estimation of what would be gained and lost by a general pardon that did not discriminate between people on the basis of their sex, rather than let the parties and the evidence speak for themselves. When Goldstone and O'Regan wrote that denying fathers the benefit of the pardon did not 'impair their rights of dignity or sense of equal worth' and 'was far from severe', they claimed a sovereignty over John Hugo, and other fathers like him, to interpret such acts of discrimination for themselves that they had no authority to make. They dismissed Hugo's own self-understanding as not worthy of the Court's respect. Rather than accepting the way Hugo and other single fathers perceived their treatment by the state, they became partisan players in the case.

Goldstone's and Mokgoro's conclusion that there were no viable, less burdensome alternatives to 'the "blunt-axe" method' of a general pardon was also an act of judicial usurpation because it was not supported by any facts. Neither Goldstone nor Mokgoro pointed to any hard evidence of how extending the amnesty to single fathers such as Hugo, whose responsibility for their children could not be in dispute, would have constituted a 'great administrative inconvenience'. If the purpose of the pardon was to alleviate the plight of young children who had no nurturing from a parent because one or the other or both were in jail, whatever additional paperwork would have been entailed in treating mothers and fathers who were primary caregivers the same would have been a trivial burden for the state.

Rulings such as *Hugo* and *Air India*, and opinions such as Scalia's in *VMI*, are painful reminders that the principle of proportionality does not provide judges with automatic, self-enforcing rules. The mistakes they made in failing to condemn the blatant acts of gender discrimination they were asked to redress shows that testing laws against the principle of proportionality is not a mindless, mechanical exercise. The principle of proportionality structures how to make informed and impartial acts of judgment. It is a formal (some say empty)[65] framework of analysis that orients judges on how to organize and evaluate conflicting factual claims that are made about the laws they are asked to review. The hard work in every case is sifting and evaluating all the evidence in a way that respects the interests of everyone who is before the Court. When judges remain completely detached from the substantive values that are at stake in a case, and take seriously all the evidence that shows what a law really means for those it affects most, the cases show that the right answer is usually pretty clear and justice wins out in the end. Mistakes occur when judges allow their own feelings to influence their estimation of how significant a law is for those involved and when they are selective and not even-handed in their accounting of the relevant facts. Only if judges always respect the perspectives and personalities of those who come before them in court, will gender discrimination become an artefact of a remote and distant past.

By the end of the century, most courts had mastered the methodology, and opinions such as Scalia's and those that carried the day in *Hugo* and *Air India* were relatively uncommon. When women complained about laws that discriminated against them on the basis of outmoded stereotypes, most judges were sympathetic to their pleas. Today it is even rare for males, who sometimes had a harder time persuading courts that they could also be victims of gender discrimination, to be told that the indignity they experience in being treated this way isn't significant enough to count. For the most part, the third branch of government has shown itself to be a pretty good check against the state practising or tolerating discrimination against either sex, at least against those men and women whose libido inclines them to act in ways that are traditional and straight. The jurisprudence of sex discrimination, when it is practised wholesale against all women (or men) looks very strong. It is more compelling evidence of the legitimacy of the review process when it is done in a principled and pragmatic way. However, when sex discrimination is aimed at only some members of the group, at the retail level so to speak, the picture is not nearly so pretty.

3. EQUAL OPPORTUNITIES FOR LESBIANS AND GAYS

When gender classifications are submerged beneath distinctions that are based on people's sexual preferences, we have already noticed that courts have been

---

[65] P. Westen, *Speaking of Equality* (Princeton: Princeton University Press, 1990).

much less willing to respond. When gays and lesbians have complained about laws that discriminate against them because of their sex, their reception from the judiciary has not been nearly as welcoming. Although gay men have had some success challenging laws that characterize their sexual behaviour as 'gross indecency' and make sodomy a crime, they have lost as many or more of these cases as they have won. Where South Africa's Constitutional Court, the European Court of Human Rights, and the UN Human Rights Committee have been sympathetic to their pleas,[66] the Supreme Courts of Ireland, the United States, and Zimbabwe, and Germany's Constitutional Court (at least initially) have not.[67] So too when they have asked the courts to overturn laws that make it impossible for them to adopt children: South Africa's Constitutional Court has voted in their favour;[68] the European Court of Human Rights against.[69] Gays and lesbians also have received conflicting opinions from established and well-respected courts on the validity of laws that denied them various employment opportunities and related benefits. The European Court of Justice has expressed its opinion that employment regulations that restrict vacation benefits to heterosexual couples do not constitute gender discrimination;[70] the Supreme Court of Israel[71] and South Africa's Constitutional Court[72] have said that they do. Canada's Supreme Court, like the country it oversees, is a house that is divided within. Within a period of four years it ruled that same-sex couples have the right to be treated the same as heterosexuals when it comes to claiming support payments from their estranged partners that are provided in matrimonial laws,[73] but not to special allowances and assistance that are given to elderly heterosexual couples by the state.[74] Most significantly, no international tribunal or court of final appeal has yet been persuaded to recognize the rights of gays and lesbians to enter contracts of marriage.[75] Two courts—Hungary's Constitutional Court[76] and New Zealand's Court of Appeal[77]—have said very emphatically that traditional marriage laws that exclude same-sex unions do not deny gays

---

[66] *The National Coalition for Gay and Lesbian Equality* v. *Ministry of Justice* [1999] 1 SA 6 (Const. Ct.); (1998) 12 BCLR 1517. *Dudgeon* v. *UK* (1981) 4 EHRR 149; *Norris* v. *Ireland* (1989) 13 EHRR 186; *Toonen* v. *Australia* (1992) UN HRC 488.

[67] *Supra* nn. 9–12.

[68] *Du Toit* v. *Minister for Welfare and Population Development* [2003] 2 SA 198; [2002] 10 B Const. LR 1006 (Constit. Ct.).

[69] *Fretté* v. *France.*

[70] *Grant* v. *South-West Trains* (1998) 1 CMCR 993 (ECJ, Case C-249/96).

[71] *El-Al Israel* v. *Danilowitz*, 4 May 1994, Supreme Court of Israel sitting as the High Court of Justice Case 721/94; <www.courts.gov.Il>. Reproduced, in part, by P. Gewirtz and I. Cogan (eds.), *Global Constitutionalism* (New Haven: Yale Law School, 1998), pp. iv, 92–113.

[72] *Satchwell* v. *President of the Republic of South Africa* [2002] 6 SA 1 (Const. Ct.).

[73] *M* v. *H* (1999) 171 DLR (4th) 577.

[74] *Egan* v. *Canada.*

[75] But see the decision of Hawaii's Supreme Court in *Baehr* v. *Lewin* (1993) 852 P (2d) 44 and two of Canada's provincial Courts of Appeal in *Egale* v. *Canada* (2003) 225 DLR (4th) 472; *Halpern* v. *Canada* (2003) 225 DLR (4th) 529.

[76] *Supra* n. 14.

[77] *Supra* n. 15.

and lesbians the equal protection of the law. Two others, the Supreme Courts of Canada and the United States have made it very clear, when they found the rights of gays and lesbians had been violated, that nothing they said in their judgments was meant to upset the traditional concept of marriage.[78] The European Court of Human Rights has not dealt directly with the issue of gay marriage, but in a series of cases dealing with the rights of transsexuals, it has consistently held to the view that the right to marry that is guaranteed in the Convention is restricted to traditional unions of two people of the opposite sexes.[79]

The treatment gays and lesbians have received from the courts is actually even less supportive than a simple tally of wins and losses might suggest. Even when they have some success, it is rare for a court to focus its analysis on the ends and means and the effects of the offending law in a rigorous and principled way. Typically their victories are narrow and incomplete. It is not uncommon when a court hands down a judgment that recognizes the right of gays and lesbians to receive various benefits and opportunities that heterosexual couples living in conjugal relationships are privileged to enjoy, to make it clear that there are limits as to how far such claims for equality can reach. Even when judges are most sympathetic to their claims, it is standard practice to disclaim any inclination or intention to challenge traditional ideas about marriage. As well, when gay men have been successful in attacking sodomy and gross indecency laws, their claims are often only partially vindicated. For example, when the European Court of Human Rights[80] and South Africa's Constitutional Court[81] struck down laws that targeted the sexual activities of gay men, neither was prepared to question the legitimacy of establishing different ages of consent for gay, lesbian, and heterosexual sex. In fact, the judges in Strasbourg made a deliberate decision not to make any reference to the question of discrimination in any part of its decision; a strategy that the United Nations Human Rights Committee also found congenial when it ruled Tasmania's sodomy laws violated the International Covenant on Civil and Political Rights. Hungary's Constitutional Court has also ruled against gays on the issue of differential ages of consent.[82]

Not only are the victories of gays and lesbians qualified and incomplete, they are also generally very limited in their reach. Gays and lesbians seem to win only the easy cases, when the evidence is so clear-cut that a court can say the offending law was the product of an irrational and/or hostile intent. In their rulings

---

[78] *M v. H* paras. 53, 55, 134; *Lawrence v. Texas.*

[79] See *Sheffield and Horsham v. UK* (1998) 27 EHRR 163; *B. v. France* (1993) 16 EHRR 1; *Cossey v. UK* (1991) 13 EHRR 622; *Rees v. UK* (1987) 9 EHRR 56. In *Goodwin v. UK* (2003) 13 BHRC 120, the Court held that defining a person's sex on purely biological criteria violated the right of transsexuals to marry and raise a family. In *Bellinger v. Bellinger* (2003) 14 BHRC 127, the House of Lords followed suit.

[80] *Dudgeon v. UK.* Twenty years later, in *L. v. Austria* (2000) 13 BHRC 594, the judges in Strasbourg ruled that different ages of consent for gay and straight sex were discriminatory and violated Article 14 of the Convention. See also *ADT v. UK* [2000] 9 BHRC 112.

[81] *The National Coalition for Gay and Lesbian Equality.*

[82] *Minimum Age for Membership of Homosexual-Oriented Associations*, Decision 21, 17 May 1996, in Sólyom and Brunner (eds.), *Constitutional Judiciary in a New Democracy*, 333.

recognizing the right of gays and lesbians to claim various benefits provided to unmarried couples under traditional family and domestic partnership laws, for example, the Supreme Court of Canada and the Constitutional Court of Hungary both made the point that the goals of such legislation would actually be compromised by excluding gay and lesbian relationships from their protection.[83] In economists' terms, treating gays and lesbians the same as heterosexuals is *pareto superior* because it enhances the objectives of the law and the constitutional rights of gays and lesbians simultaneously. Similarly, the United Nations Human Rights Committee based its ruling against Tasmania's sodomy laws in part on the fact they would work against their public health objectives of preventing the spread of AIDS by driving same-sex relationships underground.[84] So too the unanimous ruling of South Africa's Constitutional Court that gays and lesbians have a right to the same opportunities to adopt as everyone else was justified as enhancing the government's objectives and the best interests of children more generally.[85]

In some of these cases the evidence can be so strong and the targeting of gays so explicit that the court is able to base its decision on a finding of malevolent or invidious intent. That was the reason the US Supreme Court gave in *Romer* v. *Evans* when it struck down a law prohibiting municipal governments and even the state legislature from extending the protection of human rights codes to include discrimination on the basis of a person's sexual orientation. The 'sheer breadth' of the law, the Court said was 'so discontinuous with the reasons offered for it that [it] seems inexplicable by anything but animus towards the class that it affects; it lacks a rational relationship to legitimate state interests'.[86] Similarly South Africa's Constitutional Court threw out that country's sodomy laws because the evidence showed they too were motivated by nothing other than 'rank prejudice'.[87]

The narrow reasons judges give when they come down on the side of gays and lesbians contrast sharply with the strong and emphatic judgments they write when they conclude there is no merit to their claims. When courts give their seal of approval to laws that impose special burdens on gays and lesbians and/or deny them benefits and opportunities that heterosexuals are privileged to enjoy, the reasons are typically sweeping and bold. They deny it, they excuse it, and in some cases they even defend it as being reasonable and just. Some judges say sodomy and traditional matrimonial and family laws are constitutional because they simply don't discriminate as a matter of fact. Other times the argument is that the interest or activity for which protection is being sought, such as sodomy or same-sex marriages, is not something that is covered by the constitution. A third and last line of defence invokes the sovereignty of the people to pass laws for the protection of their most deeply felt moral intuitions and ideas, even if they

---

[83] *M* v. *H*, 115–16; *On the Legal Equality of Same-Sex Partnerships*, pt. III, para. 3.
[84] *Toonen* v. *Australia*.   [85] *Du Toit* v. *Minister for Welfare*.
[86] *Romer* v. *Evans* (1996) 517 US 620.
[87] *National Coalition for Gay and Lesbian Equality* v. *Minister of Justice*.

do incidentally discriminate against some people on a ground that the constitution proscribes. Typically judges who are not sympathetic to the claims of lesbians and gays will make use of more than one of these arguments in their judgments and it is not uncommon to find them making use of all three. Whatever the reason(s), whenever gays and lesbians fail to secure the relief that they seek, facts that are critical to their cases are either misunderstood or ignored.

The argument that sodomy laws and traditional matrimonial and family laws are not discriminatory has appealed to many judges and comes in two forms. The more popular of the two is based on the factual premise that sexual relations have different biological, psychological, and social meanings for men and women and for gays and straights and claims that it is entirely consistent with the principle of equality to have those differences reflected in the law. The argument purports to be a straightforward application of the general understanding that the formal principle of equality requires not only that those things, people, etc. that are similarly situated be treated the same, but that those whose circumstances differ be treated differently in proportion to their differences. So, in the same way that equality requires a person with a handicap be given a head start, it is said that it is not discriminatory to pass laws that favour heterosexual couples because their sexual relations and those of lesbians and gays are physically very different.

This argument figured prominently in the reasoning of Germany's Constitutional Court in the first reported decision on the constitutional validity of sodomy laws that explicitly targeted sexual relations between gay men.[88] For the members of that Court, in the middle of the last century, male and female homosexuality were radically different physiological and psychological states and so the constitutional principle of equality was not offended by a law that made sexual relations between men, but not women, a crime. It also appealed to a majority of the judges on Ireland's and Zimbabwe's Supreme Courts.[89] Even one of the judges who dissented, and would have invalidated Ireland's laws against buggery and gross indecency on other grounds, expressed the opinion that laws that made such practices criminal offences were not discriminatory in any way.[90] As well, the fact that same-sex couples are different from traditional heterosexual unions in their incapacity to jointly procreate and raise a family of common children has been decisive for a number of the judges who have sat on Canada's Supreme Court and, although it never has captured a majority of its members, it did have enough support to determine the outcome of the Court's seminal ruling on the scope of gay rights.[91]

The European Court of Justice has also validated an employment regulation, that limited vacation benefits paid to partners of employees to those who were of

---

[88] *Homosexuality* case.   [89] *Norris v. A.G.*; *Banana v. State.*
[90] Per Henchy J, *Norris v. A.G.*   [91] *Egan v. Canada*, per LaForest J.

the opposite sex, on the ground it did not discriminate, but its argument took a very different form.[92] Rather than emphasize the differences between same-sex and opposite-sex couples, the European Court ruled that because both men and women were equally constrained by the law no discrimination had occurred. The disqualifying condition, the Court said, applied regardless of the sex of the worker. The impugned regulation was justified as being consistent with the formal principle of equality because men and women who were similarly situated were being treated the same.

Although arguments that laws that disadvantage gays and lesbians are not necessarily discriminatory have been popular with some judges, it is rare that they are made to bear the whole weight of a decision. Typically, they are followed up with interpretative and ethical arguments to the effect that even if such laws do discriminate, either they do not constitute a violation of anyone's constitutional rights and/or they can be justified as legitimate attempts by the people to protect the moral characters of their communities. Although interpretative arguments almost never figure in cases of sex discrimination when the complainant is heterosexual, it is quite common for gays and lesbians to be told that their freedom to engage in sex and enjoy the same benefits and opportunities that the state provides for heterosexual couples, is not protected by a constitution. Often, interpretative rulings of this kind are based on historical claims about what guarantees of equality and privacy were originally understood to mean. Both Ireland's Supreme Court[93] and New Zealand's Court of Appeal[94] relied heavily on original intentions and understandings in explaining why they thought their country's laws on gay sex and traditional marriages, respectively, did not violate any constitutional norms. For the majority of judges in Dublin, it was simply 'incomprehensible' that in adopting a constitution that explicitly declared its commitment to Christian values, anyone would have thought that laws that had punished conduct that their church had taught was gravely sinful for hundreds of years would suddenly be declared to be unconstitutional and no longer of any legal force or effect.

Often historical definitions are supplemented with arguments about what the literal, natural meaning of the relevant words are commonly understood to be. Hungary's Constitutional Court[95] and the European Court of Human Rights[96] cited current understandings and popular opinion in defending laws that limited marriages to unions of people of the opposite sex, as did Zimbabwe's Supreme Court when it pointed to the conservative character of the country's moral code as a reason why it should not place 'a sexually liberal interpretation [of] the constitution [on the] country'.[97] The Americans, in their characteristic style, blended historical claims with doctrinal arguments when they validated the state of Georgia's sodomy laws in *Bowers* v. *Hardwick*,[98] and one of their most

---

[92] *Grant* v. *South-West Trains.*   [93] *Norris* v. *A.G.*   [94] *Quilter* v. *A.G.*
[95] *On the Legal Equality of Same-Sex Partnerships.*   [96] *Supra* n. 79.
[97] *Banana* v. *State.*   [98] *Bowers* v. *Hardwick.*

prominent jurists has written that current popular opinion should be decisive on the issue of same-sex marriage as well.[99]

In addition to denying the fact of discrimination and the protection of the constitution, judges who say that gays and lesbians have no basis to complain about whatever disadvantages traditional matrimonial and sexual offences laws may impose on them, almost always make what Philip Bobbitt has labelled an 'ethical' argument to support their position as well.[100] Most courts that have addressed the issue have been emphatic and unequivocal in their endorsement of states being able to give legal protection and support to the most important moral values of their people. That lawmakers may legitimately take the moral character of their countries into account in the formulation of the (criminal, matrimonial, education, etc.) laws they enact is a principle that has been endorsed by the Supreme Courts of Ireland, Zimbabwe, and the United States, Germany's and Hungary's Constitutional Courts, and the European Court of Human Rights.[101] It is uncommon to find judges equivocating about whether the enforcement of private morals can qualify as a legitimate legislative purpose.[102]

Judges who say there is nothing wrong with governments making use of the coercive powers of the state to protect the most important moral values of their people, often point to laws that make incestuous and polygamous relationships a crime, even when all the people involved have the capacity and do in fact give their consent.[103] Legislation against these and other sexual couplings has been enacted by governments all over the world. If laws against incest and polygamy are legitimate, so too, the argument goes, are injunctions against sodomy and same-sex marriages. All our laws about sexual relationships have their origins in religious and moral traditions of long standing and cannot be differentiated from each other in a way that is legally significant.

When all the rulings that have gone against gays and lesbians are added up, the raw numbers are very discouraging. In so many cases, in so many places, courts have been much less willing to set matters right when gays and lesbians are victims of state-sanctioned discrimination than when heterosexual men and women find themselves in the same position. From the perspective of a gay or lesbian person, it is as if the judiciary thinks of them as lower caste. As poorly as gays and lesbians have been treated by the courts, however, it would be prema-

---

[99] Richard Posner, *The Problematics of Moral and Legal Theory* (Cambridge, Mass.: Harvard University Press, 1999), 249–52; see also R. Posner, 'Should There Be Homosexual Marriage? And If So Who Should Decide?' (1997) 95 Mich. L Rev. 1578. Cass Sunstein, a colleague of Posner, also believes that when public opinion feels strongly about an issue such as gay marriage, it is wrong for courts to impose their will. See *Designing Democracy: What Constitutions Do* (New York: Oxford University Press, 2001), ch. 8.

[100] Bobbitt, *Constitutional Fate*, chs. 7–12; 'Methods of Constitutional Argument' 23 UBCL Rev. (1989) 449.

[101] *Norris v. A.G.*; *Banana v. State*; *Bowers v. Hardwick*; *On the Legal Equality of Same-Sex Partnerships*; *Dudgeon v. UK*, paras. 49, 57; *Norris v. Ireland*; *Fretté v. France*.

[102] But see the *National Coalition for Gay and Lesbian Equality*, paras. 25(b), 37; *Lawrence v. Texas*.

[103] See e.g. *Bowers v. Hardwick*; *Norris v. A.G.*; *Quilter v. A.G.*

ture for them to give up all hope. It is wrong to think that gays and lesbians can never receive the same protection against sex discrimination as everyone else. There is nothing in the text of any constitution or in the courts' jurisprudence that justifies judges taking a different attitude towards sex discrimination depending on the sexual orientation of the person bringing the complaint. To the contrary, what the cases again show is that rules and regulations that differentiate between people because of their sex survive only when the judges' evaluation of the details of the case is inattentive and half-hearted. Every time a court validates a law that discriminates against gays and lesbians because of their sex, their review of the facts is partial and incomplete. The flaw in the analysis is exactly the same as the inadequate accounting of the evidence that scars the few judgments that still tolerate women not being treated as equals. It happens more often when gays and lesbians are the plaintiffs but that doesn't mean it is any less amenable to being corrected and done right. In a world in which almost all judges now undertake a conscientious and comprehensive assessment of the facts when complaints about sex discrimination are made by heterosexual women, the day should not be far off when gays and lesbians get the same respect.

For judges who are willing to reflect candidly about the state of the current jurisprudence, the errors and omissions are easy to spot. The distortion of the factual record is especially clear when judges say that laws that privilege traditional marriages and family arrangements do not discriminate on the basis of sex because men and women, gays and lesbians, are treated the same. This was the basis on which the European Court of Justice ruled that gay couples were not entitled to the same employment benefits as heterosexuals,[104] and it has appealed to judges on Hungary's Constitutional Court[105] and New Zealand's Court of Appeal as well.[106] Of all the arguments that have been made in support of laws that disadvantage gays and lesbians, the claim that they are not discriminatory, because both sexes are equally burdened, is unquestionably the weakest and most difficult to defend. Even when men and women are equally disadvantaged by laws that privilege heterosexual relationships, their gender bias remains an established fact. The equal treatment of males and females describes one feature of such laws but it ignores the fact they strictly control what people can and cannot do (copulate, marry, etc.) on the basis of their sex. The fact such laws do not entail wholesale discrimination between men and women says nothing about how they treat people as individuals.

The flaw in the argument is easy to see if one changes the classification from sex to race. The fallacy is particularly poignant when the argument is that anti-miscegenation laws that prohibit interracial marriages are not discriminatory because all races are treated the same. The State of Virginia once tried to put that

---

[104] *Grant v. South-West Trains.*

[105] *On the Legal Equality of Same-Sex Partnerships.*

[106] *Quilter v. A.G.* per Gault J and Tipping J.

argument to the United States Supreme Court but didn't get very far.[107] Even though it was true to say that people of all races were equally limited in their choice of marriage partners, no one on the Court was fooled. All nine justices recognized that notwithstanding their superficial equality they were deeply racist both in their purpose and effect.

Employment regulations and traditional marriage laws that privilege heterosexual couples discriminate against people on the basis of their sex in exactly the same way. The sexist bias of our traditional rules of marriage is precisely the same as the racism that infected the anti-miscegenation laws that were struck down by the US Supreme Court. Sex, like race, determines who each person can marry. The freedom of people who want to enter same-sex and/or interracial marriages is proscribed simply because of their sex and/or race. Even though both sexes and all races are equally disadvantaged, the discriminatory character of such laws remains an undeniable, immutable fact. One judge—Ted Thomas, who sat on New Zealand's Court of Appeal—has made the connection between laws that are racist and those that are sexist notwithstanding the fact that they treat all races and both sexes the same.[108] So have some academics.[109] The fact few judges have disputed the gender bias of laws that favour heterosexual couples suggests it is a linkage that is widely understood. Denying that laws that prejudice gays and lesbians discriminate on the basis of each person's sex because males and females are equally restricted in their choice of partners is a glaring non sequitur that most people, including members of the judiciary, are able to comprehend.

The argument that traditional marriage and family laws do not discriminate on the basis of sex because men and women are treated the same is so clearly wrong as an empirical fact it is not surprising that it does not figure prominently in the jurisprudence on gay rights. Even the judges on Zimbabwe's Supreme Court who were inclined to dismiss the allegation of sex discrimination 'as a kind of chop logic' had to concede it was 'technically' correct.[110] As a result, when judges rule that laws that disadvantage gays and lesbians are not discriminatory, it is much more likely it is because they think that the defining characteristics of gay and straight relationships are so dissimilar that it is legitimate for those differences to be manifested in the law.[111] To treat people equally whose circumstances are (biologically, socially, etc.) different, these judges say, requires the law to be attentive to, not deny, those facts that distinguish and make each of them unique.

---

[107] *Loving* v. *Virginia* (1967) 388 US 1. The case and its relevance to the issue of same-sex marriage is developed at length in William Eskridge, *The Case for Same-Sex Marriage* (New York: Free Press, 1996), ch. 6.

[108] *Quilter* v. *A.G.*

[109] See e.g. Andrew Koppelman, 'Why Discrimination Against Lesbians and Gay Men is Sex Discrimination' (1994) 69 NYU L Rev. 197; A. Koppelman, *The Gay Rights Question in Contemporary American Law*; Robert Wintemute, *Sexual Orientation and Human Rights* (New York: Clarendon, 1995); Sunstein, *Designing Democracy*, ch. 8.

[110] *Banana* v. *State.*   [111] See text accompanying n. 88–91.

Like the argument that laws that disadvantage gays and lesbians are not discriminatory because men and women are treated the same, opinions that reach this conclusion because of the different biological, social, etc. characteristics of the two groups are also only as strong as the facts on which they are based. In some cases, with the passage of time, we have learned that many of the 'scientific' assumptions that were made about gays and lesbians in the past are simply not true. We now know, for example, that to say that gays and lesbians face 'a harrowing . . . life . . . of . . . loneliness and frustration'[112] is wholly at odds with modern medicine, which, though it once did, no longer characterizes homosexuality as a condition that needs to be treated.[113] Fifty years after it was made, the depiction of 'male homosexuals' by the judges on the German Constitutional Court, as 'victim[s of] an unrestrained sexual desire', bent on the seduction of others, can now be seen as the false and demeaning stereotype that it is.[114] Sometimes judges acknowledge that there is not a lot of evidence to support such negative characterizations of gay relationships and gay sex. More often, critical pieces of evidence that contradict their conclusions are simply ignored. In his judgment for his court in *Norris v. A.G.*, Thomas Francis O'Higgins, the Chief Justice of Ireland, did both. He conceded there was a lack of 'precise information' on the effects of homosexual activity on the institution of marriage and he ignored the fact that no harm had come to Ireland when its sodomy laws were not enforced or to any neighbouring countries that had decriminalized gay and lesbian sex.

Ignoring facts and making up facts are two reasons why judges have failed to protect gays and lesbians from all state-sanctioned acts of sex discrimination. Inflating the importance of facts is a third. Making a fact that was barely relevant to the parties the basis of his decision was, for example, the reason Charles Gonthier dissented from the Supreme Court of Canada's ruling that same-sex couples were entitled to make the same claims for spousal support on the break-up of their relationships as heterosexuals.[115] Gonthier refused to go along with his colleagues because he thought the fact that only opposite-sex couples were capable of jointly procreating and raising common children was critically important and justified their being singled out for special treatment in this way. For him, schemes of spousal support were aimed at remedying the plight of dependent married women who had stayed at home and raised a family and there was nothing discriminatory in the state targeting their special circumstances in this way.

Highlighting the unique procreative capacity and traditional roles of heterosexual couples gives Gonthier's opinion a measure of credibility that judgments that are based on outdated stereotypes transparently lack. It purports to ground

---

[112] *Norris v. A.G.*, per O'Higgins CJ.

[113] Neither the American Psychiatric Association nor the American Psychological Association still characterize 'homosexuality' as a mental disorder. See *Boy Scouts of America v. Dale* (2000) 530 US 640, 699, per Stevens J (Pt. VI). And see Eskridge, *The Case for Same-Sex Marriage*.

[114] *Homosexuality Case*.   [115] *M v. H.*

its conclusion on a fact that is impossible to deny. Like all the other opinions that claim it is not discriminatory to pass laws that disadvantage lesbians and gays, however, his treatment of the facts is highly subjective and partial. Gonthier makes procreation the decisive fact on which his ruling against discrimination turns even though procreation was in no way germane to a person's entitlement to claim benefits under the Act. Under the law heterosexual couples were eligible for spousal support whether or not they had any children. Older and/or sterile couples for whom procreation was a physical impossibility, for example, were not disqualified for that reason. Nor did Gonthier give any weight to the fact that gays and lesbians can and do raise families and can form relationships of dependence. Rather than base his decision on the facts as the Government and the gay community understood them, Gonthier arrogated to himself the authority of decreeing what facts mattered the most and, in so doing, forfeited the impartial perspective that is the hallmark of being a judge.

When judges say it is not discriminatory to enact laws that privilege heterosexual relationships, the factual and/or logical errors they make stand out in bold relief. By contrast, when judges rule that gays and lesbians do not have the same right to marry or even to have sex with the partner they prefer because these kinds of interests and activities are not protected by the constitution, they seem to be on much firmer ground. Especially in such countries as Ireland or Zimbabwe, where the dominant religious and cultural traditions take a very conservative and conventional approach to questions of sex, the factual description of how far those who were responsible for entrenching bills of rights into their countries' constitutions expected them to reach, seems pretty close to the mark. As a matter of fact, it is hard to argue with O'Higgins's conclusion that it would have been 'incomprehensible' to anyone involved in the adoption of the Irish constitution that they were making legal activities that their religious beliefs taught them were 'gravely sinful' and which had been outlawed for hundreds of years.

Like Gonthier's opinion that heterosexual couples are different than gays and lesbians in their capacity to procreate, O'Higgins's observation about the original understanding of those responsible for entrenching a bill of rights into Ireland's constitution is unquestionably true. Indeed, in many countries it would be accurate to say that no one expected a constitutional guarantee of equality would result in the repeal of long-standing laws on sex and marriage and a radical rethinking of the religious and moral ideas on which they were based. Once again, however, the simple truth of the assertion is not decisive because the image it depicts of the circumstances surrounding the entrenchment of the constitution is, like all false opinions, partial and incomplete. Like Gonthier's comparison of gay and straight relationships, O'Higgins's historical account of Ireland's transformation into a constitutional democracy with a written bill of rights tells only part of the story. It fails to acknowledge that in addition to whatever specific thoughts anyone may have had on issues such as gay sex and marriage, there was also a clear and conscious choice to formulate a constitutional rule against unequal and discriminatory acts by the state in the broadest possible terms.

Article 40(1) of the Irish constitution is written in a sweeping and majestic prose. It guarantees 'all citizens . . . as human persons [shall] be held equal before the law'. The way O'Higgins thinks constitutions should be interpreted is that the meaning of Article 40(1) is to be drawn entirely from the expectations people thought it would have and the words themselves (and the intention to use them) should be ignored. Such a partial privileging of the historical record is not only an inaccurate description of Ireland's constitutional history, it does not fit any modern constitution that expressly guarantees everyone the equal benefit of the law. Its distortion of text is especially egregious in such countries as Canada, Germany, and Hungary whose constitutions provide both that men and women have equal rights and that no one shall be discriminated against on the basis of their sex.[116] Courts exceed their jurisdiction when they ignore the fact that guarantees of equality and non-discrimination are written in broad and unconditional terms and base their rulings on general understandings that no one expected traditional laws governing marriage and sex would have to change. Even when constitutions (or international conventions) make explicit reference to the institution of marriage, courts assert an authority they do not have when they allow governments to ignore broad proscriptions against sex discrimination. Gays and lesbians say they are victims of sex discrimination, which the constitution expressly forbids, and it can be no answer to their claim that few if any people foresaw that traditional laws regulating sex and marriage have precisely that effect.

Privileging the expectations that people had or currently hold on what impact a constitution will have is wrong for at least two reasons.[117] As a factual account of what was going on in the minds of those who chose to express their commitment to the principle of equality and non-discrimination in strong and unqualified terms, it tells only half the story. The elevated and inspirational text that is characteristic of all modern bills of rights shows that even if no one expected they would threaten traditional laws on marriage and sex, there is in such proclamations a very clear expression of a general intention to bring the practice of people being discriminated against on the basis of their sex to an end. That is what a guarantee against sex discrimination says it protects and it would be tantamount to amending the constitution if that part of its prescription were ignored.

---

[116] Canadian Charter of Rights and Freedoms, Sections 15 and 28, German Basic Law, Article 3(1), 3(2); Constitution of Hungary, Articles 66 and 70A, in Blaustein and Flanz, *Constitutions*.

[117] In making the point that the expectations of the framers must also conform to a constitution's most fundamental principles, the German Constitutional Court has identified a third. See *Southwest State Case* (1951) 1 BVerf GE 14, in D. Kommers, *The Constitutional Jurisprudence of the Federal Republic of Germany*, 2nd edn. (Durham, NC: Duke University Press, 1997), 63.

The other mistake that occurs when judges rule that traditional laws on marriage and sex are not gender-biased, because those responsible for adopting a broad prohibition against discrimination didn't think that they were, is that it fails to address the grievances of gays and lesbians on their merits. This is why Ted Thomas of New Zealand's Court of Appeal was critical of judges who focus all their attention on what those who were responsible for adopting their bill of rights thought its consequences would be. Analysing a case from such a perspective, he pointed out, 'avoids the hard question [of] whether or not the law is discriminatory'.[118] For Thomas, reasoning from original understandings and current expectations is 'confused' because it makes the legitimacy of our traditional ideas about sex and marriage turn on what people thought the consequences of a broad commitment to equality and non-discrimination would be rather than on whether they discriminate as a matter of fact.

Interpretative arguments, that traditional laws on marriage and sex are not inconsistent with basic guarantees of equality and non-discrimination, are plagued by the same kind of empirical inaccuracies and logical flaws as conceptual claims that deny there is any discrimination going on. Both fail because they are based on incomplete and/or inaccurate accounts of the facts. Playing fast and loose with the evidence and the empirical realities of a case can develop into an attitude and habit of mind and so it is not surprising that the ethical arguments that also feature prominently in these judgments are typically marked by thin and inadequate treatment of the facts as well. Ethical arguments invariably lack hard evidence to prove that 'traditional family values' are essential to raising children and preserving the moral character of the community and make no attempt to specify what the consequences would be if gays and lesbians were just as free as heterosexuals to choose the people with whom they would have sex, join in marriage, and raise a family. No evidence is ever provided that would support the claim that if gays and lesbians had the same rights and freedoms as heterosexual couples, including the possibility of getting married, the moral character of the community and especially its young would be threatened in any way. Facts are displaced by judicial fears and vague speculation on what might just possibly be. Even worse, facts that show the contrary are brushed aside or simply ignored.[119]

Rather than making a serious effort to find out what has happened when laws that disadvantage lesbians and gays are removed from the books, judges who are of the opinion that they are constitutional, because of the moral values on which they are based, are more likely to point to laws that outlaw incestuous and polygamous relationships as conclusive analogies. Few question the legitimacy of the state making polygamy[120] or incest a crime and, so the argument goes,

---

[118] *Quilter* v. *A.G.* (New Zealand).

[119] In *Fretté* v. *France*, for example, the European Court of Human Rights upheld the decision of the French authorities not to allow gays or lesbians to adopt children without giving any consideration to evidence that showed that Philippe Fretté, the applicant in the case, had a genuine aptitude for bringing up children.

[120] *Reynolds* v. *US* (1878) SC 145.

same-sex relationships that are equally offensive to the same moral and religious traditions can also be proscribed by the state. However, drawing parallels between laws that disadvantage gays and lesbians and those that make incest and polygamy a crime is no substitute for a careful analysis of the facts. Like arguments about whether a law actually discriminates, or the intention of those responsible for the enactment of a constitutional bill of rights, the logic and force of an analogy is only as strong as that which is common to those things, states of affairs, etc. that are being compared.

The connection is often very weak. Reasoning by analogy is notoriously soft in its treatment of facts. Those who understand how important fact-finding is to the integrity of law recognize that 'analogical thinking may be an obstacle to progress'.[121] Analogical reasoning can go wrong anytime there is an inadequate inquiry into the relevant differences that distinguish the two situations, circumstances, etc. being compared. Bad analogies are misleading and unhelpful precisely because their treatment of the relevant facts is arbitrary and incomplete. Only common characteristics, features, etc. are considered important and relevant differences, no matter how significant, are ignored.

Laws banning polygamous and incestuous marriages are not good analogies or precedents for refusing to recognize same-sex marriages because they treat relatively trivial similarities between all the relationships as being of critical importance and give no weight to differences that radically distinguish all three. Drawing an analogy between polygamy, incest, and gay and lesbian marriages privileges the historical roots and widespread (though not universal) religious condemnation of all three types of sexual relations and discounts completely fundamental, biological, psychological, and moral features that are unique to each. Same sex relationships may be equally offensive to a community's religious and moral codes as incest and polygamy but they are far less threatening to the physical and psychological well being of gays and lesbians than polygamous and incestuous relationships are to women and vulnerable family members more generally. Gay and lesbian relationships certainly do not throw up any of the reproductive dangers that can threaten incestuous relationships. Nor are they susceptible to systemic exploitation and inequality as both polygamous and some incestuous unions (e.g. parent/child) have the capacity to be. If laws that outlaw incest and polygamy are constitutionally valid, it is because the risks of adverse genetic consequences, child abuse, and the subordination of women are serious and pressing and incapable of being met in any less draconian way. However instrumental religious and moral codes were in defining the boundaries of acceptable sexual

---

[121] C. Sunstein, 'On Analogical Reasoning' (1993) 106 Harv. L Rev. 741, 790. See also *Legal Reasoning and Political Conflict* (New York: Oxford University Press 1996), ch. 3. On the limits of analogical reasoning more generally, see Larry Alexander, 'Bad Beginnings'; Hutchinson, *It's All in the Game*, 152–62; Richard Posner, *The Problems of Jurisprudence* (Cambridge, Mass.: Harvard University Press, 1990), ch. 2; and Ronald Dworkin, 'In Praise of Theory' (1997) 29 Arizona State LJ 353, 371.

relationships, laws against incest and polygamy remain on the books because they can inflict a measure of harm on the people who are involved that is not characteristic of relations between lesbians and between gays. Drawing analogies to polygamy and incest obscures the specific suffering they cause. Ted Thomas of New Zealand's Court of Appeal called the comparison demeaning it is so wide of the mark.[122]

Reasoning by analogy, suffers the same limitations as traditional doctrinal analysis. Bad analogies, like bad decisions, can never legitimate action by the state that denies people rights that a constitution guarantees. Good analogies like sound precedents can serve as benchmarks or reference points to assess the soundness of one's judgment, but even they are very much secondary arguments and unavoidably superfluous at their best. Even though reasoning by analogy has played a central role in the development of the common law, in constitutional adjudication the most it can do is provide judges with the psychological comfort that comes from knowing that the way they propose to decide a particular case is consistent with how others have responded in similar situations in the past.

The lesson of the cases based on bad analogies is the same one we have drawn from all the decisions in which the injustice of sex discrimination is tolerated in court. There is simply no way for judges to be able to distinguish laws that differentiate between people on the basis of their sex that are constitutional from those that are not except by a close and careful evaluation of the facts. Moreover, the jurisprudence shows that when judges are prepared to look at all the facts of a case honestly and impartially, they have no difficulty seeing and doing what is right. There is an objectivity and determinacy in the finding of facts that is not possible in a search for the meaning of words. Two landmark rulings handed down by the judges in Strasbourg provide powerful examples of what judges can do when they devote all their energies to getting a firm grasp of the facts of a case and evaluating them as impartially and fairly as they can. In its seminal ruling in *Dudgeon* v. *UK*[123] the Court held that the laws in force in Northern Ireland that made sodomy a criminal offence violated the guarantee given by all member states, in Article 8 of the Convention, to respect everyone's family and private life. Almost twenty years later, in an equally celebrated ruling, the Court concluded that Britain's policy of excluding all gays and lesbians from its armed forces was also in violation of the Convention's right to privacy.[124]

In *Dudgeon*, the Court's decision was based on evidence elicited by the parties to show what Northern Ireland's sodomy laws really meant to them. On the one hand, most of the judges accepted as a fact that, for gay men, laws of this kind condemned 'the most intimate aspects of their lives' as criminal offences and it denied them the right to decide for themselves what moral principles they would follow when they were in the privacy of their homes and out of public view. By

---

[122] *Quilter* v. *Attorney General.*   [123] *Dudgeon* v. *UK.*
[124] *Smith & Grady* v. *UK* (1999) VI Eur. Ct. HR 45, 29 EHRR 493; (2001) 31 EHRR 620.

contrast, from the Government's side, the evidence showed that these laws were virtually irrelevant to the moral character of their community. Not only had they not been strictly enforced for a long time, they had been repealed in most neighbouring countries without any noticeable effects. The facts of the case told the judges that the harmful effects of these laws on gay men were out of all proportion to the good they accomplished for the general welfare of Northern Ireland.

In *Smith & Grady*, all the evidence ran in the same direction and, with only one partly dissenting opinion, it proved to be just as easy a case. Once again the Court recognized that people's sexual orientation involves the most intimate aspects of their private lives and commented on the exceptionally intrusive character of any process designed to uncover whether a person is gay. In addition, it took account of the 'profound effect' the exclusion would have on any gay man or lesbian who aspired to a career in the military. On the other side of the case, the Court noted the lack of 'concrete' and 'actual or significant evidence' that allowing gay men to enlist in the armed forces would prejudice its morale, fighting power, or operational effectiveness in any way. In fact, the evidence before the Court was that very few member states still maintained a blanket ban on the enlistment of gays. From their experience, and from Britain's own record integrating women and different racial groups into its armed forces, the Court was of the opinion that less draconian alternatives, such as codes of personal conduct, would be equally effective in addressing any anticipated untoward effects. In the same way that Northern Ireland's failure to enforce its sodomy laws provided the best measure of their importance to the general welfare of the 'six counties', the Court pointed to the 'robust indifference' of the military authorities to the large number of British servicemen serving alongside foreign forces whose personnel included gays, as the basis for its nearly unanimous conclusion that the 'perceived problems of integration' were not as insurmountable as the Government said they would be.

4. Liberty, Equality, and Proportionality

The judgments of the European Court of Human Rights in *Dudgeon* and *Smith* are only two examples of how responsive judges can be to the pleas of gays and lesbians when they are committed to a principled evaluation of the facts. Other cases could, as we have already noted, be added to the list. *Dudgeon* and *Smith* are important cases, however, and warrant a bit more of our attention. *Dudgeon*, in particular, holds a special place for gays and lesbians as the first major ruling by an internationally respected court in their favour and stands in sharp contrast with the judgment of the US Supreme Court five years later declaring that sodomy laws are legal.[125] It is regularly paid homage by other courts when

---

[125] *Bowers v. Hardwick*.

they are asked to adjudicate cases of gay rights,[126] and it was the basis on which the judges in Strasbourg subsequently found sodomy laws in Ireland and Cyprus to be in breach of the European Convention.[127]

In addition to their place of honour in the history of gay rights, *Dudgeon* and the Court's later ruling in *Smith* also speak to the prospects of further victories in the future. The way the judges reasoned in the two cases provides a clear template for how other issues of gay rights, including same-sex marriages, should be analysed. As well, *Dudgeon* and *Smith* offer new insights into how the principle of proportionality is related to the concept of rights and the rule of law more generally. Even though the European Court of Human Rights has not always remained faithful to the method of analysis it followed in *Dudgeon* and *Smith*, both cases highlight a connection between liberty and equality that is not widely appreciated by students of politics or law.

Judges who apply the analytical framework that was used in *Dudgeon* and *Smith* to the issue of same-sex marriage will find it a straightforward and relatively easy case.[128] Although many people would be inclined to think that making it possible for gays and lesbians to marry is much more controversial than allowing consenting adults to act out whatever sexual fantasies turn them on in private, the evidence is equally one-sided in both cases. As a matter of fact, laws that allow only heterosexual couples to get married have much more significance for the lives of those who are excluded than they do for those who are privileged to partake of the pleasures of matrimonial bliss as often as they like.

From the perspective of gays and lesbians, traditional marriage laws deny them a status which in every society is among the most valued and respected. For most of them, what is at stake is hugely more vital than being allowed to serve in their country's armed forces. People who are told they cannot get married are labelled pariahs, branded as second class. In their own words, such laws act as 'dividing practices that seek to exclude us as God's children'.[129] By contrast, those who regard conjugal relationships of people of the same sex as an immoral and grotesque perversion of the core ideas of marriage and family, have little or nothing, other than their prejudices, to lose. In an era when lesbians and gays can and do live openly in intimate relationships, and enjoy virtually all the other benefits of traditional family life, it is no longer possible to argue that allowing them to swear a legal oath of marriage will have a tangible effect on anyone else's welfare or well-being. The fact that a majority of people feel that allowing gays and lesbians to marry defiles the ideals and values that underlie the institution can't be enough to tip the scales in their favour if there are no other harmful

---

[126] See e.g. *National Coalition for Gay and Lesbian Equality*; *Banana v. State*; *Egan v. Canada*; *Lawrence v. Texas*.

[127] *Norris v. Ireland*; *Modinos v. Cyprus* (1983) 16 EHRR 485.

[128] An opinion echoed by Antonin Scalia in his dissenting judgment in *Lawrence v. Texas*. See also Eskridge, *The Case for Same-Sex Marriage*.

[129] W. Eskridge, 'A History of Same-Sex Marriage' (1993) 79 Virg. L Rev. 1419, 1511.

effects. At least in states that have rid their laws of the most egregious acts of discrimination against lesbians and gays, the fact that even a large majority of the public strongly opposes the recognition of same-sex marriages cannot by itself be decisive.[130] Because constitutions are at the apex of every legal system, popular opinion must conform to the rules they lay down, not the other way around. In exercising their powers of review, the job of the judge is to do what is legally right not what will please the crowd. The supremacy of the constitution means deferring to the will of the people is simply not an option that judges can choose. Because the contest is between the morality of the majority and the supremacy of the constitution, there is no legal basis to permit traditional marriage laws remaining in force for even one more day. Gays and lesbians should not be expected, as the Supreme Court of Canada once told the Canadian people, 'to wait patiently for the protection of their human dignity and equal rights while governments move toward reform one step at a time'.[131]

Dudgeon and *Smith* are big cases in the gay community because they represent a roadmap to a world in which the degradation of discrimination has no place and everyone always receives the justice that is their due. Their significance, however, is not limited to a vindication of gay rights. In *Dudgeon* and in *Smith* one can also find the tracings of a new understanding of the rule of law and the concept of rights and the relationship between the two that turns much conventional wisdom on its head. The cases suggest that, rather than being opposing ideas, equality and liberty give expression to a common principle of justice and conflict resolution. In both cases, the Court based its decision on a person's right to have their private and family life respected by the state that is guaranteed in Article 8 of the Convention. Importantly, at the end of both judgments, the Court said there was no need to evaluate the claims of discrimination under Article 14 because it 'amounts in effect to the same complaint'.[132] Article 14, the Court emphasized in *Smith*, 'does not give rise to any separate issue'.[133]

Although the Court did not spend any time elaborating on its observation that legal claims based on equality and privacy are essentially the same, its implication for our understanding of constitutional law and the concept of rights is quite revolutionary. It means that whether judges analyse a case under one of the substantive rights or freedoms which the Convention guarantees, or under its prohibition of state-sanctioned discrimination in Article 14, the result will be the same.[134] *Dudgeon* and *Smith* show that judges use the same analytical

---

[130] But see Sunstein, *Designing Democracy*, ch. 8; Posner, *Problematics of Moral and Legal Theory*, 249–52.

[131] *Vriend* v. *Alberta* (1998) 156 DLR (4th) 385, para. 122. Although states must treat gays and lesbians the same as heterosexual couples, it does not follow that religious groups, for whom gay sex is a sin, would have to abandon the traditional concept of marriage. On a test of proportionality, they would do no wrong by refusing to marry two people of the same sex.

[132] *Dudgeon* v. *UK*, para. 69. [133] *Smith and Grady* v. *UK*, para. 116.

[134] South Africa's Constitutional Court has also discussed the close connection between equality and privacy. See *National Coalition for Gay and Lesbian Equality*. The Americans, characteristically, do not. See e.g. *Lawrence* v. *Texas* in which O'Connor and Kennedy thought the differences between the two were so significant as to warrant their writing separate opinions to reach the same result.

framework in every case regardless of which right or freedom is in play. Conceptually, the principle of proportionality dissolves what are widely thought to be antagonistic concepts within a common method of analysis. In law, liberty and equality share a common structure and, as a practical matter, mean exactly the same thing. Regardless of whether a law is attacked under the banner of equality or liberty, its legitimacy and its life depend on whether it can pass a rigorous evaluation of its ends, its means, and its effects against the principle of proportionality that connects all three.

Testing the legitimacy of all state action against a common measure of proportionality, no matter what right or freedom is at stake, means the whole focus of the review process is dedicated to trying to get as true a picture of the facts as is possible in every case. Rather than acting as an expositor of text, or a philosopher king, the job of the judge is critically to evaluate all the evidence that is brought to his or her attention in order to get the most accurate assessment of what the parties really think. In *Dudgeon* and again in *Smith*, the judges in Strasbourg took note of the inaction and indifference of the responsible government officials to the aberrant behaviour they said was so threatening to the well-being of their communities. They looked at the experience of other member states when similar laws were repealed. In both cases the Court thought the evidence showing how the laws worked in practice and what actually happened when they were no longer in force was a better measure of how vital they really were than what was said about them in court.

When *Dudgeon* and *Smith* are put alongside all the other cases of sex discrimination we have encountered in this chapter, constitutional adjudication emerges as a very different social practice from how it is usually understood. None of the ways lawyers are taught to reason in other areas of public and private law are much help. Interpretative strategies prove to be as subjective and indeterminate on issues of gender discrimination as they were at providing meaning to all the different religious rights and freedoms constitutions characteristically guarantee. Doctrinal and analogical reasoning are at best redundant except in providing the psychological relief that comes when a person's considered judgment has been embraced by someone else. Ethical and prudential arguments make no sense even from the perspective of the (moral, institutional) values they are intended to promote. The only conceptual apparatus judges have, and all that they need, to harmonize the autonomy of each person with the general will of the community is the formal principle of proportionality. With it and nothing else, the European Court of Human Rights was able to restrain the British Government from abusing its lawmaking authority in *Dudgeon* and again in *Smith*.

The unity of method that proportionality forges between liberty and equality leaves us with an intriguing possibility. What if not just liberty and equality but all rights can be reduced to a common analytical framework? What if all rights—positive, negative, individual, and group, first, second, and third generation—were always evaluated in exactly the same way; liberty, equality, and fraternity all variations on the same theme? Whether a case was packaged as a claim of 'free speech' or 'private property' or 'life, liberty, and equality' or even 'the minimum standards of wholesome and cultural living'[135] would be of no practical importance to the judge. If liberty and equality are simply two different ways of expressing the idea of proportionality it might also, even more grandly, be a universal principle of distributive justice that is controlling in all constitutional democracies and determinative of all human rights.

To discover whether the principle of proportionality is capable of effecting a perfect, global synthesis of liberty, equality, and fraternity—the three defining virtues of just societies—means that we must head back to the law reports. First on the list must be the cases in which people whose circumstances are less fortunate than others invoke the moral force of 'fraternity' and demand that their governments make adequate provision for their health, education, and general well-being. So far our focus has been on cases in which courts have acted as a constraining force, imposing limits on what the people and their elected representatives can legitimately do and staking out the boundaries they are not allowed to cross. Now it is time to examine what courts have told those in power about the positive obligations that come with the political authority that they wield.

Social and economic rights pose one of the most difficult challenges for any theory of constitutional law that aspires to provide a coherent and comprehensive account of modern bills of rights. They represent the brave new world of relations between the citizen and the state and between politicians and the courts. Commonly referred to as 'second- or third-generation', or 'positive' rights, they are meant to take the idea of guaranteeing a basic equality of autonomy and opportunity for every person to a richer and more meaningful plateau. The idea is that first-generation rights and freedoms are practically worthless if a person's essential physical and material needs are not met. On the same logic that 'ought' implies 'can', social and economic rights guarantee that measure of security and well-being that is required for the actualization of first-generation rights.

The problem with guaranteeing everyone a set of basic entitlements to such things as healthcare, housing, education, and material well-being is that it seems to run roughshod over the principle of separation of powers that governs the relations between the courts and the two elected branches of government. Assigning judges the role of enforcing social and economic rights seems to transfer the power of the purse to the one part of government that is unelected and therefore accountable only to itself and, in so doing, transform it from being 'the least dangerous branch' to the one with the potential to be most autocratic. As proceduralists such as Ely, Monahan, and Sunstein argued in Chapter 1, whatever the logic and moral force of social and economic rights, their enforcement seems to compromise the democratic character of government and the sovereignty of the people to determine for themselves what the collective, public character of their communities will be.

---

[135] Constitution of Japan, Article 25, in Blaustein and Flanz, *Constitutions*.

The complexities and ambiguities of social and economic rights are well known to the judiciary. This is another part of the comparative constitutional jurisprudence that is large and rapidly expanding. The US Supreme Court has been offering its opinion on the right to work for more than a hundred years and urgent claims for food, shelter, and medical care are being added to dockets every day. Studying these cases will allow us to see whether the principle of proportionality plays the same role in deciding whether governments have done enough for those who are subject to their rule as it does when the question is whether they have done too much. They should tell us whether in law all rights are derivative concepts, legal conclusions that appear only after all the hard (pragmatic) thinking has been done.[136]

[136] Michael Ignatieff, *Human Rights as Politics and Idolatry* (Princeton: Princeton University Press, 2001), 20: 'we cannot speak of rights as trumps . . . at best rights create a common framework that can assist parties in conflict to deliberate together.'

4

Fraternity

1. Philosophical Objections to Social and Economic Rights

Bad luck, bad judgement, and (for the moment) bad genes are all part of the human condition. Every community that has ever existed has had its share of sick and disabled, weak and less fortunate people in its midst. Homelessness, malnutrition, illness, and illiteracy have plagued the earth since the beginning of time. What has changed over the course of human history is the language people use when they talk about the poverty and misfortune that surrounds them. For a long time the discussion centred on the moral obligations of the strong and successful towards those who had, often for reasons beyond their control, fallen on difficult times. Religious and ethical imperatives—commanding love of one's neighbours—were the dominant idioms through which images of destitution and disadvantage were understood.[1]

Over time, in many parts of the world, the vocabulary of moral duties and charitable obligations was supplemented and largely replaced by a rhetoric of rights. The right to food, housing, healthcare, education, and a basic measure of general well-being are now part of a 'lingua franca' everyone speaks.[2] Critical to this shift in thinking were the writings of pamphleteers, philosophers, and legal scholars in the seventeenth and eighteenth centuries who made powerful arguments in their tracts and treatises that a right of subsistence—an entitlement to take from others what is needed to avoid starvation—was everyone's natural right.[3] Although it took time, by the end of the twentieth century the natural rights of Grotius, Hobbes, Locke, and Paine had found their way into most constitutions of both socialist and liberal democratic states and were the subject of international treaties as well.[4]

Most of the constitutions that were written after the Second World War make some mention of social and economic rights, although they vary greatly both in substance and style. Sometimes the recognition is tentative, as in India, where the entitlements are written as directives to Government rather than as legally

---

[1] G. Himmelfarb, *The Idea of Poverty* (New York: Alfred Knoff, 1986).

[2] *The Economist*, 18/24 August 2001, 18–26.

[3] Thomas A. Horne, 'Welfare Rights as Property Rights', in J. Donald Moon (ed.), *Responsibility, Rights and Welfare* (Boulder: Westview Press, 1988).

[4] United Nations International Covenant on Economic, Social and Cultural Rights, 993 UNTS 3 (03/01/76).

enforceable claims.[5] In other places, such as Japan, a single, all-encompassing guarantee 'to maintain the minimum standards of wholesome and cultured living' was entrenched.[6] More recently, and especially after the fall of the Berlin Wall in 1989, it has been more common for specific guarantees to housing, food, healthcare, schooling, etc. to be recognized as separate rights. Emerging from very different histories, many of the countries of central and eastern Europe[7] and South Africa[8] have favoured this approach, and have provided for an especially rich menu of social and economic rights.

As a result of this proliferation of 'positive' entitlements over the course of the last fifty years, rights talk has moved out of the classrooms and conference halls and into the courts. No longer the stuff of high moral philosophy and/or deep religious faith, in our time claims for social and economic support have become the subject of lawsuits and lawyers' pleas. By the end of the millennium, the poor and the powerless in most parts of the free and democratic world could force their governments into court if they felt they did not get what the constitution said they were entitled to receive. So, for example, just in the last ten years: (1) HIV-infected mothers and the homeless in South Africa sued the state for its failure to provide an antiretroviral drug and temporary emergency shelter respectively;[9] (2) Canadians whose hearing was impaired went to court demanding provincial governments provide sign-language interpreters when they receive treatment in publicly funded hospitals;[10] (3) the Constitutional Court in Hungary was asked to stop the Government from dismantling the country's major programmes of social assistance so that its beneficiaries would have more time to adjust;[11] and (4) the right of all Indian children to receive a primary school education has been the subject of a landmark ruling by their Supreme Court.[12] Even in the United States, the Supreme Court has played an important role in determining what education[13] and welfare assistance[14] Americans receive. On

[5] Constitution of India, Part IV; see also Constitution of Ireland, Article 45. Up-to-date versions of all constitutions can be found in A. P. Blaustein and G. H. Flanz, *Constitutions of the Countries of the World* (loose-leaf) (Dobbs Ferry, NY: Oceana).

[6] Constitution of Japan, Article 25, in Blaustein and Flanz, ibid.

[7] See e.g. Constitution of Hungary, Articles 16 (Youth), 17 (Social Security), 18 (Healthy Environment), 70(B) (Work), 70(D) (Health), 70(E) (Welfare), 70(F) (Education), in Blaustein and Flanz, ibid.

[8] Constitution of South Africa, sections 24 (Environment), 26 (Housing), 27 (Healthcare, Food, Water, Social Security), 28 (Children), 29 (Education), in Blaustein and Flanz, ibid.

[9] *Treatment Action Campaign v. South Africa (Min. of Health)* [2002] 5 SA 721 (CC); *Grootboom v. The Republic of South Africa* (2000) 11 BCLR 1165; [2001] 1 SA 46 (CC).

[10] *Eldridge v. A.G. British Columbia* (1997) 151 DLR (4th) 577.

[11] *On Social Security Benefits*, Decision 43/1995, 30 June 1995, trans. and reported in L. Sólyom and G. Brunner (eds.), *Constitutional Judiciary in a New Democracy* (Ann Arbor: University of Michigan Press, 2000).

[12] *Unni Krishnan v. State of Andhra Pradesh* AIR 1993 SC 2178.

[13] *Brown v. Board of Education* (1954) 347 US 483; *Plyler v. Doe* (1981) 457 US 202. Also see *Hudson Central School District v. Rowley* (1982) 458 US 176 and *San Antonio Independent School District v. Rodriguez* (1972) 411 US 1.

[14] See e.g. *Saenz v. Roe* (1999) 526 US 489; *Califano v. Wescott* (1979) 443 US 76; *United States Dept. of Agriculture v. Moreno* (1973) 413 US 528; *New Jersey Welfare Rights Organization v. Cahill* (1973) 411 US 619; *Shapiro v. Thompson* (1969) 394 US 618; *Goldberg v. Kelly* (1969) 397 US 254.

these and related issues courts and the law have come to play an increasingly active and influential role.[15]

Rights talk is a much tougher language when it is spoken by lawyers and judges than when it is invoked in polite conversation. In legal briefs, rights have a critical edge. When judges rule that a constitution provides that those who suffer some misfortune have a right to some benefit or service from the rest of the community, their decision is backed with the force of law. No longer are the destitute and disadvantaged at the mercy of those whose well-being is secure to know what morality requires of them and to be inspired to do the right thing.

The shift in the way we think and talk about the suffering and misfortune of others has always been and remains highly controversial.[16] For many, the idea that people have 'a right' to claim relief from others for deprivations and disadvantages for which the latter bear no responsibility is nonsensical. It is a contradiction in terms. Among philosophers it is perceived by some to be a 'category mistake'; a confusion about what it means to have a right.[17] For others, the concept of social and economic rights is inconsistent with and even imperils the value of liberty and freedom that rights are supposed to protect.[18] And, beyond these conceptual and normative flaws, lots of people worry that if constitutions and international treaties guarantee people legally enforceable rights to their health, education, welfare, and whatever else is necessary for a decent human life, the democratic character of their governments and their sovereignty as a people will be lost.[19]

The conceptual objection to social and economic rights is based on the idea that a right is a unique moral claim, concerned exclusively with the freedom of people to do with their lives as they wish and with a corresponding obligation of others not to interfere. Having a right to speak or practise one's religion freely,

[15] D. M. Beatty, 'The Last Generation: When Rights Lose their Meaning', in Beatty (ed.), *Human Rights and Judicial Review* (Dordrecht: Kluwer, 1994).

[16] Thomas A. Horne, 'Welfare Rights as Property Rights'.

[17] Cécile Fabre, *Social Rights Under the Constitution* (Oxford: Clarendon Press, 1999); R. Plant 'Needs, Agency and Welfare Rights', in Moon, *Responsibility, Rights and Welfare*; M. Cranston, *What are Human Rights* (London: Bodley Head, 1973), ch. 7; A. I. Melden, 'Are There Any Welfare Rights?' in Peter Brown, Conrad Johnson, and Paul Vernier (eds.), *Income Support* (Totowa, NJ: Rowman & Littlefield, 1981); H. L. A. Hart, 'Are There Any Natural Rights?' 64 Philosophical Review (1955) 175; Rodney Pfeffer, 'A Defense of Rights to Well-being' (1978) 8 Phil. & Pub. Aff. 65.

[18] C. Fried, *Right & Wrong* (Cambridge, Mass.: Harvard University Press, 1973). R. Nozick, *Anarchy, State & Utopia* (Cambridge, Mass.: Harvard University Press, 1974).

[19] D. Davis, 'The Case Against the Inclusion of Socio-Economic Demands in a Bill of Rights Except as Directive Principles' (1998) 14 SAJHR 475; K. D. Ewing, 'The Human Rights Act and Parliamentary Democracy' (1999) 60 Mod. LR 79; G. Bognetti, 'Social Rights, a Necessary Component of the Constitution? The Lesson of the Italian Case', in R. Bieber and P. Widmer (eds.), *The European Constitutional Area* (Instit. Suisse de Droit Comparé) (Zurich: Schulthess Polygraphischer Verlag, 1995), 85; G. Frug, 'The Judicial Power of the Purse' (1978) 125 U Pa. L Rev. 715; P. Monahan, *Politics and the Constitution* (Toronto: Carswell, 1987), ch. 6.6; R. Winter, 'Poverty, Economic Equality and the Equal Protection Clause' (1972) Sup. Ct. Rev. 41. For some, social and economic rights are not unique in the threat they pose to democracy: see e.g. J. Waldron, *Law and Disagreement* (Oxford: Clarendon, 1999), pt III; M. Walzer, 'Philosophy and Democracy' (1981) 9 Political Theory 391.

for example, means others must respect the behaviours it protects. They have a duty to forbear. Rights, it is said, endow those who hold them with a power to control how others behave.[20] So, the right to life is understood as the right not to be killed; freedom of speech, the right not to be censured. On this account, rights function defensively as shields against unjustified intrusions by others. In constitutional texts and international agreements, they are aimed primarily at governments and restrict what kind of rules and regulations they can enact. In this sense, rights define the limits of legitimate coercion. They tell governments when they have gone too far. They serve as signposts marking out the boundaries between the sovereignty of each person and the lawmaking powers of the state.

Rights as protective shields is the standard metaphor and it accords with the way most of our traditional civil and political rights, such as freedom of expression, association, and religion, and the right to life, liberty, and security of the person, etc. actually work. It does not, however, do very much for social and economic rights. Claims for food, shelter, healthcare, and schools do not speak defensively. They demand more than forbearance. Social and economic rights are claims for scarce resources, not just for the space and the authority to make decisions for oneself. They purport to protect people not only against what is done to them, but what happens to them as well. Rather than telling governments what they can and cannot do, social and economic rights purport to impose positive obligations of assistance and support.

It is the conceptual difference between negative and positive rights that makes the legal recognition of the latter so controversial and contested. First, there is the logical point, made by Charles Fried and others that social and economic rights are constrained by natural limits of scarcity in a way that classical rights, which call only for forbearance, are not. The duties to which classical civil and political rights give rise can all be met without conflicting with or compromising each other. As Fried explains, 'we can fail to assault an infinity of people every hour of the day. Indeed, we can fail to lie to them, fail to steal their property, and fail to sully their good names—all at the same time.'[21] Social and economic rights, by contrast, are plagued by serious problems of scarcity. Rights to food and shelter and healthcare and to be able to go to school are not cheap. Everyone can restrain himself or herself from assaulting other people, but no one can render assistance to everyone in need. For Fried, the scarcity limits that are inherent in all positive rights means it is logically impossible to define them categorically and unconditionally. In his words, 'It is not just that it may be too costly to provide a subsistence diet to the whole Indian subcontinent in time of famine—it may be simply impossible.'[22]

In addition to highlighting their conditional and contingent character, Fried also worries that the recognition and legal enforcement of social and economic rights could extend the limits of personal responsibility in arbitrary and

---

[20] H. L. A. Hart, 'Are There Any Natural Rights?'   [21] Fried, *Right & Wrong*, 112.
[22] Ibid. 113.

irrational ways. If people are given a right to whatever resources are necessary to live a decent and fully human life, for example, society could become hostage to those (very sick, very poor, etc.) with insatiable needs. 'If needs create rights to their satisfaction', Fried warns, 'how are we to prevent them from claiming so much that there is no energy left to pursue other goals?'[23] Fried's concern is that because social and economic rights have the potential to make excessive demands on those against whom they are made, there is a serious risk that the value of freedom, which the concept of rights is meant to protect, will be lost. 'Surely', he writes, 'I . . . have a right to do something else with my life than devote it wholly to feeding those whose starvation I might prevent if I worked at it night and day.'[24]

Fried is not alone in his fear that social and economic rights could threaten the freedom of those who would be obliged to provide the resources that such entitlements require. Most classical liberal philosophers, including Hayek[25] and Nozick,[26] regard social and economic rights as the antithesis of liberty and freedom. Nozick believed that taxing the rich to relieve the suffering of the poor was on a par with 'forced labour'.[27] As he saw it, taking from the haves to provide for the have-nots allows government to become 'part owner' of those whose earnings and profits are taxed.[28] From Nozick's perspective, positive and negative rights are polar opposites. Negative rights advance the cause of freedom. Social and economic rights do the reverse.

Concerns about the conceptual coherence and normative integrity of social and economic rights, such as Fried's and Nozick's, are not simply academic quibbles. Doubts are also expressed about their legitimacy and viability in practice. The limits on resources that are available for distribution and on the extent to which people can legitimately be forced to provide for their neighbours give rise to very difficult problems of definition and enforcement. The question of how social and economic rights should work in practice is and has always been one of their most controversial and challenging features.

For the most part, modern constitutions have not tried to specify precisely and in detail what services and resources people have a right to expect. Although a catalogue of specific, very narrowly defined rights is one way of addressing the problems of scarce resources and excessive obligations, constitutions that are written in this manner run the risk, as time goes by and circumstances change, of becoming obsolete and even counterproductive.[29] As the saying goes, a constitution that is written in the style of a last will and testament is doomed to become one. The preferred strategy that has been followed in most modern constitutions, therefore, has been to write in the same inspirational and elevated style that is characteristic of all bills of rights and to delegate to the courts the task of

[23] Ibid. 122.   [24] Ibid. 114.

[25] Freidrich Hayek, *The Constitution of Liberty* (Chicago: University of Chicago Press, 1960).

[26] Nozick, *Anarchy, State & Utopia*, 169.   [27] Ibid.   [28] Ibid. 172.

[29] Cass Sunstein, 'Against Positive Rights' (1993) 2 East European Constitutional Review 35; Bognetti, 'Social Rights, a Necessary Component of the Constitution?'

deciding what the rights that have been guaranteed are actually worth. What the right to 'the minimum standards of wholesome and cultured living' actually means in the lives of Japanese people, for example, is decided by their Supreme Court. Similarly, the Constitutional Court in South Africa has been given the power of telling governments what specific obligations are entailed by the right to 'a basic education' and 'further education that the state must make progressively available and accessible'. So too in Hungary, where the judges in Budapest have been made responsible for defining what the right to 'the highest possible level of physical and mental health' actually means. Typically, entitlements are made conditional on resources being available, and here again, the authority for deciding whether there is enough to go around is assigned to the courts.

Even though the judicial definition of social and economic rights has the advantage of ensuring constitutional texts are always sensitive to a country's capacity and wealth it still strikes a lot of people as a singularly bad idea. In Chapter 1, we saw proceduralists such as Ely, Sunstein, and Monahan argue very strongly that those who sit on the Bench have neither the qualifications nor the moral authority to do the job. People who don't think the legal enforcement of social and economic rights is a good idea invariably make the point that judges are not trained to decide how much healthcare or what kind of shelter people are entitled to receive and that the judicial process is not designed to answer such questions. Moreover, even if they were, they say, these are issues about the way a community distributes its resources and expresses its character as a collectivity which are properly for the people and their chosen representatives, not for a professional elite, to make. The critics contend that the judicial enforcement of social and economic rights is not only ill advised, it is fatally undemocratic as well.

The first argument against courts having the authority to spell out what social services and economic benefits states are under an obligation to provide is a claim about their institutional competence and design. The assertion is that courts simply don't have the procedures, tools, talents, etc. that are required for the job. The judicial process is said to be an adjudicative procedure designed, in the main, to settle questions of right or wrong (such as criminal or civil liability) on the basis of findings of fact and the application of clear principles of law. Negative rights—such as the right to be free of gender discrimination or the right to practise one's religion freely—raise issues of this kind but, the argument goes, social and economic rights do not. Rights to housing, healthcare, education, and 'to the minimum standards of wholesome and cultured living' are all claims for scarce resources, not for tolerance from the state. They ask whether government acted fairly in distributing the largesse of the state, not whether in doing what it did it committed a wrong.

The limits of the judicial process were famously described by Lon Fuller more than thirty years ago.[30] Fuller saw adjudication as a process that is ideally suited to resolve disputes that affect a limited number of people and to which some

---

[30] Lon Fuller, 'The Forms and Limits of Adjudication' (1978) 92 Harv. L Rev. 353.

overarching principle or set of rules applies. He argued that other kinds of disputes, that affect a lot of different interests and to which several competing principles might be relevant—he called them polycentric—can be handled better by other methods, such as the legislative process or negotiation which are designed to find solutions by compromise and give and take.

In Fuller's terms, social and economic rights classically manifest all the characteristics of polycentric claims and they demonstrate the ineptness of the judiciary trying to find a way to distribute the state's resources that is fair to everyone. In deciding, for example, whether people have a right to life-saving treatment such as dialysis or antiretroviral drugs, or whether those who are hearing-impaired have a right to a sign-language interpretation service when they are receiving medical advice, there is no one principle that can tell the judges how a government should spend its money. Need, merit, and compensation may all have something to say. Moreover, there will be an endless line of other claimants who can also say the Government should look after them, many of whom will never be heard in court. The fact there are so many different ways that healthcare, housing, education, etc. can be legitimately organized—in terms of what services are provided, to whom, and for how long—means that adjudication is not well suited to resolve claims of this kind and the fact that so many others can make competing claims for the contested funds means that neither are the courts. There are so many causes on which governments can spend their money and so many individuals and groups on whom it can be spent that any judgment a court proposes will be arbitrary and incomplete.

The institutional critique of the judicial enforcement of social and economic rights raises serious questions about the capacity of the courts to do a good job. For many, there is an even more basic question of whether they should even try. The argument that it is undemocratic for courts to tell the elected representatives of the people how much money they must raise through taxes and how it should be spent challenges the very integrity of social and economic rights. The idea that the legal enforcement of social and economic rights is illegitimate because it conflicts with our commitment to democratic forms of government has been made by commentators of all political stripes. This is one point on which the left, right, and centre of the political spectrum are agreed. For all of them, the judicial definition and enforcement of social and economic rights constitutes a serious derogation of the principle of separation of powers. Investing judges with the authority to tell the elected branches of government what services and benefits they are under a constitutional duty to provide allows them to take over final responsibility for the budget and the financial affairs of the state.

By extending the power of the judiciary over the purse, social and economic rights transforms what has historically been thought to be the 'least dangerous branch' of government[31] into potentially the most autocratic. Rather than

---

[31] In the Federalist Papers 78, Alexander Hamilton famously argued the judiciary was incontestably the weakest of the three branches of government precisely because it had no powers over the

people deciding which precepts of (distributive) justice will define the characters of their communities, a 'junta of lawyers'[32] decrees whose needs must be met by the state and ultimately, if one follows Nozick's thinking, by the forced labour of others. Judicial control of the fiscal affairs of the state means a return to a system of 'taxation without representation'—a method of coercion infamous in the annals of tyranny. Ordinary citizens lose the opportunity to engage in a full debate about what rights they will recognize and what obligations they will bear. Questions about the moral character of a community are moved out of parliament and into the courts where only those who are professionally trained are allowed to speak. Technical legal argument replaces ordinary party politics as the way communities decide whether and/or the extent to which they will feed the hungry, shelter the homeless, and minister to the sick.

2. RETHINKING OLD IDEAS IN A NEW MILLENNIUM

In theory, all the arguments against the recognition of social and economic rights are serious and substantial. Collectively they make a convincing case. In practice, however, their impact has not been so strong. In court, the voices of those who oppose positive rights often have failed to persuade. Indeed, when one examines how judges have responded to constitutional claims of fraternity, answers for most, if not all, doubts about their coherence and integrity can and have been found. At least that seems to have been the experience of Cass Sunstein and Dennis Davis, two prominent legal scholars who have written a lot in the area of social and economic rights and about comparative constitutional law in general. Sunstein, as we learned in Chapter 1, is one of America's most prolific legal scholars. Davis is a legal giant in South Africa who left a position in the academy for a seat on the Bench. At one time, both had written very strongly against the idea that a constitution should contain social and economic guarantees that were legally enforceable, but both underwent profound conversions on the basis of a single case.

Initially Sunstein told the people of central and eastern Europe they should break with the legacy of their socialist pasts and leave social and economic rights out of their new constitutions. To include them would be, he warned, 'a large mistake, possibly a disaster'.[33] He argued that entrenching positive rights to assistance from the state would interfere with the development of market economies, foster a culture of dependence, and in most cases be impossible to enforce. For him the idea of guaranteeing everyone in Hungary the 'highest possible physical and mental health' was 'absurd'. Seven years later, Sunstein's take on

'sword or the purse'. Alexander Hamilton, James Madison, and John Jay, *The Federalist Papers* (New York: Bantam Books, 1982), 393. See also Alexander Bickel, *The Least Dangerous Branch* (New Haven: Yale University Press, 1962).

[32] Winter, 'Poverty, Economic Equality and the Equal Protection Clause', 43.

[33] Sunstein, 'Against Positive Rights'.

social and economic rights shifted 180 degrees. In the new millennium he was upbeat and enthusiastic about the good they could do. In addition to providing tangible relief to those most in need, constitutional rights to shelter and food would, he (like Habermas) now believes, enhance the quality of deliberation in ordinary political life. Even poor countries cannot afford to ignore them completely.[34]

Davis's shift was written more softly but it was no less definitive in the end. In 1992 Davis wrote a measured and scholarly essay arguing the case against the inclusion of social and economic rights in South Africa's new constitution except (following India's example), as non-justiciable directive principles.[35] Although he rejected the idea that social and economic rights were categorically different than traditional civil and political rights in the extent of their polycentricity or in the duties to which they gave rise, he still thought their legalization was a mistake because it 'removes politics to the courtroom . . . [and] . . . place[s] far too much power in the hands of the judiciary'. At the moment when his country was debating whether to entrench a catalogue of social and economic rights in their new constitution, Davis's advice was that following central and eastern Europe's example would endanger the democratic process. It 'elevates judges to the role of social engineers, concentrates power at the centre of the state and consequently erodes the influence of civil society'.[36]

A few years later, after he had been appointed to the Bench, Davis co-authored a piece in which the judiciary in South Africa, Canada, and Israel were criticized for not enforcing social and economic rights as rigorously as they might.[37] Davis and his co-authors argued that judges should recognize a social dimension in all the traditional civil and political rights and interpret whatever social and economic rights were entrenched broadly as well. Although they recognized 'social citizenship' could be advanced in a number of ways, they had no doubt that 'ceteris paribus, a constitution with social rights is better than one without them'.

One of the most remarkable aspects of Sunstein's and Davis's conversion is that it was inspired not by another philosophical or political piece in some academic tome, but by their reflections on a specific case. What caught their eye was a judgment of South Africa's Constitutional Court which ruled that the national, provincial, and municipal governments in their country had a collective responsibility to develop programmes that would provide emergency shelter and relief for Irene Grootboom and her fellow squatters who were living in 'crisis conditions'.[38] Sunstein hailed the Court's judgment as 'an extraordinary

---

[34] Cass Sunstein, 'Social and Economic Rights? Lessons from South Africa' (2000/1) 11 Constitutional Forum 123; *Designing Democracy* (Oxford: Oxford University Press, 2001), ch. 10.

[35] Dennis Davis, 'The Case Against the Inclusion of Socio and Economic Demands'.

[36] Ibid. 489.

[37] Dennis Davis, Patrick Macklem, and Guy Mundlak, 'Social Rights, Social Citizenship and Transformative Constitutionalism: A Comparative Assessment', in Joanne Conaghan, Michael Fischl, and Karl Klare (eds.), *Labour Law in an Era of Globalization* (Oxford: Oxford University Press, 2002).

[38] *Grootboom* v. *Republic of South Africa*.

decision' which 'for the first time in the history of the world' might show those who object to the legal enforcement of social and economic rights that it is possible for courts to provide meaningful relief to the least fortunate members of a society in a way that does not place them in an 'unacceptable managerial role'.[39]

What impressed Sunstein about the Court's decision in *Grootboom* was its carving out a middle ground between making social and economic rights fully enforceable individual entitlements and denying them any recognition in law. According to the Court, what the constitution guaranteed was not housing on demand but rather a 'coherent and coordinated programme' to make housing accessible to the poor, including an infrastructure to provide emergency relief for those living in the worst conditions. Although the Court recognized that the state's obligation to provide 'access to adequate housing' would vary between geographic (urban/rural) areas and between people of different economic means, it insisted that those whose needs were most urgent could not be completely ignored. Those whose circumstances were most desperate had a kind of collective entitlement that, even if not all of them could be taken care of immediately, a 'significant number' of them would receive some form of emergency shelter and relief.

Irene Grootboom and her family and friends also figured critically in Davis's epiphany and his coming to endorse the legalization of social and economic rights as positively as he has. As it happened, Davis was the judge of first instance to whom Grootboom prayed for relief and so he was acutely aware of all of the details of her case. Indeed, he was so moved by her plight that the order he made directing the state to supply land, tents, portable toilets, and a regular supply of water went further than the remedy the Constitutional Court authorized in the end. Being faced with the squalor and deprivation of those who came to his court clearly caused him to see the issues in a new light.

Grootboom is undoubtedly another of those pivotal cases that will be read for generations and Sunstein's effusive praise for it doesn't seem misplaced. His characterization of the Court's conception of social and economic rights as entitlements to 'sensible priority-setting with particular attention to the plight of those who are neediest',[40] is an accurate reading of the case, and his intuition that it avoids many of the normative and institutional concerns of those who object to their legal enforcement is a fair and measured appraisal as well. Rather than try to spell out a set of categorical, core entitlements of all homeless people, the Court defined the right as a duty of the state to devise a 'comprehensive and workable' housing policy that paid due regard to 'the most vulnerable group', those 'whose needs were most urgent', 'desperate'.[41] At the same time that it recognized that 'foundational values' of human dignity, freedom, and equality are denied those who have no food, clothing, or shelter,[42] it was sensitive to the

[39] Sunstein, *Designing Democracy*, 221–2.   [40] Sunstein, 'Social & Economic Rights', 229.
[41] *Grootboom v. Republic of South Africa*, paras 31, 38, 44, 63, 66.   [42] Ibid. para. 23.

fact that there were many ways governments might respond to the needs of the homeless which would meet the requirements of the constitution. The Court expressly contemplated the possibility of finding governments to have acted constitutionally even if they could not provide relief to everyone immediately.[43]

Grootboom is a landmark case in part because the horrible history of homelessness in South Africa is so evocative and in part because the Court was able to help people whose situation was truly desperate in a way that respected the traditional roles of the judiciary and the elected branches of government. It is, however, only one decision, and even allowing for its effect on Sunstein and Davis, there is no reason to exaggerate its importance. As remarkable as it is, it is not so exceptional as to be one of a kind. In fact, it turns out that there is an impressive collection of judicial opinions that have been written over the course of the last fifty years that mirrors much of the thinking that animated the Court's reasoning in *Grootboom*. Overall, this comparative jurisprudence shows that a lot of judges think that the legal enforcement of social and economic rights isn't so different from the protection that is provided by the more traditional civil and political guarantees. The reasoning that the judges employ in the two sets of cases, in fact, is virtually the same. South Africa's Constitutional Court has commented explicitly on the common function performed by the two sets of entitlements[44] and there is a lot of evidence in judgments written by other courts around the world that proves it is right.[45]

3. Legal enforcement of social and economic rights

3.1. The Right to Work

The first wave of claims for social and economic rights that came to the courts were brought by people who were not looking for any assistance from government beyond respecting their right to make it on their own. By and large these cases are identical, in shape and structure, to those in which civil and political rights are at stake. Most of them involve claims by people to be allowed to work and pursue a livelihood of their own choosing. In a few of these cases the right to work might require some positive action on the part of the state. For example, in *Lovett* v. *Grogan*[46] the Supreme Court of Ireland ruled that a person whose business was threatened by the illegal activities of others was entitled to insist the state protect his rights by issuing an injunction against those who conducted

---

[43] Ibid. para. 68. The Court subsequently reaffirmed the possibility that governments may be found to have acted consistently with the constitution even when they are unable to satisfy everyone's rights all at once, in *Treatment Action Campaign* v. *South Africa*.

[44] *Re Certification of the Constitution of the Republic of South Africa* [1996] 4 SA 744; (1996) 10 BCLR 1253, para. 78.

[45] The European Court of Human Rights has made the same observation. See e.g. *Airey* v. *UK* (1970) 2 EHRR 305, para. 26; *Lopez-Ostra* v. *Spain* (1995) 20 EHRR 277.

[46] (1995) 1 ILRM 13.

their affairs in violation of the law. Most of the cases in which a right to work is at stake are not, however, like *Lovett*. Rather, they challenge the legitimacy of laws that regulate and restrict people's freedom to take up and practise a particular vocation. They speak to the limits of legitimate state action rather than to what positive initiatives governments must undertake.

Like many of the most important first generation, political and civil rights,[47] recognition of a right to work has not required its explicit entrenchment although many modern constitutions do now contain guarantees of this kind.[48] Where they don't, the right to work is simply drawn from other parts of the text. In some instances, the right is located in the most inspirational parts of the text. So, for example, Hungary's Constitutional Court has expressed the opinion that a right to work would be enforced as part of 'the general right of personality' if it wasn't explicitly guaranteed.[49] Similarly, South Africa's Constitutional Court struck down a law restricting the availability of work permits to foreign nationals on the ground that it offended the 'human dignity' of those affected.[50] Undoubtedly the practice of the American Supreme Court, at the turn of the century, in protecting people's freedom to contract as part of their right (in the 14th Amendment) not to be deprived of their 'liberty without due process of law' is the most famous (and for many most scandalous) example of first-generation rights being extended in this way.[51] The recognition by Ireland's Supreme Court of 'an unspecified right to work' is certainly the most sweeping.[52]

In other jurisdictions, a wide range of more specific guarantees has been invoked to protect people's right to work. In Canada, lawyers relied on their mobility rights successfully to attack laws that limited their ability to practise in different parts of the country.[53] The European Court of Human Rights has ruled that the right to 'the peaceful enjoyment of [a person's] possessions' includes the right to practise a profession[54] and has relied on the Convention's guarantees of freedom of expression[55] and freedom of association[56] to protect people's right to work and pursue their business interests even though, in the latter case, it was

---

[47] Especially in the United States where rights of privacy (*Griswold* v. *Connecticut* (1965) 381 US 479); travel (*Shapiro* v. *Thompson* (1960) 394 US 618) and free association (*NAACP* v. *Alabama* (1964) 377 US 288) are not explicitly guaranteed; but also in other countries including, as we saw in the last chapter, Israel (implying a right to equality in *Miller* v. *Minister of Defence* (1998)) 32 Israel L Rev. 159 and Canada (freedom from discrimination on the basis of sexual orientation, *Egan* v. *Canada* (1995) 124 DLR (4th) 609 (SCC)).

[48] e.g. in the constitutions of Germany (Article 12), Japan (Article 22), India (Article 19(g)), Hungary (Article 70B), South Africa (Article 22), in Blaustein and Flanz, *Constitutions*.

[49] *On the Freedom of Enterprise and on the Licensing of Taxis*, Decision 21/1994; 16 April 1994—trans. and reproduced in Sólyom and Brunner, *Constitutional Judiciary*, 292, 296.

[50] *Booysen* v. *Min. of Home Affairs* [2001] 4 SA 485 (CC).

[51] *Lochner* v. *New York* (1905) 198 US 45.

[52] *Lovett* v. *Gogan*.

[53] *Black* v. *Law Society of Alberta* (1989) 58 DLR (4th) 317. See also a parallel ruling by the European Court of Justice in *Vlassopoulu* v. *Ministerium für Justiz* (1993) 2 CMLR 221.

[54] *Van Marle* v. *Netherlands* (1986) 8 EHRR 483.

[55] *Informationsverein Lentia* v. *Austria* (1993) 17 EHRR 93.

[56] *Sigurjonsson* v. *Iceland* (1993) 16 EHRR 462.

clear that those who drafted the Convention never intended it to have this effect. Even the concept of 'culture' that is guaranteed in Article 27 of the International Covenant on Civil and Political Rights is broad enough, in the mind of the United Nations Human Rights Committee, to protect the 'traditional means of livelihood for national minorities'.[57]

Rather than being dependent on the particular words that are used in a text, the scope and the substance of the right to work have been fixed, for all practical purposes, by the principle of proportionality. Facts, not texts or authoritative sources of meaning, are the key. The more extreme and restrictive the terms of the law, the more likely it is to fail. Invariably restrictions that limit people's choice and access to particular vocations are regarded as more serious and invasive and so more vulnerable than those that regulate how a profession or a trade can be practised. Similarly, laws that regulate how people do their work are more likely to be found wanting where it cannot be shown that they advance the well-being of the community in some significant way. When laws interfere with people's occupational freedom more than is necessary to secure whatever public interest they were enacted to promote, they are almost certain to be found wanting no matter the style or the words of the constitution.

Laws that prevent people pursuing the careers of their choice, even when they are qualified, come closest to a total negation of a right to work and are least likely to be able to pass a test of proportionality. Germany's Constitutional Court[58] and the Supreme Court of Japan[59] have both struck down laws that imposed numerical and geographic limits on the number of pharmacies that could operate in a given area and Hungary's Constitutional Court has invalidated a similar legislative regime controlling the licensing of taxis.[60] For all three courts, the adverse impact on the lives of those who were not allowed to pursue the careers of their choice was out of all proportion to whatever enhancement in the well-being of the community policies of this kind could effect. On one side were the interests of those people for whom being a pharmacist or taxi-driver were fundamental acts of self-expression (entailing, for the former, years of preparation and study) critical to their whole personalities and, simultaneously, the primary activity by which they would contribute to the social welfare of the communities in which they lived. On the other side, the suitability of using such barriers to entry to achieve safe and healthy pharmaceutical and transportation standards was ambiguous and uncertain, especially in comparison to alternative strategies that would interfere with people's occupational freedom much less.

---

[57] *Länsman v. Finland*, UNHR Committee Communication 511/1992, UN Doc. CCPR/C/52/D/511/1, 1992.

[58] *Pharmacy Case* (1958) 7 BVergGE 377, trans. and reproduced in D. Kommers, *The Constitutional Jurisprudence of the Federal Republic of Germany*, 2nd edn. (Durham, NC: Duke University Press, 1997).

[59] *Sumiyoshi Inc.* v. *Governor, Hiroshima Prefecture* (The Hiroshima Pharmacy Location Case) 29 Minshū 4, 572; SC 1975, trans. and reproduced in L. Beer and H. Itoh, *The Constitutional Case Law of Japan 1970–1990* (Seattle: Washington University Press, 1996).

[60] *On the Freedom of Enterprise and on the Licensing of Taxis*. See also *Sigurjonsson v. Ireland*.

In all these cases, the net effect of the law was that one group of people was given ironclad protection against economic competition while another was not even allowed on the field.

Even restrictions that target the practice, rather than the choice, of a trade or profession can fail the test of proportionality where it can be established that they work against the public interest they were meant to achieve. So, for example, India's Supreme Court once struck down a law that banned the slaughter of all cows as an unjustified interference with the right of Muslim butchers to carry on their trade because, by extending the lives of useless animals, it actually frustrated one of the law's primary purposes which was to improve the breed of cattle in the country.[61] Similarly, in Canada, the Supreme Court invalidated a rule that prevented lawyers in different provinces forming partnerships for the reason that, rather than helping local law societies police the competence and ethics of those providing legal services in their communities, it actually made things worse.[62]

Occupational and trade restrictions that impose unnecessary and insurmountable barriers against new entrants, or which frustrate the larger purposes of the regulatory regimes of which they are a part, have not received favourable reviews from judges anywhere. Laws that calibrate the interests of those who aspire to particular careers and the public at large more evenly do much better. Thus, at the same time as it ruled that numerical quotas on the number of taxis that could operate in an area were unconstitutional, Hungary's Constitutional Court upheld regulations requiring would-be entrants to establish their creditworthiness and pass a road test. Similarly, when Germany's Constitutional Court gave its opinion on Bavaria's 'Apothecary Act', it also said that entrance qualifications that certify a person's knowledge and capacity to practice as a pharmacist safely, and in a way that is compatible with the public interest, will generally have no difficulty passing the (proportionality) test. However, as the European Court of Justice has pointed out, even regulations of this kind must not be applied in a way that blocks the legitimate career aspirations of people for little or no gain to the state.[63]

Although the cases show that courts analyse claims of a right to work in exactly the same way as they evaluate other civil or political rights, some will be dubious as to how relevant they are to resolving the question of what obligations, if any, states owe to people who are vulnerable and in need. After all, most of the cases that recognize a right to work are about stopping the state from interfering with people's career ambitions; they are not demands for a job. On closer inspection, however, important similarities between the two sets of

---

[61] *Moh'd Hanif Quareshi* v. *State of Bihar* AIR 1958 SC 731. Germany's Constitutional Court has also come to the defence of Muslim butchers in ruling that their religious freedom entitles them to an exemption to an animal protection law that made their method of slaughter unlawful. *International Herald Tribune*, 16 January 2002; cf. Sami L. Aldeeb Abu-Sahlieh, 'Faux débat sur l'abbattage rituel en Occident' (2003) Revue de Droite Suisse 247.

[62] *Black* v. *Law Society of Alberta.*   [63] *Vlassopoulu* v. *Ministerium.*

cases, and between positive and negative rights more generally are apparent. In fact, the way in which courts have assessed laws that restrict people's freedom to pursue the careers of their choice closely tracks the reasoning South Africa's Constitutional Court followed when it ruled in favour of Irene Grootboom, and the 900 other homeless people with whom she lived, in two important respects. Analytically, *Grootboom* and 'right to work' cases share a common conception of rights that is grounded in an idea of 'fair shares' rather than in categorical, core guarantees. Normatively, both are very attentive in ensuring governments remain free to pursue the values and goals and social and economic policies that got them elected.

Fair shares in the allocation of shelter and in the distribution of work opportunities is the common—and dominant—theme running through all the cases. In *Grootboom*, the state was found to be in dereliction of its duty because the resources of the country that were dedicated to housing were distributed in a very inequitable, regressive way. Whereas some people enjoyed the benefits of subsidies and housing from the state, others such as Irene Grootboom, who were most in need, were left out in the cold. Laws that erect insuperable barriers against those who aspire to be pharmacists or taxi-drivers are flawed by the same distributive inequity. All the benefits to be gained in taking up either vocation are reserved for the people who are already reaping substantial rewards and nothing is left for others who are trying to launch their careers. In both cases the injustice in the law consists in paying no attention to those who have the least.

The other striking similarity in the way courts generally think about a right to work and the approach South Africa's Constitutional Court developed in *Grootboom* is how generously both draw the line separating their own powers and those of the elected branches of government in a way that shows great respect for the latter. In *Grootboom*, the Court acknowledged that there were many ways a government might design its housing policies that would meet its constitutional obligations and it was the responsibility of the legislative and executive branches, not the courts, to decide which one to adopt. Similarly, when courts tell governments they have improperly interfered with someone's right to work, they rarely question the legitimacy of the goals or purposes that are being pursued. Health, safety, and the moral and economic well-being of the community are all recognized as legitimate reasons to enact trade and employment regulations. Only laws passed for naked self-interest and self-dealing are condemned on the basis of the purposes that they pursue.[64]

This common understanding of both (positive and negative) dimensions of social and economic rights, as entitlements to fair shares of whatever is being legislated, but allowing governments an almost unlimited choice in whether and/ or how to regulate in any area of social and economic policy, accounts for almost all the leading cases in which someone's right to work has been vindicated. It 'fits' the cases, as Ronald Dworkin would say. But it doesn't account for them all.

---

[64] *Pharmacy* case.

Most notably, it leaves out a significant number of judgments the US Supreme Court has handed down on this issue including *Lochner* v. *NY*,[65] universally regarded as one of the defining (and most notorious) cases of American constitutional law, as well as *West Coast Hotel* v. *Parrish*,[66] which reversed it.

The American take on people's right to pursue vocations and careers of their own choosing is unlike that followed by courts anywhere else in the world.[67] Like so much of American constitutional law, there have been huge swings in the jurisprudence. For its first hundred years and for the last seventy-five, the US Supreme Court was and is now again exceedingly deferential to Congress and state governments when it has been asked to review laws that control people's freedom to work and pursue their career aspirations. In between, for a period of about thirty years around the turn of the last century, during the so-called *Lochner* era, the Court went to the other extreme of imposing very stringent limits on the kinds of vocational and labour laws politicians could enact. However, even in this period, when it actively defended people's right to work, the freedom it secured did little for those who needed protection most.

Compared to a right to work that is tied to the principle of proportionality and the idea of fair shares, neither of the approaches the Americans have tried looks very attractive. Most of the time, the US Supreme Court has been very unsympathetic if not downright hostile to the idea of a right to work. In the beginning the Court validated laws that denied women the right to practise law[68] as well as legislation that granted government monopolies over whole trades for extended periods of time,[69] regardless of how seriously they interfered with people's freedom to pursue their careers. Today the Court adheres to the rule that it will not even provide relief (except to lawyers)[70] against laws that gratuitously and irrationally interfere with people's freedom to decide for themselves what roles they will play in the communities in which they live.[71] For more than half a century, judicial protection of all economic liberties has been practically non-existent. In the minds of many, the Court's position is essentially that government is free to abuse its citizens' freedom to pursue their livelihoods pretty much whenever and however it pleases.[72]

[65] *Lochner* v. *New York*.   [66] *West Coast Hotel* v. *Parrish* (1937) 300 US 379.

[67] In its earlier rulings on the right to choose an occupation, the Japanese Supreme Court took a similar deferential approach. See e.g. *Koizumi* v. *Japan* (The Gypsy Taxi Cab Case) (1963) 17 Keishū 12, 234, trans. and reproduced in Itoh and Beer, *The Constitutional Case Law of Japan 1961–1970* (Seattle: Washington University Press, 1978); and *Marushin Industries* v. *Japan* (The Osaka Small Business Restraint Case) (1972), trans. and reproduced in Beer and Itoh, *The Constitutional Case Law of Japan 1970–1990*.

[68] *Bradwell* v. *The State* (1872) Sup. Ct. 130.

[69] *Slaughterhouse Cases* (1872) Sup. Ct. 36.

[70] See e.g. *Supreme Court of New Hampshire* v. *Piper* (1985) 470 US 274; *Schware* v. *Board of Bar Examiners* (1956) 353 US 232.

[71] *Williamson* v. *Lee Optical* (1955) 348 US 483; *West Coast Hotel* v. *Parrish*; see also *New Orleans* v. *Dukes* (1976) 427 US 297.

[72] Jonathan R. Macey, 'Some Causes and Consequences of the Bifurcated Treatment of Economic Rights and Other Rights under the United States Constitution', in Ellen Frankel Paul, Fred D. Miller, and Jeffrey Paul (eds.), *Economic Rights* (Cambridge: Cambridge University Press, 1992).

Even when, during the *Lochner* era, the Court did invalidate laws that interfered with people's right to work, its approach to the issues is widely regarded to have done more harm than good. Although defences have been written on its behalf[73] *Lochner* has become an object of widespread condemnation by lawyers of every political stripe.[74] For many, *Lochner* represents one of the low points of American law. Certainly for those who are struggling to stand on their own feet, *Lochner* is not much of a crutch. What the Court said in *Lochner* was that the State of New York could not restrict the liberty of people to work more than ten hours a day in a bakery if that is what they wanted to do. The freedom it protected—to enter contracts of employment on whatever terms one's talents will command—is, however, much more valuable for the strong and those with marketable skills than it is for those who are relatively weak and vulnerable to exploitation. Compared to the opportunities created by a principle of proportionality and a rule of fair shares, the freedom of contract that was guaranteed by *Lochner* is largely formal and empty and distributively perverse towards those who need it most.[75]

Not only does a freedom of contract approach provide less meaningful protection for a right to work than one that tests for proportionality and fair shares, it is also profoundly undemocratic. In *Lochner*, the Court took the position that the people of New York had no authority, through their elected representatives, to pass labour legislation establishing maximum hours and/or minimum wages for ordinary kinds of work. Labour laws, said the Court, did nothing to promote the health, safety, morals, or welfare of the community and so fell outside the legitimate lawmaking powers of the state. For many who have commented critically on the case, *Lochner*'s complete disregard of the principle of separation of powers and the Court's limited authority is its greatest sin.

Defining a right to work as a right to fair shares does a better job of protecting liberty and respecting democracy than *Lochner*'s idea of guaranteeing pure freedom of contract. It can also give a better account of the decision in the case. Had the Court tested New York's labour law for its fairness in restricting the hours of some bakeries while allowing others to work as long as they please, it seems likely it would have been able to reach the same result without compromising the separation of powers principle as egregiously as it did. On the facts before the Court, almost half the bakeries in the state, including all the larger establishments that were unionized, were exempted from the

---

[73] See e.g. Macey, 'Some Causes and Consequences . . . ', ibid.; Richard Epstein, 'Toward a Revitalization of the Contract Clause' (1980) 51 U Chic. L Rev. 732; Bernard H. Seigan, 'Constitutional Protection of Property and Economic Rights' (1992) 29 San Diego L Rev. 161.

[74] Note: 'Resurrecting Economic Rights: The Doctrine of Economic Due Process Reconsidered' (1990) 103 Harv. L Rev. 1363; John Hart Ely, *Democracy and Distrust* (Cambridge, Mass.: Harvard University Press, 1980), 14–15; R. Dworkin, *Law's Empire* (Cambridge, Mass.: Harvard University Press, 1986), 389; R. Bork, *The Tempting of America* (New York: Free Press, 1990), 46–9.

[75] Cass Sunstein, 'Lochner's Legacy', 87 Colum L Rev. (1987) 873; 'Naked Preferences and the Constitution', Colum. L Rev. (1984) 1689.

regulations.[76] The effects of the law were largely borne by smaller, family-run bakeries, many of whom were put out of business. As *Lochner* argued in his pleadings, the law was highly discriminatory in restricting the hours of workers in some bakeries and allowing others, 'including many who [were] competitors . . . to work their employees as long as they choose'.[77] The large number of exemptions from the regulation also suggested that long hours posed no greater threat to the health of people employed in bakeries than they did in any other line of work. Moreover, if it could have shown that related sections of the law controlling ventilation, drainage, cleaning, and inspection were effective ways to ensure bakeries were healthy work environments, the Court could have said the limit on the hours of work was unnecessary—gratuitous—as well.

Defending the decision in *Lochner* as an appropriate application of the principle of proportionality and fair shares puts the case in a much more flattering light. It incorporates the insights of those on the left who criticize the anti-democratic bias of the judgment and those on the right who lament the Court's current position of refusing to provide any protection for such an important dimension of human freedom. It is the argument Lochner's lawyers pushed hardest when they had their day in court and had it been accepted Americans would be as free doing business in the marketplace as they are when they are engaged in politics or giving a speech. Rehabilitating *Lochner* would be a jurisprudential event of almost miraculous proportions. It would be the legal equivalent of resurrecting Lazarus from the dead. It might even be enough for other students of the law, following Sunstein's and Davis's example, to convert. As impressive as it is, however, a fair-shares account of the right to work is only part of the story of the judicial enforcement of social and economic rights, and in some respects the least important part. The fact is that in most of these cases the ruling of the court was limited to setting restrictions on what kinds of regulations governments can pass and so does not speak directly to the conceptual, normative, and institutional concerns that put in question the integrity of the more recent wave of positive social and economic rights.

3.2. The Right to the Necessities of Life

Claims that governments have positive duties to guarantee basic necessities of life to everyone under their jurisdiction have been coming to the courts for more than twenty-five years, and have been a regular part of their dockets for the past ten. The caselaw is rich in the intensity and diversity of the claims that have been made. The cases tell the stories of people with powerful and painful pleas. Street-dwellers in Mombai insist they have a right to erect shacks on city sidewalks so

---

[76] Richard A. Epstein, 'The Mistakes of 1937' (1988) Geo. Mason UL Rev. 5; Note: 'Resurrecting Economic Rights'; Norman Karlin, 'Back to the Future: From Nollan to Lochner' (1988) 17 South Western UL Rev. 627.

[77] *Lochner v. New York*, 48.

they can live within commuting distance of their work.[78] Pregnant women in South Africa testing HIV positive want access to a drug that will significantly reduce the chances of their foetuses being infected.[79] Men dying of kidney failure in Durban, South Africa and Whangarei, New Zealand say their governments have a constitutional duty to ensure they receive the dialysis treatment they need to survive.[80] Hearing-impaired people on Canada's west coast demand public hospitals have sign-language interpreters on staff so they can understand what is happening to them when they receive medical care.[81] All over the world, students and their parents have been especially litigious, claiming access to all levels of public education as well as funding for special religious and linguistic schools.[82] Welfare laws have been attacked in Canada and the United States as discriminatory and in Hungary the Constitutional Court was asked to stop a massive restructuring of its social welfare system that was an integral part of its transition to a market economy.[83]

Even though most constitutions now contain provisions guaranteeing some set of social and economic rights, again it is rare that the particular way they are written in the text is the critical or determining factor in how cases are resolved.[84] Even when the language of the text is strong and categorical, it is never understood to provide an absolute, ironclad guarantee. In Japan, for example, the Supreme Court has rejected the claim that the unqualified commitment that 'compulsory education shall be free', in Article 26 of its Constitution, means parents can insist that governments must pay for everything, including textbooks and school supplies.[85] Similarly, the unqualified prescription in Section 27 of South Africa's constitution that 'no one may be refused emergency medical treatment' was not enough to ensure that Thiagraj Soobramoney (or anyone else who was facing imminent death as a result of kidney failure) would be provided with a dialysis unit.[86] In both cases, in fact, the claims were rejected because they could not pass a proportionality test.

Not only is there no set of magic words that can guarantee satisfaction in every case, it turns out that, because of the interpretative strategies that are favoured by most courts, it isn't essential that a constitution make specific provision for social and economic rights. In the same way courts have been able to draw a

---

[78] *Olga Tellis v. Bombay Municipal Corporation*, AIR 1986 SC 180.

[79] *Treatment Action Campaign v. South Africa.*

[80] *Soobramoney v. Minister of Health* (Kwazulu-Natal) [1998] 1 SA 765; (1997) 4 BHRC 308; *Shortland v. Northland Heath Ltd.* (1998) 1 NZLR 433.

[81] *Eldridge v. A.G. British Columbia.*

[82] See the text accompanying nn. 101–7 and *infra*, Ch. 5 s. 5.

[83] See the text accompanying nn. 108–13.

[84] The comparative unimportance of how constitutional texts are actually written has not gone unnoticed by those who are familiar with the jurisprudence. See e.g. Dennis Davis, Patrick Macklem, and Gay Mundlak, 'Social Rights, Social Citizenship . . . '; David Currie, 'Positive and Negative Constitutional Rights' (1986) 53 U Chic. L Rev. 864.

[85] *Kato v. Japan* 18 Minshū 2 p. 343 26/02/64, trans. and reproduced in part in Itoh and Beer, *Constitutional Case Law of Japan 1960–70.*

[86] *Soobramoney v. Minister of Health*, paras. 19, 26, 28–9.

right to work from basic guarantees of liberty and life, the fact a constitution is silent with respect to social and economic rights need never be fatal to a case. Traditional first-generation rights of liberty and equality are all any judge who is inclined to read constitutional texts to give effect to their overarching values and purposes really needs. Indeed, in India the 'right to life' has proved to be more important as a source of positive claims against government than it has in protecting people from being put to death by the state. Thus, at the same time that it has ruled that capital punishment is not per se a violation of the right to life,[87] it has also said such a guarantee logically entails 'the basic necessaries of life . . . [including] . . . adequate nutrition, clothing and shelter, and facilities for reading, writing and expressing oneself in diverse forms . . . '.[88] As well, it has interpreted the right to life to include a right to earn a livelihood,[89] a healthy, non-hazardous environment,[90] and guaranteed access to primary school education.[91]

The judges in Delhi are certainly among the most dedicated to the method of reading constitutions to give maximum effect to their highest, overarching purposes but they are by no means all alone. Hungary's Constitutional Court also understands the right to life to impose a duty on government to maintain 'the natural basis of human life', including a healthy environment.[92] So far Canada's Supreme Court has shied away from such a robust definition of the 'life, liberty' clause of its Charter of Rights,[93] but in two major rulings it has made equivalent use of its strongly worded guarantee of equality and freedom from discrimination. In one case the Court invoked the equality clause to sustain the right of senior citizens to claim unemployment insurance benefits when they were put out of work.[94] In another, they upheld the claim of people whose hearing was impaired to be provided with sign-language services when they were receiving treatment in public hospitals.[95] Even the Supreme Court of the United States has come to the aid of the poor and least advantaged using 'first-generation' rights. Most famously, it relied on the equal protection clause of the Fourteenth Amendment to bring segregated education to an end and subsequently it recognized a right of children of illegal immigrants to attend state schools.[96] It has also responded to the pleas of welfare recipients by treating

---

[87] *Bachan Singh* v. *State of Punjab*, AIR 1980 SC 898, 1980 2 SCC 684; cf. *Mithu* v. *State of Punjab* AIR 1983 SC 473.

[88] *Frances C. Mullen* v. *Administrator, Union Territory of Delhi*, AIR 1981 SC 746 para. 7.

[89] *Olga Tellis* v. *Municipal Corporation of Bombay*.

[90] See e.g. *Vellore Citizens Welfare Forum* v. *Union of India* AIR 1996 SC 2715; *Consumer Education and Research Centre* v. *Union of India*, AIR 1995 SC 922; *Subash Kumar* v. *State Bihar*, AIR 1991 SC 420; see also *Narmada Bachao Andolan* v. *Union of India* AIR 2000 SC 3751.

[91] *Unni Krishnan* v. *State of Andhra Pradesh*.

[92] *On Environmental Protection*, Decision 28/1994 20/05/94 trans. and reproduced in L. Sólyom and G. Brunner (eds.), *Constitutional Judiciary in a New Democracy*.

[93] See *Gosselin* v. *Québec* (2003), 221 DLR (4th) 257.

[94] *Canada Employment and Immigration Commission* v. *Tétreault–Gadoury* 81 DLR (4th) 359 (1991).

[95] *Eldridge* v. *A.G. British Columbia*.   [96] *Supra* n. 13.

social assistance like a property right and creating a constitutional right of mobility out of whole cloth.[97]

Much more important than the words or vintage of the text is the distributive fairness of the claimant's case. Whether it is a demand for healthcare, schooling, or just straight cash, the critical fact is how a claim measures up against the principle of proportionality and the idea of fair shares, not whether it finds explicit recognition in words on a page. Sometimes, as in *Grootboom*, the focus is on how whatever service or support is being claimed is distributed. In other cases what is decisive are the proportionalities that hold between those who claim they have a constitutional right to be supported in a certain way by the state and those who will be forced to bear the cost. When courts are inclined to rule in favour of a claim for social and economic rights it is not uncommon for whatever law or regulation is under review to be found wanting on both. Both measures of fair shares figure prominently in two judgments, handed down within days of each other, by the highest courts in Canada and South Africa, which illustrate the sorts of claims people can make against their governments to help them regain good health. In the first, *Eldridge v. A.G. of British Columbia*,[98] the Supreme Court of Canada held that governments have an obligation to fund sign-language interpretation services in public hospitals. In the second, *Soobramoney v. Minister of Health*[99] (Kwazulu-Natal) all the members of South Africa's Constitutional Court were agreed that no one had a right to receive dialysis treatment from the state even when going without meant they would die.

Eldridge was also a unanimous opinion, which was remarkable for a Court on which there has always been a wide divergence of views about what equality means.[100] In *Eldridge*, however, all nine judges thought the failure to fund was distributively perverse in both senses. Compared to people who could communicate about and understand the diagnosis of their condition and the treatment that was being prescribed, those whose hearing was impaired received a standard of medical care that was significantly inferior. Those who already suffered a disadvantage got less (in terms of the quality of the medical care they received from the state) than those who did not. From the perspective of those who were deaf it was a straightforward case of discrimination, of not respecting their right to the equal benefit and protection of the law. Compared to the position of the state and those who would be called on to pay for the extra service, the proportionalities were equally clear-cut. On the one side of the case were those in need of medical services for whom miscommunication and misunderstanding could mean misdiagnosis and maltreatment. On the other, was an annual cost to taxpayers of $150,000 or .0025 per cent of what the government spent on the health of its citizens.

---

[97] *Shapiro v. Thompson.*   [98] (1997) 151 DLR (4th) 577.   [99] [1998] 1 SA 765.

[100] For an introduction to the Supreme Court's early approach to equality see D. Beatty, 'Canadian Constitutional Law in a Nutshell' (1998) 36 Alta L Rev. 605.

In *Soobramoney* the numbers were almost exactly the reverse. In contrast with the relatively trivial sums that were involved in the Canadian case, a ruling that everyone with acute kidney failure has a right to receive dialysis treatment as a matter of 'emergency treatment' would have made it very difficult, if not impossible, for the South African state to fulfil its obligation to provide basic health-care services to the population at large. No one, said the Court, has an absolute and unqualified right to expensive medical treatment even when their own life is at stake because in a world of limited resources, it would mean many others who depend on government to provide for their health and well-being would have to do without even the most basic services and care. Even though he asked for no more than what was needed to save his life, Soobramoney did not succeed because, like the claim of any 'utility monster', what he believed was his right was in fact much more than his fair share.

The same two measurements of proportionality and fair shares feature prominently in cases in which courts have been asked to evaluate claims that governments owe their citizens and other residents (even including the children of illegal immigrants) an education. When claimants can show they have not been as well treated as others in similar or even more prosperous circumstances they are almost certain to prevail. That is also the case if they can prove that the education they demand does not entail substantial financial and/or other costs to the state. If, however, neither of these distributive inequities can be made out, it is much more likely they will not succeed even if, as in *Kato* v. *Japan*[101] the constitutional guarantee is absolute and unqualified.

Two landmark rulings of the US Supreme Court opening public schools to blacks and the children of illegal immigrants illustrate the two scales of fairness judges use when they assess claims that states have a responsibility to educate those who are living inside their borders. *Brown* v. *Board of Education*,[102] arguably the most important judgment the US Supreme Court has ever written, is all and only about fair shares. Separate schools for whites and blacks were unequal schools because however similar they were in bricks and books and teachers who make learning a joy, the latter received an inferior education. Separate schools gave less to those who needed the most. By systematically attacking black children's self-esteem they could never match the education that white or integrated schools could provide. Systems of education that are drawn on racial lines are unjust and unfair and at odds with constitutional guarantees of equality because the schools they create are caste societies and the differences in the quality of education they deliver are distributively perverse.

Almost thirty years after it handed down its judgment in *Brown* v. *Board of Education*, the Court opened classroom doors that had been barred to children of illegal immigrants. The reason the Court gave for coming to their aid entailed a different calculation of fair shares than the one that motivated its ruling in *Brown*. Rather than equating the educational rights of 'undocumented' children

---

[101] 18 Minshū 2 p. 343 26/02/64.   [102] (1954) 347 US 483.

with those who were legally resident in the state, in *Plyler* v. *Doe*[103] the Court focused on the fact that giving these children the same education as everyone else would make a huge difference in their lives while imposing hardly at all on anyone else. On one side of the case the Court saw public schools as a vital civic institution, exclusion from which presaged a lifetime of illiteracy and hardship. On the other side, the Court noted that whatever reallocation of funds was required to educate the children who had previously been excluded was such 'a proportionately small' diminution of resources spent on each child, it would not have a 'grave impact' on the quality of their education. Denying people very basic educational opportunities that matter enormously to them but very little to those who already have access to them is the very antithesis of fair shares.

The idea that the rights that people have to be educated by their governments are rights to a fair share of whatever resources are invested in the training and development of a community's 'human capital' is one that has appealed to judges all over the world. Canada's Supreme Court adopted what it called 'a sliding scale approach' in defining the ways in which and the extent to which linguistic minorities could control the education of their children and insisted they receive the same, proportional funding that the majority, linguistic group receives from the state.[104] Germany's Constitutional Court has explicitly rejected the suggestion that 'the right freely to choose . . . their place of training' imposed a 'duty to supply a desired place of education at any time to any applicant', in favour of a right to fair shares.[105] '[E]very citizen qualified for university studies', the Court said, has the right to 'share equally in the opportunities being offered'. On this understanding, the Court invalidated government regulations that imposed rigid quotas and absolute numerical limits on the number of students that could be admitted to various programmes because, in its words, such restrictions 'lead to the glaring inequality that one class of applicants receives everything and the other receives nothing'.

India's Supreme Court also thinks about the right to education in terms of fair shares and indeed has pushed the logic of that understanding as far as any court in the world. In a long (though far from uniform), series of cases, the Court has expressed its approval of 'reserving' a limited number of places for students from the most disadvantaged sections of society in post-secondary institutions that otherwise would not be as accessible.[106] Most recently, in *Unni Krishnan* v. *State of Andhra Pradesh*,[107] led by B. P. Jeevan Reddy, a majority of the judges sitting on a five-person Bench ruled that all Indian children have a right to receive a primary school education for the first fourteen years of their lives, and it based its

---

[103] (1981) 457 US 202.   [104] *Mahe* v. *Alberta* (1990) 68 DLR (4th) 69.

[105] *Numerus Clausus* case (1972) 3 BVerfGE 303, trans. and reproduced in part in Kommers, *Constitutional Jurisprudence of Germany*.

[106] See e.g. *Balaji* v. *State of Mysore*, AIR 1963 SC 649; *Chitra Gosh* v. *Union of India*, AIR 1970 SC 35; *D. N. Chanchala* v. *State of Mysore*, AIR 1971 SC 1762; *AIIMS Students Union* v. *AIIMS* AIR 2001 SC 3262.

[107] AIR 1993 SC 2178.

decision very explicitly on an argument of fair shares. The Court cited the work of Gunnar Myrdal, the Swedish social scientist, and in particular his criticism of the fact that even though India spent proportionately much less on education than other constitutional democracies, it allocated a disproportionate share of what it did spend to secondary and tertiary institutions of higher learning. As a matter of distributing the community's scarce resources, the Court thought that giving more to those who already have was an 'inversion of priorities'. In the same way that South Africa's housing programme didn't provide anything for those who were most in need, India's approach to the education of its people violated the rights of 'the weaker sections of society' because it allocated much more money to the secondary and post-secondary institutions of higher learning where the children of 'the upper strata' and 'politically powerful' went to school than it did to primary education that caters to rich and poor students alike.

More cases, in which claims for social and economic rights have been vindicated as entitlements to fair shares, could be added to the list. Important claims for welfare assistance and income support, for example, have been analysed in this way. Once again, in cases of this kind, judges typically focus their attention on how well the claimants are treated compared to others whom the government supports and how expensive, overall, the claim will be. The Supreme Courts of the United States and Canada have both written major opinions with this orientation invalidating, respectively, welfare laws that restricted or denied people benefits because of their residency status and their age. The Canadian judges explicitly tested the ineligibility of people over 65 to collect regular unemployment insurance benefits against the principle of proportionality and found it wanting. As a solution to potential problems of fraudulent claims being made by people who were really retired and not looking for work, the Court found the absolute exclusion of everyone over the age of 65 was more draconian and heavy-handed than it needed to be.[108] Although 'proportionality' and 'fair shares' are not part of the mainstream vocabulary of American constitution law, the Court's insistence that new residents are entitled to the same welfare benefits as people who have lived in a state for a long time, is based on the same idea.[109] Need, not length of residence, is the proper criterion for distribution. If the purpose of the differentiation was to save money and guard against the creation of large budget deficits, the Court said it would have been fairer to reduce everyone's benefits by 72c. a month than make new residents bear the whole cost.

A particularly evocative set of decisions defending the rights of those who rely on social programmes for their physical and emotional security were handed down by Hungary's Constitutional Court soon after it began to exercise its powers of review.[110] In half a dozen rulings the judges in Budapest declared invalid large parts of a massive austerity package (known locally as the 'Bokros

---

[108] *Canada Employment and Immigration Commission* v. *Tétreault-Gadoury.*
[109] *Saenz* v. *Roe; Shapiro* v. *Thomson.*   [110] *On Social Security Benefits.*

laws' after the finance minister who formulated them), passed by the Hungarian Government, radically overhauling (and sharply reducing) the old communist system of social security and welfare rights, in order to stave off bankruptcy and ultimately to facilitate the country's transition to a market economy. Overturning laws that envisaged severe structural and economic reform and that were passed at the insistence of the country's creditors, including the International Monetary Fund, is unquestionably one of the boldest and most controversial defences of social welfare rights that has been written to date.[111]

The core of the decision is based on a principle the Court called 'legal certainty', which effectively adds a temporal gloss to the idea of fair shares. What bothered the Court most was not so much that assistance had been slashed, and its payment made conditional on proving need rather than as of right, but that the reforms had been introduced so quickly, 'practically overnight' and 'without any transition'. The unfairness lay more in the speed than the substance of the change. The principle of legal certainty, the Court said, guaranteed those affected by the reforms a period of time to adjust to the new conditions. For benefits such as pregnancy and maternity allowances, that were provided for a fixed and relatively short period of time in the immediate future, the Court required the Government to continue to assist those who had reasonably relied on the expectation that the benefits would be paid. In the longer term, however, the Court recognized that the Government was entitled to amend the entire system of social security and welfare assistance, including the legal grounds of entitlement and the basis on which it is paid. What the Court said was that, in pursuing its objectives and restructuring legal relations in the state, it was wrong for the Government to ignore the disruption and dislocation that people face when they lose the systems of support that have sustained them in the past.

As dramatic as the Bokros cases undoubtedly were, they are not categorically different than other rulings defending people's social and economic rights. In building a temporal dimension into the idea of fair shares, the Hungarian Court followed a path marked out by other courts that have defended welfare rights in a similar way. The American Supreme Court, for example, made a similar move in this direction when it ruled that welfare recipients could not be summarily cut off from their benefits without notice and without an opportunity to plead their case.[112] India's Supreme Court acted on the same impulse when it refused to allow the city of Mombai to remove slum and pavement dwellers who had illegally erected shelters on streets and sidewalks near their places of work until after the monsoon season had passed in order to minimize the hardship that would be caused by their immediate eviction.[113] The principle that a state

---

[111] For a sharp criticism of the Court's ruling see Andras Sajo, 'How the Rule of Law Killed Hungarian Welfare Reforms' (1996) 5 East European Constitutional Review 31. Cf. S. Zifzak, 'Adjudicating Social Rights: Lessons From the Hungarian Constitutional Experience' (1998) 4 East European Rights Review 53.

[112] *Goldberg v. Kelly.*   [113] *Olga Tellis v. Bombay Municipal Corp.*

owes the beneficiaries of a public service a duty to give reasonable notice of its intention to bring it to an end is also well established in the jurisprudence of the South African Constitutional Court.[114]

The Bokros cases fit the pattern in which courts have generally not defined social and economic rights as categorical and unconditional entitlements beyond minimum subsistence levels of support. When courts uphold the pleas of those who say they have a constitutional right to be supported by the state it's not because they think there is a set of fundamental, core entitlements that everyone has a right to claim. Courts respond positively when they are shown governments have not acted fairly in how they make their services available to the public and distribute the riches of the state.

4. The Justice of Fair Shares

When the Bokros and other welfare cases are put alongside those in which courts have ordered governments to educate, medicate, and generally take care of people in their communities, the collection makes for an impressive body of jurisprudence. The cases are not huge in number but they cover a wide variety of quite different claims and, collectively, they tell a story of not inconsiderable force. One of the most striking features of this body of judicial opinions is its thoroughly global character. Even though there is not a lot of explicit cross-referencing between courts, all over the world judges have converged on a common understanding and method of evaluating claims of support from the state. The idea of fair shares and the principle of proportionality through which it is expressed are universals that transcend radically different legal cultures and political traditions. They account for virtually every case in which courts have responded positively to protect people's general welfare and well being and many others, like *Soobramoney*, in which they have not. Certainly no other conception of social and economic rights fits the cases as well.

The global appeal of a fair-shares account of positive rights should not come as a great surprise. Even Fried has argued the case for fair shares at some length.[115] Fair shares ensure governments respect basic principles of justice in the distribution of their wealth. A right to fair shares also speaks directly to all of the conceptual, normative, and institutional concerns that have been expressed about legalizing what historically have been understood as matters of personal morality and private charity and entrusting the only branch of government that is unelected and unaccountable to the public to define and enforce them. To those who say positive and negative rights are different concepts, the cases show that all rights are identical in the duties and obligations they create. To liberals and democrats who worry that social and economic rights simultaneously threaten the liberty and lawmaking powers of the people, the cases show suc-

---

[114] *Premier, Mpumalanga* v. *Executive Committee* [1999] 2 SA 91 (CC).
[115] C. Fried, *Right & Wrong*, ch. 5.

cessful claims are calibrated precisely to ensure they do not significantly interfere with either the sovereignty of the people to shape the public character of their communities or the liberty of those who end up paying the bills. Institutionally, against those who think issues of distributive justice are inherently polycentric and beyond the capacities of legally trained judges to resolve, the cases paint a picture of courts assessing factual claims of unfair distribution against neutral principles of equality and proportionality, which makes them ideally suited for adjudication. Even linguistically the cases bring the larger moral issues of poverty and disadvantage back full circle by translating the rhetoric of rights into a vocabulary of duties that governments must meet whenever they seek to impose their philosophy using the coercive authority of the law.

Conceptually, the jurisprudence of social and economic rights and the caselaw protecting political and civil rights are all of a piece. Both rely on the principle of proportionality to distinguish claims that are legitimate from those that are not and both impose the same obligations—positive and negative—on government. In their enforcement of social and economic rights courts do not demand anything of government that is conceptually different from what they have ordered governments to do when they protect traditional political and civil rights. Although judicial enforcement of social and economic rights does force government to pass laws and spend against its will, courts make similar demands in their enforcement of civil and political rights all the time. Governments cannot fulfil their constitutional duty to respect the rights of their people simply by not interfering. We have already seen in Chapter 2, for example, both the Supreme Court of Japan[116] and the German Constitutional Court[117] ruling that the state has an obligation to do whatever is necessary to ensure that religious groups show each other tolerance and respect. For the Germans, the idea that traditional rights such as religious freedom give rise both to negative and positive duties (to forbear and to protect) runs through all their jurisprudence. So, for example, the right to choose one's occupation is understood to impose on the state a duty to establish educational facilities in which the right can be realized.[118] Similarly, the guarantee of freedom of expression and a free press carries with it an obligation to ensure that laws that establish a broadcasting system guarantee that the full spectrum of opinion in the community will be heard.[119] In one of its most remarkable rulings, the German Court once held the country's abortion law to be unconstitutional because it wasn't satisfied that it provided strong enough deterrents to ensure proper protection of human life.[120] For judges in Germany,

---

[116] *Japan v. Nakaya (Serviceman Enshrinement* case) 1988, trans. and reproduced in Beer and Itoh, *Constitutional Case Law of Japan 1970–1990.*

[117] *Classroom Crucifix II* case (1995) 93 BVerfGE 1 trans. and reproduced in Kommers, *Constitutional Jurisprudence of Germany.*

[118] *Numerous Clausus.*

[119] *Television* cases (1961, 1981) trans. and reproduced in part in Kommers, *Constitutional Jurisprudence of Germany,* 404–15.

[120] *Abortion I* case (1975) 39 BVerfGE 1, trans. and reproduced in part in Kommers, *Constitutional Jurisprudence of Germany.* See also 9 John Marshall Journal of Practice and Procedure (1975) 551.

human rights that are guaranteed in constitutions and international treaties presuppose that whatever laws are necessary to ensure they will be respected will be enacted and enforced. Entrenching human rights in constitutional and international texts would be an irrational, cynical gesture if the state were not required to put in place the laws and legal apparatus (i.e. the police and the courts) on which their existence depends.

The judges in Strasbourg have been especially emphatic about the positive duties that attach to traditional, first-generation rights. To live up to their obligation that no one be subjected to 'inhumane and degrading treatment', for example, the Court has ruled that member states must enact laws that will provide effective protection for children from sexual and other physical abuse.[121] They have also held states must take positive action and provide whatever police protection is necessary to enable people to exercise their basic rights of association, expression, and lawful assembly.[122] Governments have been told they must take effective action against industrial pollution if they are to satisfy their obligation to respect people's family and private life.[123] Even though these are traditional first-generation civil and political rights, they demand more of states than the purely negative obligation of forbearance. Protective legislation must be passed and enforced and lots of money must be spent. Indeed, in one major ruling, the Court required the Irish Government to provide free legal assistance to a woman seeking a legal separation from her husband even though the text of the Convention recognized such an entitlement only in criminal proceedings and notwithstanding the fact that in signing the Convention the Irish Government had expressly demurred from assuming any obligations of this kind.[124]

The duty of governments to provide some system of legal aid for people caught up in a state's legal system is widely recognized by courts all over the world. In addition to the European Court of Human Rights, Germany's Constitutional Court,[125] the Swiss Federal Court,[126] and the Supreme Courts of India,[127] Canada,[128] and even the United States,[129] all have read traditional first-generation guarantees of equality and due process of law to include a positive

---

[121] *E v. United Kingdom* (2003) 36 EHRR 519; *Z v. United Kingdom* (2002) 34 EHRR 97; *A. v. United Kingdom* (1998) 27 EHRR 611; *X and Y v. The Netherlands* (1986) 8 EHRR 235; see also *Stubbings v. United Kingdom* (1996) 23 EHRR 213.

[122] *Platform 'Ärtze für das Leben' v. Austria* 139 ECHR (Series A) (1988) 1.

[123] *Guerra v. Italy* (1998) 26 EHRR 359; *Lopez Ostra v. Spain* (1995) 20 EHRR 277.

[124] *Airey v. Ireland* (1979) 2 EHRR 305.

[125] [1967] 22 BVerfGE 83, trans. and reproduced in part in M. Capelletti and W. Cohen, *Comparative Constitutional Law* (New York: Bobbs Merrill, 1979).

[126] Decision of 9 July 1952 (BGE 78 I 193).

[127] See e.g. *Hoskot v. State of Maharashtra* AIR 1978 SC 1548; *Khatoon v. Bihar*, AIR 1979 SC 1360; *Dwivedi v. Union of India*, AIR 1983 SC 624; *Barse v. State of Maharashtra* AIR 1983 SC 378; *Suk Das v. Union Territory of Arunachal Pradesh* AIR 1986 SC 991.

[128] *J.G. v. New Brunswick* (Min. of Health and Community Services) (1999) 177 DLR (4th) 124.

[129] e.g. *Gideon v. Wainwright* (1963) 372 US 335; *Miranda v. Arizona* (1966) 384 US 436; *Vitek v. Jones* 445 US (1980) 480.

obligation to provide legal counsel for people who need it but cannot afford to pay. Although there are differences of opinion about the circumstances in which and the extent to which the duty binds the state,[130] there is virtually universal agreement that positive duties are an essential part of first-generation civil rights, even if they are written in the negative and with the purely defensive purpose of limiting the state's capacity to interfere.[131] Because a constitution depends on a government putting in place institutions and services such as the courts and the police, it can fairly be said, as Holmes and Sunstein have, that all rights are in important respects positive rights.[132]

At the same time as they have ordered governments to take care of the health, education, and/or general welfare of their people in way that preserves a conceptual unity with traditional first-generation political and civil rights, the judges have also shown great sensitivity in ensuring that neither the democratic powers of the people nor the liberty of any its citizens are unduly constrained. Governments are given wide discretion to determine the areas of social and economic policy they will emphasize and what overarching goals they will pursue. In none of the cases are governments told how much they must spend. The duties that have been imposed by the courts in their enforcement of social and economic rights only constrain the distributive patterns of government policy, not the decisions on whether to spend, on what projects, or how much. So too with personal liberty. When courts order governments to provide care and assistance to people, the amount of money and resources that are involved is typically comparatively small. *Eldridge* and *Plyler* were cases in which many people were made a whole lot better off for relatively little cost. The loss of liberty of those whose taxes would be used to pay the extra bills can be measured in terms of minutes and hours of their lives. These are not cases in which courts could fairly be described as legitimating 'forced labour' or allowing some individuals to be 'sacrificed' for the benefit of others.

Its conceptual coherence, normative strengths, and global appeal makes the fair shares account of social and economic rights very attractive. What should make it practically irresistible is the fact that it works. Applying the principle of equality or proportionality to a discrete set of facts is, even in Fuller's terms, what adjudication is all about and what judges do best. To test laws and regulations against a basic and widely accepted principle of fairness, judges have no reason to engage in high moral philosophy or deep historical

---

[130] Cf. *J.G.* v. *New Brunswick* and *Lassiter* v. *Dept. of Social Services* (1981) 452 US 18.

[131] An outstanding exception to the broad consensus is Richard Posner, the distinguished American scholar and jurist. In his judicial capacity, Posner has written strongly against the recognition of all positive duties. See e.g. *Bowers* v. *Devito* (1982) 686 F (2d) 616 618, 'The constitution is a charter of negative liberties . . . it does not require . . . government . . . to provide services, even so elementary a service as maintaining law and order . . . ' See also his opinions in *Jackson* v. *City of Joliet* (1983) 715 F (2d) 1200, and *Deshaney* v. *Winnebago County Dept. of Social Services* (1987) 812 F(2d) 298.

[132] S. Holmes and C. Sunstein, *The Cost of Rights: Why Liberty Depends on Taxes* (New York: Norton, 1999) 48; see also Sunstein, *The Partial Constitution* (Cambridge, Mass.: Harvard University Press 1993), 69–75.

investigations or any other line of intellectual inquiry that draws on disciplines other than the law. Nor, because all constitutional cases are focused on specific laws and actions taken by the state, need courts worry about other unjust and arbitrary distributions that may be the subject of another case.

Testing government programmes to ensure they don't treat some people worse than others who are in similar situations or even better off is a task ideally suited for adjudication. When disputes about fair shares are settled with a principle of proportionality they fit Fuller's model like a glove. Cases examine the distributive fairness of spending patterns of specific policies and programmes and not how budget priorities between different areas of social policy are set. Anyone whose interests are affected by a law that is under review can be assigned to one of the opposing sides of the argument and accommodated in a single case. The analysis parallels the courts' traditional role in settling private disputes; of deciding what is just in a controversy between two (or more) contending parties. The cases show that the principles are clear and familiar and capable of being applied in an impartial and objective way. Measured against a principle of proportionality it is possible to say, as the judges did, that the failure of India's government to ensure all its children received a primary school education; or the South African state to distribute antiretroviral drugs that inhibit the transmission of HIV from mother to child as widely as possible; or Canada's healthcare system to provide a sign-language service for people whose hearing was impaired; or America's welfare system to treat new and old residents the same, all were distributively perverse.

5. THE LAW OF FAIR SHARES

Although the comparative jurisprudence that has been written on the rights that people have to claim support from their governments is still in its adolescence, on any measure it is an impressive beginning. Few judgments can claim perfection, but collectively they extend the range of government action to which the principle of proportionality applies considerably. They constitute another important chapter in the pragmatist's story about judicial review. The cases show the principle and the method are just as effective in settling questions about the extent of government's responsibility to provide the basic necessities of a decent human life as it is identifying the liberty and space states must respect if everyone is to be truly free. In the few cases in which courts have not responded positively to a claim of fair shares, it is never because the principle has been held up for examination and found to be wanting. When courts give their seal of approval to acts and regulations that are distributively perverse, they tend to make the same mistakes that cause them to miss cases of sex discrimination and intolerance of religious freedom.

Sometimes fair shares don't figure in a case because a court feels the Government isn't responsible, in fact or in law, for the circumstances of the person claiming its support. Invariably those cases are flawed by the same sorts of empirical inaccuracies and interpretative errors that spoil the jurisprudence of gender discrimination and religious liberty we encountered in the previous two chapters. On other occasions judges have been won over by arguments about democracy and separation of powers and, without regard for the supremacy of the constitution, they have abandoned the principle of proportionality in favour of a weaker, more deferential standard of review. In either case, the injustice that goes unremedied is again the product of human error, not a defect in the law.

So far, very few judges who have been asked to order government to provide some economic benefit or social service have had difficulty with the facts. Occasionally it happens and when it does the resulting injustice cries out, like the right of gays and lesbians to get married, for immediate relief. Unquestionably, one of the most notorious examples of such a ruling was the early decision of the European Court of Human Rights, in which it declared valid a Belgian law that required all education in both the French and Flemish parts of the country to be conducted in the language of the majority; French in the Walloon region and Flemish in Flanders where the linguistic heritage is Dutch.[133] Except in and around Brussels, practically no minority language education was allowed. The Court recognized the law meant that some children whose mother tongue was not the language of the region in which they lived would have to leave their families and/or travel long distances to find schools where the language of instruction was the same as their own. It even conceded that the consequences in individual cases could be 'harsh'. However, it ruled that there was no violation of Article 8 of the Convention, which guarantees everyone respect for their 'private and family life' because, it said, if children were separated from their families in order to be educated in their mother tongue it was the choice of their parents, not the terms of the legislation, that was to blame. Contrary to the facts, it made those who suffered most from the territorial language regime the authors of their own misfortune and completely ignored the law that made all minority language education illegal. Contrary to all precepts of fairness, it wrote a judgment that told only half the story.

The same argument was once made to the Supreme Court of Canada, in a case (*Adler*) in which various religious groups claimed that the state had an obligation to fund their schools so long as they met the relevant educational standards, but it was not nearly as well received.[134] Although a majority of the Court decided that the claim was not well founded, only one of them, John Sopinka, said it was because whatever burdens and inequities (of having to pay for the entire cost of their children's education) these religious groups were required to bear were the result of their spiritual choices and not by command of the state. Invoking the same logic that appealed to the European Court of Human Rights, Sopinka was of the opinion that the Government had done nothing to prevent anyone sending

---

[133] *Belgian Languages in Education* case, ECHR, 23 July 1968, 1 EHRR 252.
[134] *Adler* v. *Ontario* (1996) 140 DLR (4th) 385.

his or her children to the local public schools. No one else on the Court found the argument persuasive and Beverly McLachlin and Claire L'Heureux-Dubé, the two women on the Court, explained why. For McLachlin it was a matter of simple logic. If a charge of discrimination could be rebutted by saying the person discriminated against chose the religion (or language) and so must assume responsibility for the consequences, discrimination could never be stopped. For L'Heureux-Dubé, the idea that people choose their religion was implausible as a matter of fact. From the claimants' perspective, ensuring their children received an education that was compatible with their religious beliefs was a moral imperative, not something over which they had any control.

The error and injustice of 'blaming the victim' and absolving the state of all responsibility is especially clear in such cases as *Adler*[135] and *the Belgian Languages in Education* case where the legitimacy of government policy is at stake. It is less evident when someone tries to hold government accountable for remaining passive; when the state actually has done nothing to damage or interfere with the victim's rights. But it is still there. Consider the case of Joshua Deshaney, who was beaten and abused so severely by his father that he suffered profound and permanent retardation.[136] At first blush, it seems the US Supreme Court was on firm ground in its conclusion that this was a case in which the state was in no way responsible for the tragedy of Joshua's life. It was after all the father, not some state official, who committed the assault. On reflection, however, it is evident that even if the state did not administer the beatings, it was deeply implicated in Joshua's fate. Joshua's father was only able to abuse his son as he did because the state's department of social services had not removed him from his home as it was empowered to do. Even though state social workers were aware of the threatening environment in which he lived, they allowed his father to retain custody of him. Had they been more vigilant in doing their job, Joshua could still look forward to normal human life rather than the sad and tragic future he must endure.

Nor can the state evade responsibility by arguing that however inadequately its officials handled Joshua's case, they had done nothing to put him in a worse situation than he would have been in if the state had not acted at all. Although it is true, as a fact, that the state had not aggravated Joshua's situation, it is not a fact that is pertinent to the resolution of the case. As a matter of constitutional law, the critical fact is what the state of Wisconsin actually did. It had established an extensive programme of social services and it was questions about their operation that the Court was asked to review. To rely on the truth that the state had not harmed him any more than if it had never got involved is to substitute counterfactuals for the real thing. It is an overt and egregious attempt to rewrite the facts of the case.

---

[135] The Supreme Court's decision was subsequently found to be in violation of Article 26 of the International Covenant on Civil and Political Rights by the UN Human Rights Committee in *Waldman* v. *Canada*, 05/11/99 Communication No 694/1996.

[136] *DeShaney* v. *Winnebago County Dept. of Social Services* (1988) 489 US 189.

Once the state got into the business of providing social services, its duty to respect the prescriptions and principles of the constitution was engaged. As a matter of constitutional law, the decision to create a social services department was an act of the state that automatically brought all the principles of the higher law, including proportionality, into play.[137] Acting unjustly (in failing to give Joshua's case its best attention), is legally worse than not acting at all. It is an act of misfeasance, not just nonfeasance, for which it is answerable in court. Like Irene Grootboom and the homeless more generally, Joshua Deshaney and victims of violence have a right to rank at the very top of the state's priorities. Without any guarantee of his physical security he, like she, had no life, no liberty, no freedom in any meaningful sense. In failing to hold the state to account for not protecting those whose rights to their life and liberty were most at risk, the Court compounded the injustice Joshua was made to suffer and abdicated its own responsibility of ensuring that all aspects of the constitution were fully respected and enforced.

So far rulings like *Deshaney* and the *Belgian Languages in Education* case, in which courts fail to recognize the fact of a state's involvement in the violation of people's rights, have been the exception rather than the rule.[138] More often, when courts certify laws that are distributively perverse, one of two things is going on. Either they are of the opinion that the constitutional guarantees they are authorized to enforce do not include positive rights of any kind, or they think they should defer to the legislative and executive branches of government when it comes to formulating social and economic policy and making decisions about how the state's resources should be spent. At this stage of our inquiry into the real world of judicial review, it should come as no surprise that a high percentage of the judges who feel this way are American. For every such decision as *Brown v. Board of Education*, *Plyler v. Doe*, and *Saenz v. Roe* in which the US Supreme Court has defended social and economic rights of less-privileged Americans, it has also handed down judgments validating educational systems that favoured the rich over the poor[139] and welfare laws that excluded children who, on a test of pure need, should have qualified for assistance.[140] When the US Supreme Court gives it seal of approval to laws that are distributively unjust, typically it explains that the American Constitution is about the negative liberty to be free from coercive and arbitrary treatment by government and not positive entitlements to government assistance and support. Invariably it follows its standard

---

[137] The idea that state action must conform to the principle of proportionality even when no other constitutional (or conventional) rights are at stake is well accepted in European law. The approach of the European Court of Human Rights is discussed by Nicolas Bratza in the opinion he wrote in *Fretté v. France* <http://hudoc.echr.coe.int/>.

[138] But see *Harris v. McRae* (1980) 448 US 297 in which the Court, by a bare 5 : 4 majority, upheld a federal medicare law that denied all funding for therapeutic abortions on the ground that the government had done nothing to aggravate the circumstances of indigent women who couldn't afford to pay.

[139] *San Antonio Independent School District v. Rodriguez* (1972) 411 US 1.

[140] *Dandridge v. Williams* (1969) 397 US 471.

practice of pointing to the language and the history and its own prior interpretations of the text to justify its unwillingness to intervene. If it can, as it did in
Deshaney, it will make use of all three.

Although historical, doctrinal, and institutional arguments are especially
popular with Americans, they are not unknown in other parts of the world.
There have been many judges on the Supreme Courts of Canada,[141] Ireland,[142]
and Japan,[143] for example, who share the belief that it is inappropriate for the
judiciary to interfere with the prerogatives of the legislature when issues of social
and economic policy are at stake. In all three countries, the courts have adopted
much softer, more deferential standards of review when big money is on the line.
At the extreme, the Chief Justice of Ireland, Thomas Aloysius Finlay, once
pronounced the courts to be 'a wholly inappropriate' institution to decide
whether governments have distributed their resources unfairly.[144]

Occasionally, historical arguments—that no one understood the relevant constitutional text or treaty to impose positive obligations on governments to
provide specific public services—have also appealed to judges outside the United
States. In its judgment in the *Belgian Languages in Education* case,[145] for
example, the European Court of Human Rights thought the intentions of those
signing the first protocol to the European Convention in 1952 were decisive. In
addition to denying the state's involvement in the disruption it caused to people's
family life, the Court was emphatic that the claims for state support of minority
language schools could not succeed because the specific purpose of the protocol
was only to guarantee everyone equal access to whatever educational opportunities were provided in each state. It was never intended to force all governments
in Europe to adhere to a common standard on minority education that didn't
even exist.

The historical, doctrinal, and institutional arguments that courts conventionally make when they say constitutions don't impose affirmative duties on the
state to help people in need or to treat people fairly in the distribution of its
resources should sound quite familiar. They are, after all, the same ones we saw
judges invoke when they say that gays and lesbians are not entitled to the same
protection against discrimination as heterosexuals or that religiously minded
people have fewer rights in public places than those whose spiritual orientation is
secular. Reasoning from original understandings, prior cases, and institutional
modesty we know could not justify the results in those cases. Nor, it turns out,
can they do any better when social and economic rights are at stake.

Arguments based on precedent can immediately be put to the side. It would be
repetitive to explain again why when constitutional cases are argued in a coun-

---

[141] *Irwin Toy Ltd.* v. *A.G Québec* (1989) 58 DLR (4th) 577.
[142] *Mhicmhathúna* v. *Ireland* [1995] ILRM 69, *Re Employment, Equality Bill* [1997] 2 IR 321
(SC).
[143] *Marushin Industries* v. *Japan: Sumiyoshi* v. *Hiroshima.*
[144] *Mhicmhathúna* v. *Ireland.*
[145] ECHR 23 July 1968, 1 EHRR 252.

try's highest court, reasoning by precedent is either redundant or unconstitutional.[146] Judicial doctrine cannot have any more force in the adjudication of social and economic rights than they exert in the resolution of first-generation rights. In either case, if an earlier decision comes to be understood as being in conflict with the constitution it is the latter, because of its supremacy, that logically must prevail. No matter what the substantive issue may be, precedent can never justify extending any claimant less protection than a constitution or convention guarantees. Indeed, as we have seen, even precedents that can pass the test of constitutional legitimacy can never be primary sources of authority. They are always secondary and derivative at best. Precedents that possess any authority do so only because they are consistent with and give expression to a more fundamental principle in the constitution. Without the principle, precedent can never be decisive on its own.

Although arguments against the recognition of social and economic rights that are based on precedent suffer the same fatal contradiction that affects all judge-made doctrine in constitutional law, those that are based on the words and history of the text do look stronger here than when they are used to clarify other parts of a constitution. Certainly constitutions modelled on the American Bill of Rights, that are written almost entirely in the negative, seem incapable of giving rise to positive obligations on the part of the state. ('Congress shall make no laws . . . nor shall any state deprive any person of life, liberty . . . ') Moreover, whereas historical arguments about original understandings of first-generation rights were plagued with gaps and indeterminacies, there can be little doubt that many constitutions, including the German as well as the American, were written with the very clear understanding that no social and economic rights were being guaranteed. Unlike cases of sex discrimination, where the words of the constitution and the intention that underlies them pulled in opposite directions, when it comes to issues of social and economic rights the words reflect very precisely the thinking that caused them to be written as they were.

Even though the negative style of a text such as the US Bill of Rights seems definitive, it isn't and it could never be. No matter what the words read literally and/or historically may seem to imply, their logic insists that all constitutional rights unavoidably and inevitably give rise both to negative duties of non-interference and positive duties of effective protection. Even in a minimalist nightwatchman state, the entrenchment of the most basic civil and political rights in a country's constitution necessarily imposes a duty on government to enact and enforce whatever laws are required to guarantee their efficacy. Without laws making assault and trespass and nuisance legal wrongs, neither security of the person nor private property could exist. It is their recognition in and enforcement by law that distinguishes legal rights from claims that are founded in morality. Constitutional rights that cannot be defended in court, like the Directive Principles in India's Constitution, are moral, not legal, claims. The

---

[146] See discussion in Chapter 3, 87–91.

logic of constitutional rights being legal entitlements means they require a lot of attention and investment from government. Police, courts, and codes of correct conduct are the bare essentials that all traditional first-generation rights, even those written in the negative, presuppose. Being legally enforceable implies, at a minimum, a functioning legal order, which can ensure the words on the page match the events of real life.

A functioning legal order means that a sufficient number of independent judges must be appointed,[147] fair procedures put in place,[148] and legal counsel paid[149] to ensure the review process and the adjudication of people's rights are carried out on a level playing field. Free legal aid is a constitutional right, as we have seen, that has been recognized all over the world. The fact it isn't mentioned in a text doesn't mean it isn't there. Effective participation is as essential to the integrity of a legal system as emergency shelter is to government programmes designed to ensure people are adequately housed. Anyone forced to fight for their rights in court without the aid of someone trained in the law faces a huge disadvantage. Although the kind of assistance people have a right to expect will vary with the complexities and resources of each legal system, when someone's most fundamental rights (to their life, liberty, and the security of their person) are at stake, their claims for assistance merit the highest priority.

The logic that requires the state to provide the means by which people can vindicate their rights when they are threatened by others, also insists that governments must be proactive in preventing violations before they occur. Even if the primary purpose of a right is to insulate people from having the state arbitrarily interfere in their lives, remedial initiatives designed to rectify the infringement of a right after the fact will rarely be enough. Except when the costs are prohibitive, prevention is always better than the cure. Especially when a fundamental aspect of a person's life or liberty is at stake, states must be held to be partially responsible if the laws they enact allow others to attack people's rights and freedoms with impunity. Having a right not to be subjected to inhuman or degrading treatment, or to have one's family and private life respected, carries with it an entitlement to state protection, in the form of effective deterrence, against serious breaches of such guarantees.[150] Governments do interfere with religious liberty if they allow it to be attacked in the daily routines of community life by crafting a legal system that is tolerant of such abuses. The lesson of the caselaw is that a legal regime that allows the indiscriminate infringement of constitutional rights by anyone acting in a private, unofficial capacity is in fact and law in material breach of a state's basic obligation of non-interference.

The idea that all rights, even negative liberties, necessarily give rise to positive duties of protection and enforcement is, as we have just seen, one few judges anywhere contest. As a practical matter, in the twenty-first century of the social

---

[147] See e.g. *R.* v. *Askov* (1990) 2 SCR 1199.
[148] See e.g. *Singh* v. *Minister of Employment and Immigration* (1985) 1 SCR 177.
[149] *Supra* nn. 124–30.   [150] *E.* v. *UK; Z* v. *UK; A.* v. *UK.*

welfare state, for most of them it is no longer a question of whether government has a duty to act, only whether in what it did it went too far or didn't do enough. In a world in which all space is subject to some legal rule(s), it is now almost always and only a question of the quality of the state's intervention, not whether any regulation has or must take place.

Undoubtedly India's Supreme Court has understood better than most that the distinction between positive and negative rights is false and misleading. They have followed the logical method of reading a constitutional text as far as any group of judges and further than most. On the premise that 'that, which alone makes it possible to live . . . must be deemed to be an integral component of the right to life'[151] the judges in Delhi have derived a right to livelihood, education, and to the health and safety of its working population from a constitutional text that is written as a guarantee of non-interference.[152] However, although the Indians have been pioneers in staking out a broad range of positive obligations states must meet in order to satisfy their constitutional commitments not to interfere with the lives and liberties of their people, like-minded judges can be found coming to similar conclusions all over the world.

On environmental issues, for example, jurists in Europe have been particularly alert to the connection. On more than one occasion the European Court of Human Rights has not hesitated to find that governments interfere with the rights of privacy and family life of their citizens when they allow the environment in which these people live to be poisoned by industrial pollution.[153] In a parallel ruling, László Sólyom, the first President of Hungary's Constitutional Court, emphasized that even if the Hungarian Constitution did not explicitly commit the state to guaranteeing that the country maintain a healthy environment, the obligation could be deduced directly from the basic right to life. Like the Germans twenty years earlier,[154] the Hungarians have taken the position that states have an obligation 'to guarantee the physical conditions that are necessary to implement the right to human life'.[155] For all three courts, a safe and clean environment is as much a precondition to respecting a person's right to life, as laws that make the intentional infliction of harm a crime, and states have a responsibility to provide both.

Even in the United States, the distinction between positive and negative rights has been fudged. For a long time the judges in Washington have been saying that due process rights of non-interference may require states to provide free legal assistance.[156] The idea that governments have an obligation to protect people's rights from being abused by private parties is also well known in American

---

[151] *Olga Tellis* v. *Bombay Municipal Corp.*, para. 32.

[152] *Supra* nn. 88–91.

[153] *Supra* n. 123.

[154] *Aircraft Noise Control* case (1981), trans. and reproduced in part in Kommers, *Constitutional Jurisprudence of Germany*, 128–31.

[155] *On Environmental Protection*, Decision 28/94, 20/05/94, trans. and reported in Sólyom and Brunner, *Constitutional Judiciary in a New Democracy*.

[156] See e.g. *Johnson* v. *Zerbst* (1938) 304 US 458; *Gideon* v. *Wainwright*; *Miranda* v. *Arizona*.

constitutional law.[157] Indeed, when a state's restriction of a person's life and liberty is an established fact, the US Supreme Court has ruled that government is responsible to provide for his or her basic needs including food, clothing, and medical care.[158] Even though the American Bill of Rights is only and exclusively a catalogue of injunctions against government interference with a basic set of negative liberties, no one doubts that when a state causes someone to be put in jail it is obliged, at a minimum, to provide the basic necessities of life.

The comparative jurisprudence that courts have written ordering governments to provide whatever is required for people to live their lives with dignity, puts the lie to the claim that negative rights of non-interference do not give rise to affirmative duties to provide for people's material and spiritual well-being. It shows that in law all rights are, to varying degrees, positive rights, and that the distinction between acts and omissions of governments is false and misleading. Still, and despite the factual and legal responsibility of states for the most fundamental aspects of the health, education, and welfare of their people, some will want to resist the conclusion that this inevitably leads to the wholesale enforcement of a broad range of social and economic rights. There are, as we have noted, many judges around the world who think the social and economic character of a community is for the elected branches of government not the courts to decide. For most judges who share this opinion, entrusting courts with jurisdiction over social and economic policy is objectionable because it is seen to be a radical departure from the principle that the powers of the judiciary and elected branches of government are separate and distinct and a serious limitation on the sovereignty of the people to govern themselves democratically.

Debates about what role courts should play in the economy and the governing structure of a state are a staple in the science and philosophy of politics. They have, however, no place in either the theory or practice of law. Even though the habit of deferring to the elected branches of government on issues of social and economic policy has appealed to many judges, it has no support in any text and it constitutes a flagrant violation of the principle of constitutional supremacy. Being deferential means not doing the job. It purports to give laws that cannot meet the test of fair shares a legitimacy they can never have. When courts argue there are sound political and practical reasons why broad guarantees of equality and liberty should not be rigorously enforced when issues of social and economic policy are at stake, they claim an authority they do not possess. Rather than apply and enforce the terms of the constitution, as its logic requires, they assert a power to rewrite and amend the text.

The logic of constitutions being the supreme law in a legal system means all laws and activities of government must be subject to the same standard of review. No person, nor any law, can be exempt. There is no historical, doctrinal, or institutional argument that can challenge or override its supremacy. The judge's

[157] *Shelley* v. *Kraemer* (1948) 334 US 1.
[158] *Youngberg* v. *Romeo* (1982) 457 US 307; *Estelle* v. *Gamble* (1976) 429 US 97.

job is to ensure no person is denied the equal protection of the law regardless of what those who drafted a constitution or enforced it in an earlier era might have thought, and no matter the personal characteristics of those seeking the protection of the court, nor the subject matter of their complaint. The unavoidable and irreducible lesson of the cases is that judges behave unconstitutionally if they validate laws they know cannot pass the test of fair shares and the principles of proportionality and equality by which it is applied.

Standards of review that are less demanding than the principle of proportionality are not only illegitimate tests of what is constitutionally valid, they are practically misplaced as well. Even if they could be squared with the supremacy of the constitution, principles that employ weaker, more deferential tests are premised on a misunderstanding of the way the idea of fair shares and the principle of proportionality actually work. Deference would be appropriate if courts were asked to tell governments what areas of social policy they should emphasize most, or how much money they should spend. But that is not, as the cases show, what the enforcement of social and economic rights is all about. When courts insist governments distribute their resources fairly and in ways that respect basic principles of proportionality, they give the people free rein to choose which aspects of community life will receive the highest priority and how much, globally, they will spend. Just as classical Greece and Rome pooled their resources to build temples, theatres, and public baths, modern states may promote the health and welfare of their people by building houses, hospitals, and schools. Except for invidious and discriminatory purposes, courts have deferred to the values and goals that the people and their elected representatives choose. Questions about whether and/or the extent to which a state should fund a comprehensive healthcare system or post-secondary education are left for politics and the people to decide.

Analysing whether government policy respects people's right to fair shares calls on judges to apply the same principle and follow the same pattern of reasoning that they use when traditional, first-generation, political and civil rights are at stake. If deference is wrong in the latter case, it must be equally mistaken in the adjudication of social and economic rights. In both sets of cases the character and magnitude of the disputes they are asked to resolve are the same. The scales of justice—and the principle by which they are calibrated—never change. In the same way we observed Aharon Barak refusing to be drawn into a debate between the orthodox and secular communities in Jerusalem about the possibility of other street closings in the future,[159] the focus of the judge faced with an allegation that someone's share of a government programme is not fair, is concentrated exclusively on the laws or policies that are said to be distributively perverse. Each area of public expenditure is the subject of its own case. Judgments are made about how the resources that are dedicated to

---

[159] See Ch. 2, n. 54.

health or education or housing are distributed, not on how the funding between all three compare.

The fact that the logic of every constitution with an entrenched bill of rights requires judges to assess claims of social and economic assistance from the state in precisely the same way they adjudicate cases involving political and civil rights suggests that the principle of proportionality can sustain a comprehensive and coherent theory of judicial review all by itself. As a matter of constitutional law, the cases show that contrary to what many philosophers and political leaders have thought, liberty, equality, and fraternity all mean the same thing. Ensuring everyone who is authorized to exercise the powers of the state always acts moderately and with respect for others is the one and only function judges are authorized and competent to perform.

The idea that all constitutional law can be reduced to a single principle or framework of analysis is so at odds with how judicial review is conventionally understood, we need to pause and catch our breath. To assess its credibility we need to know how it would measure up against the standards constitutional theories are expected to meet. Does, for example, proportionality qualify as a neutral principle that would satisfy Herbert Wechsler or Robert Bork? How does it fare on Dworkin's twin criteria of fit and justice? What is the deep moral value on which it is based? We must also assess how relevant a proportionality model of judicial review is in different parts of the world. How does it play, for example, in the United States, where, as we have seen, the word is less well known and its method only inconsistently employed? Is it a universal principle of constitutional law that can flourish as well in America as anywhere else?

Before reading more cases we need to attend to these questions. We must stand back and get a perspective on the larger picture that the cases have brought into focus. It is necessary to adopt a more theoretical orientation towards the principle of proportionality that will parallel the stance that we took at the beginning of the book. We have spent a lot of time looking at the principle of proportionality and the way it works in practice, from the inside looking out. We must now take its measure externally, from the outside, and bring our inquiry back to where it began.

5

Proportionality

1. PROPORTIONALITY AND THE PARADOX

At the end of the twentieth century constitutional democracies, in which courts sit in judgment on the decisions that are made by the elected representatives of the people, remain something of an anomaly, their politics plagued by a paradox that seems to defy resolution. On the one hand, this form of government has emerged as the pre-eminent model of structuring the powers of the state all over the world. Whenever and wherever people have been able to throw off the shackles of arbitrary and unjust regimes, they have, more often than not, embraced the American model of constitutional democracy in which judges are made guardians of people's basic human rights. Constitutional and international bills of rights have been embraced by most countries in Europe and the Americas and have established roots in Asia, Africa, and the Middle East as well. An example, some might say, of the globalization of a good idea.

On the other hand, this flourishing of a 'judicialization of politics' has come about without a satisfactory account having been provided for why so much power should be entrusted to a small group of lawyers who are unelected and virtually unaccountable to anyone but themselves. The unprecedented globalization of judicial review has occurred despite the fact that an adequate justification for making judges so powerful has still to be written. As we saw in the first chapter, a number of theories have been offered but none has been able to explain how giving judges the authority to stop politicians acting on the platforms that got them elected is compatible with our core ideas of democracy and the power of people to control their own destinies.

To unravel this paradox we have undertaken an extensive, though far from exhaustive, review of what the judges have been doing while the theorists have been trashing each other's work. There is a lot more jurisprudence to read but in the last three chapters we have made the following discovery. Despite the carnage that the theorists have made of each other's ideas, judges all over the world have converged on a framework of analysis that allows them to evaluate the work of the political branches of government from a common perspective and without regard to their own political and moral philosophies. With only scant notice of (and from) the high priests of constitutional law, and not without dissent in its own ranks, the judiciary has constructed a working model of judicial review that relies, almost entirely, on the principle of proportionality to tell them when the elected representatives of the people and their officials are acting properly and when they are not. In all areas of government regulation, no matter the nature of the right or freedom that is alleged to have been violated, and regardless of the personal characteristics of those bringing the case, on what might be called the jurist's model, the test is always the same. Laws—indeed any act undertaken in the name or with the authorization (explicit or tacit) of the state—must respect a basic principle of proportionality in the way they deal with the different interests and values they affect. Whether judges are faced with a claim of religious freedom, sex discrimination, or for material support from the state, more often than not they have done their job by trying to get as accurate an assessment as possible of what the disputed state action actually means to those it affects the most. When it is applied properly, proportionality requires judges to assess the legitimacy of whatever law or regulation or ruling is before them from the perspective of those who reap its greatest benefits and those who stand to lose the most.

The idea that judicial review can be reduced to the enforcement of a principle of proportionality will strike a lot of people as counterintuitive, if not foolish and even regressive. It smacks of being a throwback to a 'mechanical jurisprudence' that has been discredited for almost a hundred years.[1] A theory based on the principle of proportionality bears little resemblance to the common understanding that judicial review is a process in which judges protect people's basic constitutional rights by elaborating and elucidating a sacred text. It entails very little interpretation and makes the concept of rights almost irrelevant. It has the effect of turning a lot of conventional wisdom on its head.

The more familiar we have become with how judges go about making their decisions, however, the more a theory of judicial review organized around a principle of proportionality gains credibility. The jurisprudence courts have written on religious freedom, sex discrimination, and social and economic rights has demonstrated that judges have found a way to define their own role in the governance of their communities that actually makes a lot of sense. With a principle of proportionality, judges are able to resolve conflicts between majorities and minorities in a way that is equally respectful of both. With it, a compelling justification for entrusting the judiciary with the power of overseeing the legislature and executive is possible. Making proportionality the critical test of whether a law or some other act of state is constitutional or not separates the powers of the judiciary and the elected branches of government in a way that provides a solution to the paradox that has confounded constitutional democracies for so long. Building a theory of judicial review around a principle of proportionality, it turns out, satisfies all the major criteria that must be met for it to establish its integrity. It qualifies both as a 'neutral principle' in Herbert

---

[1] R. Pound, 'Mechanical Jurisprudence' (1908) 8 Colum L Rev. 605.

Wechsler's famous turn of phrase[2] and it meets Ronald Dworkin's tests of 'fit' and 'value' as well.[3]

2. THE NEUTRALITY OF PROPORTIONALITY

Of all the criteria that a theory of judicial review must meet none is tougher than the requirement of neutrality. As we saw in the first chapter, it is so demanding that until now no theory has been able to satisfy it in every respect. Even the US Supreme Court in its finest hour when it ordered the desegregation of American schools has been judged as falling short of its mark. Herbert Wechsler's powerful critique of the Court's judgment in *Brown* v. *Board of Education*[4] illustrates how stringent the requirement of neutrality can be. For Wechsler, neutrality meant that the criteria a theory uses to distinguish acts of government that are constitutional from those that are not has to 'be framed and tested as an exercise of reason and not merely as an act of willfulness or will'. For him, neutrality required the process of review to 'be genuinely principled, resting with respect to every step that is involved in reaching judgment on analysis and reasons quite transcending the immediate result'. Even though he thought segregated schools were morally wrong, he argued that the Court had not provided a principled reason why the blacks' right to associate should trump the whites' and how its ruling was anything more than the 'ad hoc evaluation of a naked power organ'.[5]

More recently, Robert Bork has pushed the logic of requiring judges to base their decisions on the even-handed application of neutral principles, to emphasize that the latter must be neutrally derived and neutrally defined as well.[6] To avoid being 'a naked power organ', Bork pointed out, the principles must not only be capable of being applied 'consistently and without regard to [the judge's] sympathy or lack of sympathy with the parties before him', they must also be expressed or implied by the words of the constitution and articulated at a 'level of generality that . . . the words and the structure and the history of the constitution fairly supports'.[7] Neutral principles must be drawn from the constitution and formulated in a way that allows them to be applied consistently. To reconcile democracy and judicial review in a principled way a theory must demonstrate its neutrality in all three respects.

The jurisprudence that courts have written in resolving disputes about religious freedom, sex discrimination, and social and economic rights shows that

---

[2] H. Wechsler, 'Toward Neutral Principles of Constitutional Law' (1959) 73 Harvard L Rev. 1.

[3] R. Dworkin, *Law's Empire* (Cambridge, Mass.: Harvard University Press, 1986), ch. 6; *Freedom's Law* (Cambridge, Mass.: Harvard University Press, 1996), ch. 1; *Life's Dominion* (New York: Vintage Books, 1994), 111.

[4] (1954) 347 US 483.

[5] Wechsler, 'Toward Neutral Principles of Constitutional Law', 11–15, 32–5; see also A. Bickel, 'The Original Understanding and the Segregation Decision' (1953) 69 Harv. L Rev. 1.

[6] R. Bork, *The Tempting of America* (New York: Free Press, 1990), 151.   [7] Ibid. 150.

proportionality is certainly more neutral than any of the theories we considered in Chapter 1. The caselaw we have encountered over the course of the last three chapters establishes the impartiality of the principle in all the required dimensions. The fact that every major court with the power to review the decisions of the two elected branches of government has employed its pragmatic method of analysis, albeit with varying degrees of commitment, and often under different names, attests to the integrity of its derivation. Proportionality is a universal criterion of constitutionality. It is an essential, unavoidable part of every constitutional text. Even the US Supreme Court relies on a test very similar to the metric of proportionality when it subjects state action under the First, Fifth, and Fourteenth Amendments to 'strict scrutiny', although it only applies the standard to laws that draw distinctions on the basis of suspect classifications (e.g. race) or derogate from what it deems to be fundamental rights (e.g. to travel, vote, privacy).[8]

Different courts have emphasized different words and structural features of the relevant texts in explaining their derivation of the principle. For the German Constitutional Court proportionality is a principle of long standing whose roots reach back to the 'rule of law'.[9] In Canada,[10] Israel,[11] and South Africa[12] proportionality has been found to be embedded in values of pluralism and toleration that underlie the most basic understandings of 'democracy'. The European Court of Human Rights uncovered proportionality in the Convention's rules against discrimination and inequality.[13] Judges in Japan and Hungary have found the principle in specific rights to religion[14] and expression[15] that are separately and unconditionally guaranteed and the High Court of Australia has drawn the principle from a right to political expression that isn't even mentioned in the text.[16]

---

[8] L. Tribe, *American Constitutional Law*, 2nd edn. (New York: Foundation Press, 1987), ch. 16:6–13

[9] N. Emilou, *The Principle of Proportionality in European Law* (Dordrecht: Kluwer, 1996), ch. 2; D. Kommers, *The Constitutional Jurisprudence of the Federal Republic of Germany*, 2nd edn. (Durham, NC: Duke University Press, 1997), 46.

[10] *Regina v. Oakes* (1986) 26 DLR (4th) 200.

[11] *Lior Horev v. Ministry of Communication/Transportation*, April 1997, trans. and reproduced in part in P. Gewirtz (ed.), *Global Constitutionalism* (New Haven: Yale Law School, 1997).

[12] *S v. Makwanyane* [1995] 3 SA 391 (Const. Ct.); see also D. van Wyk, J. Dugard, B. de Villiers, D. Davis (eds.), *Rights and Constitutionalism* (Cape Town: Juta, 1994).

[13] *Belgian Linguistic* case (1968) 1 EHRR 252 para. 10; *Marckx v. Belgium* (1979) 2 EHRR 330, para. 33; *Rasmussen v. Denmark* (1985) 7 EHRR 371 para. 38, and see generally P. van Dijk and G. J. H. van Hoof, *Theory and Practice of the European Convention on Human Rights* (Antwerp: Kluwer, 1984).

[14] *Kakunaga v. Sekiguchi* (1977), *Shinto Ground Breaking Ceremony Case*, trans. and reproduced in part in L. Beer and H. Itoh, *The Constitutional Case Law of Japan, 1970–1990* (Seattle: University of Washington Press, 1996).

[15] Decision 30/1992, 26 May 1992 on Freedom of Expression in L. Sólyom and G. Brunner, *Constitutional Judiciary in a New Democracy* (Ann Arbor: University of Michigan Press, 2000), 229–38.

[16] *Australian Capital Television Ltd. v. Commonwealth* (1992) 66 ALJR 695; *Nationwide News P/L v. Wills* (1992) 66 ALJR 658, and see generally B. Fitzgerald, *Proportionality and the Australian Constitution* (1993) 12 U Tasmania L Rev. 263.

The fact is that proportionality is an integral, indispensable part of every constitution that subordinates the system of government it creates to the rule of law. It is constitutive of their structure[17] an integral part of every constitution in virtue of their status as the supreme law within a nation state.[18] A constitution without some principle to resolve cases of conflicting rights would be incoherent: it just wouldn't make any sense. As Wechsler's critique of *Brown* v. *Board of Education* made clear, without a principled way of reconciling the competing interests and values that are part of every case, a constitution would quickly become encrusted in a jurisprudence of confusion and contradiction and courts would themselves become one of the 'naked power organs' they were meant to suppress. The idea that a constitution could exist without some standard of proportionality is a logical impossibility. It serves as an optimizing principle that makes each constitution the best it can possibly be.[19]

The jurisprudence puts the pedigree of proportionality beyond any question or doubt. In tracing its roots beneath the words on the page, judges have found that proportionality runs to all four corners of every constitutional text. Collectively, their judgments establish the neutrality of its definition as well. Although, as we have seen, it often goes by different names, 'reasonableness' in India[20] and Japan, 'toleration' in Israel, 'strict scrutiny' in the United States, its meaning never changes. The caselaw shows proportionality can be and usually is formulated at the highest level of generality that the words and structure of the constitution logically support. Although it is commonly broken down into three distinct principles, testing the 'rationality' (suitability), 'necessity', and 'proportionality' in the 'strictest' or 'narrowest' sense,[21] the first two are really just clear and easy applications of the third. Tests of rationality (suitability) and 'necessity' mark out cases when, in effect, no legitimate reasons of any kind can be identified to justify what was done. Laws that can't pass the necessity test constitute gratuitous infringements on people's constitutional rights because they are broader and more burdensome than they need to be. There is no (rational) reason, no (legitimate) interest for not pursuing a less restrictive and less draconian alternative which would accomplish all the Government's objectives, while lightening the burden on, or discrimination of, those they adversely affect. However it is defined, in all its formulations, it is all about moderation and mutual respect from beginning to end. As a general principle,

[17] On the logical character of structural arguments in constitutional law, see Philip Bobbitt, *Constitutional Fate* (New York: Oxford University Press, 1982), ch. 6.

[18] Emilou, *The Principle of Proportionality*, 47.

[19] R. Alexy, '*Rights, Legal Reasoning and Rational Discourse*' (1992) 5 Ratio Juris 143; 'Jurgen Habermas's Theory of Legal Discourse' (1996) 17 Cardozo L Rev. 1027, 1030–1.

[20] Although the Supreme Court of India included the idea of proportionality in its earliest definitions of reasonableness, at the end of the century at least two members of the Court were less certain of the connection. See *State of Madras* v. *A.H. Row*, AIR 1952 SC 196, 200; cf. *Union of India* v. *Ganayutham*, AIR 1997 SC 3387, p. 125.

[21] Emilou, *The Principle of Proportionality*, ch. 2. See also J. Jowell and A. Lester, 'Proportionality Neither Novel Nor Dangerous', in J. Jowell and D. Oliver (eds.), *New Directions in Judicial Review* (London: Stevens, 1988), 53.

proportionality tells governments and their officials that they have to have stronger and more compelling reasons for decisions that inflict heavy burdens and disadvantages on people than when the infringements of rights and liberties are not as serious or painful.

Whether it is understood as a three-pronged test, or one overarching evaluation of how fairly governments reconcile the competing interests and values of their constituents, most judges define its reach at the broadest level of generality possible so as to embrace every order and edict that is backed with the coercive force of the law. Legislation, regulations, executive orders, administrative rulings, and local bylaws are all subject to the standard of fairness and even-handedness that proportionality sets. So too in most places, most of the time, are the declarations and the decisions of the courts.[22]

2.1. Proportionality and Private Law

A few judges have struggled with the idea that the law they create and the remedies they provide to resolve disputes between private individuals are subordinate and must conform to the highest standards of the constitution, including the principle of proportionality. The Canadian Supreme Court and (following Ottawa's lead) South Africa's Constitutional Court have both written major opinions that 'private law' is not as strictly bound by the requirements of proportionality as other kinds of law. In both countries it was granted a kind of partial immunity.[23] In South Africa, the Court's ruling was nullified soon after by a decision to make specific reference to the judiciary in the final version of the country's first democratic constitution.[24] In Canada, however, the judges continue to insist they can develop the rules of the common law, like defamation or trespass, without having to meet the same standards as officials who work in the legislative and executive branches of government.[25] The Canadians still think that private law is something special and distinct.

The position of the Canadian judges is completely at odds with mainstream opinion in the rest of the world and makes no logical or practical sense. Very simply, putting any aspect of the legal system beyond the reach of a constitution undermines the supremacy of the latter. Because only one law can be paramount, everything else that has legal force must be subordinate. The logic of a consti-

---

[22] A. Barak, 'Constitutional Human Rights & Private Law' (1996) 3 Review of Constitutional Studies 218; A Clapham, *Human Rights in the Private Sphere* (Oxford: Oxford University Press, 1994).

[23] *Retail, Wholesale and Department Store Union, Local 580 et al.* v. *Dolphin Delivery* (1986) 33 DLR (4th) 174; *Du Plessis* v. *De Klerk* [1996] 3 SA 850 (Const. Ct.); see also *Khumalo* v. *Holomisa* [2002] 5 SA 401.

[24] Section 8 of the South African Constitution says explicitly it binds the judiciary and that the rules of the common law must conform to section 36 which entrenches the principle of proportionality. See A. P. Blaustein and G. H. Flanz, *Constitutions of the Countries of the World* (loose-leaf) (Dobbs Ferry, NY: Oceana).

[25] See e.g. *Hill* v. *Church of Scientology* (1995) 126 DLR (4th) 129.

tution's supremacy is inescapable. There can be no species of law that is of equal rank, and all branches of government must be bound in virtue of its status at the top of the legal order. Even the US Supreme Court has recognized that when judges decide to enforce private agreements between two people that discriminate against a third, their order qualifies as action taken in the name and with the force of the state.[26] If any judicially created rule of private law (contract, property, tort, etc.) cannot satisfy the principle of proportionality, there is no logical way it can be saved.

Exempting judge-made rules that regulate how people interact personally and privately in civil society from having to conform to the principle of proportionality is worse than incoherence. It not only turns the hierarchical relationship between supreme and subordinate laws on its head, it also threatens the values of privacy and personal autonomy the exemption is supposed to foster. People who deny the logic of the supremacy of the constitution sometimes argue that if the judicial development of those areas of law that are concerned with personal and private affairs had to measure up to the principle of proportionality no space of individual liberty and freedom would be secure from meddling by the state. They worry no one would be able to deny access to their homes to people whose cultural practices, religious beliefs, or sexual orientation etc. offended them. Nor, it is said, would people be able to differentiate between their children on the basis of their sex when they divided up their estates.[27]

In fact, the principle of proportionality is calibrated in a way that makes it acutely sensitive to the personal spaces and values people care about most. The right to discriminate in how one deals with one's property, for example, is strongest when it concerns places and objects that are most private and personal and weakest when what is at stake is generally accessible to the public at large. Property and contract regimes that are well proportioned recognize a person's right to refuse to rent a room to someone of a different race, religion, or sexual orientation if it is situated in his or her home, but not if it is in a large apartment complex.[28]

The most intimate and private aspects of a person's life are more at risk when the law that lays down the rules is not subject to the principle of proportionality than when it is. When judges don't have to show that the legal rules they devise to resolve interpersonal conflicts are well proportioned, liberty and freedom

---

[26] *Shelley* v. *Kraemer* (1947) 334 US 1.

[27] Gerald Gunther, *Cases and Materials on Individual Rights in Constitutional Law*, 3rd edn. (New York: Foundation Press, 1981): 'a broad application of *Shelley* would have left no private choices immune from constitutional restraints', 622; Aharon Barak, 'Constitutional Human Rights and Private Law', 230–1: 'If we apply the Basic Laws provisions also to relations between private parties, we will find that Basic Laws do not only grant rights, but they also negate rights—since the right of one private party is the obligation of another private party.' See also L. E. Weinrib and E. J. Weinrib, 'Constitutional Values and Private Law in Canada', in D. Friedmann and D. Barak-Erez (eds.), *Human Rights and Private Law* (Oxford: Hart Publishing, 2001), and Katherine Swinton 'Application of the Canadian Charter of Rights and Freedoms' in W. Tarnopolsky and Gerald Beaudoin, *The Canadian Charter of Rights and Freedoms—Commentary* (Toronto: Carswell, 1982).

[28] A. Barak, 'Constitutional Human Rights', 273–4.

receive selective protection and many do not fare well. Left to their own devices, Anglo-American courts, for example, developed a set of common law rules in contract and tort to regulate relations between workers and their employers that consistently sacrificed the liberties and freedoms of the former to the pursuit of wealth by the latter. Doctrines were developed that exposed workers to huge liabilities whenever they engaged in strikes or took other collective action against their employers and, simultaneously, made it almost impossible for them to claim compensation when they were injured or suffered illnesses as a result of working in an environment that was polluted with hazards and risks.[29] Indeed, in the minds of some, over the course of the nineteenth and early twentieth century the whole of the common law in the United States was transformed to favour the welfare and well-being of the ruling class.[30]

Most judges who have considered the relationship between constitutional and private law have understood that the principle of proportionality is an essential part of all constitutional texts and international human rights instruments. They also know that, as its most important principle, proportionality must be defined at a level of generality that will encompass and discipline all law. To meet the highest standards of neutrality that distinguish good constitutional theory from bad, proportionality cannot be defined in a narrower or more limited way. When six judges on Canada's Supreme Court ruled the principle had limited application to the rules of the common law, they arrogated to themselves a power to restrict the supremacy of the constitution they had no authority to assert.

2.2. Proportionality and Perspective

Even with its imperfections, the caselaw leaves no doubt about the neutrality of proportionality's derivation and definition. It also shows its capacity to meet Herbert Wechsler's test of neutrality in how it is applied. As we have seen, properly enforced, courts judge the relevant proportionalities in a case from the perspectives of those who are most affected by whatever law or government action is under review. Judgments are based on findings of fact about the parties' own evaluation of the significance of whatever government initiative or decision is before the court. Applied in this way, proportionality offers judges a clear and objective test to distinguish coercive action by the state that is legitimate from that which is not. When they stick to the facts, the personal sympathies of the judges towards the parties in the case never come into play.

That was the important lesson to be drawn from the debate between Kate O'Regan and Albie Sachs in *Lawrence, Negal and Solberg* v. *State* over how much weight should be given to the public interest of regulating alcohol consumption

---

[29] I. Christie, *The Liability of Strikers in Tort* (Toronto: Carswell, 1967). T. Ison, *The Forensic Lottery* (London: Staples Press, 1967); P. S. Atiyah, *Accidents, Compensation and the Law* (London: Weidenfeld and Nicolson, 1975).

[30] M. Horowitz, *The Transformation of American Law* (Cambridge, Mass.: Harvard University Press, 1977).

when deciding on the validity of a law restricting its sale on Sunday.[31] Even though most people are likely to identify with Sachs's instinct to value very highly any effort to reduce the terrible human suffering caused by excessive use of alcohol, the fact that the state allowed liquor to be sold on non-Christian holidays, when the consumption of alcohol was just as high, showed it did not regard the consequences so seriously. When it suited its purposes, the state was quite willing to let people purchase as much liquor as they pleased regardless of the cost.

Solberg will never be heralded as one of those landmark cases like *Brown* v. *Board of Education* or *Grootboom*,[32] which probe the soul and history of a nation. And yet, jurisprudentially, the lesson it teaches—that judges fail in their duty to apply the rules of constitutional law neutrally when they base their rulings on their own personal opinions about the competing values at stake—is huge. It identifies a perspective from which judges can view every case impartially. Like scales of justice, judges have no say on the worth of what is put on each side of the balance. When reviewing the legitimacy of laws that make having an abortion a crime, for example, when life and death issues really are at stake, it tells judges they have no authority to second-guess how a community thinks about the deep philosophical and spiritual meanings of life. It is, as Hungary's Constitutional Court has ruled, the responsibility of the people to decide the value of prenatal life.[33] To maintain their neutrality, judges must respect the fact that societies can and do value foetuses very differently. The fact is that foetal life is regarded as more sacred by people who try to live their lives according to the basic teachings of the Roman Catholic church than by liberal Darwinists who are inclined to more secular and scientific understandings. Judges forfeit their neutrality when they say they know better or more than their communities about the sanctity of human life. A community's moral character is for its people to define. Sometimes, as in *Solberg*, when it looks like the general welfare can be enhanced by a judge's imposition of his or her own views, a transgression such as that of Albie Sachs seems excusable, even worthy of praise. The lesson of the abortion cases, however, is that judges taking over a community's moral choices can never be right.

The requirement that the rules and principles of constitutional law be applied neutrally is more than just a negative injunction against their selective and inconsistent enforcement. It doesn't mean simply not taking sides. Neutrality also entails recognizing that what is just, what is in proper proportion, in any case is particular to each community. Unlike the concept of law, justice is a local, not a universal ideal.[34] Proportionalities vary directly with the weight and values

---

[31] (1997) 4 SA 1176; see Ch. 2, 62–4.

[32] *Brown* v. *Bd. of Education*; *Grootboom* v. *Republic of South Africa* [2001] 1 SA 46; (2000) 11 BCLR 1165.

[33] *On the Regulation of Abortion*, Decision 64/1991, 17/12/91, in Sólyom and Brunner, *Constitutional Judiciary*, 178–99.

[34] Cf. J. Habermas, *Between Facts & Norms* (Cambridge, Mass.: MIT, 1996), 60, 153–4, 256; Michael Walzer, *Spheres of Justice* (New York: Basic Books, 1983); 'Philosophy and Democracy' (1981) 9 Political Theory, 391.

people place on the relevant interests. So, in the case of abortion, more restrictive laws can be justified in Ireland, where the religious faith of the people attaches infinite value to human life from the moment of conception, than in Japan where the morality of foetal life and death is understood very differently. Even though Japanese women have more freedom to control their reproductive destinies than their sisters in Ireland, there is no basis in law to say the politicians in Dublin have acted unjustly or abused the powers of the state. Because the effects of an abortion are so much more profound for the foetus (its death) than they are for the woman (except in life-threatening situations), in places in which both have the same moral status, the rights of the unborn must trump. When all the relevant interests are measured against the principle of proportionality, the results in both cases are right. Making the perspectives of the parties the vantage point from which courts judge each case means no particular philosophy or moral vision is privileged over any other. Applied impartially, proportionality is a formal principle that is capable of being used anywhere in the world. On a shrinking planet, it is appropriately multicultural. It structures an integration of the real and the ideal, the local and universal, by integrating a fundamental principle of distributive justice into each community's understanding of itself.

Even though it respects every society's right to define its collective character for itself, proportionality does not countenance judges always rubberstamping everything a state says is important to its identity. In many cases, including those reviewing laws that prohibit women from terminating their pregnancies, the evidence of the significance of the law for those it affects most is clear and unambiguous and not a matter of dispute. No one doubts the sincerity and intensity of Irish Catholics regarding the sanctity of foetal life. Sometimes, however, because parties can become too caught up in a case and so liable to exaggerate their claims, it is necessary for a court to make its own evaluation of how significant the relevant law is for both its defenders and detractors. That was what happened, it may be recalled, when the military authorities in Israel and Virginia claimed that training women to be pilots or admitting them to military academies that used physical and psychological methods that were designed for males, would jeopardize the security of the country and/or the mission of the school. Neither Israel nor Virginia could point to any hard, factual evidence that could justify their fears. In both cases, the country's highest court stepped in and, on the basis of experience in other parts of the world and in other coeducational academies, concluded that the significance of giving women the same access as men to training opportunities in the military was not as harmful as those defending their exclusion claimed them to be.[35]

---

[35] *Miller v. Minister of Defence* [1998] 32 Isr. L Rev. 157; *US v. Virginia* (1996) 518 US 515.

3. THE LOGIC OF PROPORTIONALITY

Testing the legitimacy of laws through the prism of proportionality creates a framework of analysis around which a very powerful theory of judicial review can be built. Impartially applied, proportionality permits disputes about the limits of legitimate lawmaking to be settled on the basis of reason and rational argument. It makes it possible to compare and evaluate interests and ideas, values and facts, that are radically different in a way that is both rational and fair. It allows judgments to be made about ways of thinking that are as incommensurable as reason and faith.[36] It provides a metric around which things as dissimilar as length and weight can be compared.[37] Across a broad spectrum of cases, touching complex and controversial issues of religious liberty, sexual equality, and social and economic rights, we have seen proportionality able to solve conflict between fundamentally antagonistic moral values in a way that shows equal concern and respect to everyone involved.

A surprising number of these cases turned out to be relatively easy because they involved what the American legal theorist David Luban has called 'large-small trade offs'.[38] Admitting women to military academies,[39] providing sign-language translation services in public hospitals,[40] asking motorists to take a two-minute detour during hours of prayer,[41] making antiretroviral drugs available to pregnant woman who are HIV positive,[42] were all cases of this kind. Even when two sides of a case are more evenly balanced and more difficult to decide, the analysis remains the same. In either case, proportionality turns the review process into a relatively straightforward exercise of logical or syllogistic reasoning. A court begins with the major premise that states that all law must be proportional to be constitutional. The minor premise is its ruling that a particular law or act of government is proportional or not. The conclusion that follows is that in the first case the law is constitutional but in the second it is not.

On this model of judicial review, it is in the formulation of the minor premise, where the facts and details of the government's behaviour are scrutinized and probed, that all the hard work is done. Once the major (interpretative) premise is established, it can be (and usually is) taken for granted. There is no need for

---

[36] Cf. Albie Sachs, *Christian Education South Africa* v. *Minister of Education* [2000] 4 SA 757; *Lawrence, Negal and Solberg*, para. 171.

[37] Cf. Antonin Scalia in *Bendix Autolite Corp.* v. *Midwesco Enterprises Inc.* (1988) 486 US 888, 897, arguing the impossibility of saying whether a particular line is longer than a particular rock is heavy.

[38] David Luban, 'Incommensurable Values, Rational Choice and Moral Absolutes' (1990) 38 Cleveland St. L Rev. 65, 75. Cf. Cass Sunstein, 'Incommensurability and Valuation in Law' (1994) 92 Mich L Rev. 779.

[39] *US* v. *Virginia.*

[40] *Eldridge* v. *A.G. British Columbia* (1977) 151 DLR (4th) 577.

[41] *Lior Horev* v. *Ministry of Communication/Transportation.*

[42] *Treatment Action Campaign* v. *South Africa (Minister of Health)* [2002] 5 SA 721 (CC).

judges to rely on history or semantics or philosophy to tell them whether or not the state has acted in a way that respects the constitution. On a proportionality model, the day-to-day practice of judicial review has nothing to do with solving interpretative puzzles. It is not about defining the reach of a constitution or about whether a particular case (e.g. taking peyote) falls within the parameters of a larger category (religious liberty). It is, as Habermas emphasizes, a process of rule or norm application pure and simple. It is all and only about proportionality. Because all laws limit liberty, and/or discriminate among people in some way, and because, as the jurisprudence shows, proportionality is what basic rights of liberty, equality, and fraternity actually guarantee, it sets the standard that every law, every act of government, must meet.

With its focus on the particulars of each act of government, proportionality transforms questions that in moral philosophy are questions of value into questions of fact. It stimulates a distinctive kind of discourse that operates, in Habermas's terms, in an intermediate zone between facts and norms. In deciding whether a law on abortion, or sex discrimination, or housing, or health care, is constitutional or not, everything turns on the facts. Whether a state can legitimately punish women who abort their foetuses, or treat people differently on the basis of their religion or sex, or withhold resources they need to survive, depends entirely on the factual details of each case. Strict abortion laws can be justified in societies such as Ireland whose religious traditions equate pre- and post-natal life. Some forms of discrimination may be tolerated in the home that could not be practised on the street. The resources each person can legitimately claim from the state vary directly with the affluence of their communities and the number of people who are in need.

Habermas and others have called the reasoning process that judges follow when they measure acts of government against the principle of proportionality, a special discourse of rule or norm application.[43] It is, in fact, a particularly powerful example of a method of analysis known as 'casuistry', which involves the application of ethical rules to cases of conflicting obligations by emphasizing the factual distinctions of each. Proportionality allows casuistry to operate at its best.[44] Its supremacy, as part of every constitution, means there are no exceptions and no competing principles that can limit its reach. There can never be a question of the legitimacy or extent of its application to any dispute about the authority of the state to act. All cases are always settled on the basis of the same universal principle being applied to their particular set of facts.

---

[43] J. Habermas, *Between Facts & Norms*, 217–19, 265–6. See also R. Alexy, 'Rights, Legal Reasoning and Rational Discourse'; 'Justification and Application of Norms', 6 Ratio Juris (1993) 157; and, generally, *A Theory of Legal Argumentation* (Oxford: Clarendon, 1989).

[44] Casuistry, as a general method of argument, has received more mixed reviews. Cf. A. R. Jonsen and S. Toulmin, *The Abuse of Casuistry: A History of Moral Reasoning* (Berkeley: University of California Press, 1988); C. Sunstein, *Legal Reasoning and Political Conflict* (New York: Oxford University Press, 1996), ch. 5; R. Posner, *Overcoming Law* (Cambridge, Mass.: Harvard University Press, 1995); *Problematics of Moral and Legal Theory* (Cambridge, Mass.: Harvard University Press, 1999).

Legal reasoning about human rights contrasts sharply with the way economists and philosophers think about these issues. Whether someone's rights have been violated in law is not computed by some utilitarian, mathematical calculation. It is not about adding and subtracting people's preferences. Nor is it a process in which factors are catalogued and quantified and balanced against each other. Hypothetical arguments also play no role because they assume rather than evaluate the really critical facts. Indeed, when judges rely on the principle of proportionality to structure their thinking the concept of rights disappears. Proportionality transforms the meaning of rights from assertions of eternal truths into what human-rights advocate Michael Ignatieff has called 'a discourse for the adjudication of conflict'. In law, they are just 'common . . . reference points . . . that can assist parties in conflict to deliberate together'.[45] When rights are factored into an analysis organized around the principle of proportionality, they have no special force as trumps.[46] They are really just rhetorical flourish.

Because proportionality refuses to accord either rights or numbers any special status, it can claim an objectivity and integrity no other model of judicial review can match. It avoids the subjectivity and indeterminacy that plagues interpretation and cost/benefit calculations alike. Turning conflicts about people's most important interests and ideas into matters of fact, rather than matters of interpretation[47] or matters of moral principle,[48] allows the judiciary to supervise a discourse in which each person's perception of a state's course of action is valued equally and for which there is a correct resolution that can be verified empirically. Making proportionality the litmus test of legitimacy guarantees, to borrow another of Ignatieff's apt descriptions, 'that individuals are deliberative equals whose views are entitled to a respectful hearing in all moral discussions about how universal standards should apply in each instance'.[49]

4. THE JUSTICE OF PROPORTIONALITY

As well as possessing a neutrality and a capacity for rationality that guarantees its integrity in solving very basic issues of social co-operation, proportionality supports a theory of judicial review that meets Dworkin's criteria of 'fit' and 'value' as well. As a practical matter, proportionality is a legal standard that is very familiar to the judiciary. It has a proven record of success. Of all the theories that have offered justifications for a process of judicial review, the proportionality model is unquestionably the most compatible with current practice. There

---

[45] Michael Ignatieff, *Human Rights* (Princeton: Princeton University Press, 2001), 20.

[46] Cf. Ronald Dworkin, *Taking Rights Seriously* (Cambridge, Mass.: Harvard University Press, 1977).

[47] Antonin Scalia, *A Matter of Interpretation* (Princeton: Princeton University Press, 1997).

[48] Ronald Dworkin, *A Matter of Principle* (Cambridge, Mass.: Harvard University Press, 1985).

[49] Michael Ignatieff, *Human Rights*, 170.

is a very extensive, if not perfect, fit. One reason for the coincidence and why proportionality is a better theory of judicial review than its interpretivist rivals is partly because it doesn't call on judges to master methods of analysis such as archival research or moral philosophy that are foreign to the law. Rival theories, like originalist and moral readings of the constitution, face serious practical contradictions. Both insist judges master disciplines and ways of thinking in which they have no special knowledge or expertise. It is a fatal weakness of his theory that Dworkin needs a superhero to make it work. It is no accident his model jurist is named Hercules and not Antonin, Itsuo, or Kate.

Proportionality not only provides an account of judicial review for which the judiciary has already shown considerable sympathy, and which plays to its institutional strength to make work, it tells a very compelling story as well. The fact that proportionality qualifies as a neutral principle does not mean it is value free. The principle assumes that all who participate in a debate about the legitimacy of some course of action carried out by or with the blessing of the state are, at least for the purposes of the debate, each other's equal. Each point of view carries the same moral weight in the analysis. There is no universal, a priori answer to the question whether abortion is murder, or whether people of the same sex can marry each other that holds true all over the world. For the purposes of determining what rights foetuses, gays, and the poor can claim against the state, each ethical perspective that respects the equal standing of conflicting opinions is entitled to have its position evaluated fairly and according to the evidence that shows it in the best possible light.

The normative conception of equality that underlies the principle of proportionality will not be difficult for most societies to embrace. Only those that stigmatize others as inferior could object. In every area of law we have examined, the cases show that when judges test the decisions of politicians and their officials against the principle of proportionality, human rights are better protected and the sovereignty of the people more respected simultaneously. Proportionality establishes a metric to resolve conflicts between majorities and minorities that renders justice to both. It integrates law and politics in a way that maximizes the authority of each. It formulates the principle of separation of powers between the judiciary and the elected branches of government so that all three work co-operatively to facilitate each community being as just and fair as it is possible for a group of strangers to be. Because it is able to evaluate the intensity of people's subjective preferences objectively, it can guarantee more freedom and equality than any rival theory has been able to provide.

Human rights are best protected when courts are vigilant in their insistence that those who are invested with powers of the state respect the principle of proportionality in everything they do. In societies where the principle is strictly enforced, liberty, equality, and fraternity all flourish. The jurisprudence shows that in societies where the principle of proportionality prevails there is more religious freedom, less arbitrary discrimination, and greater recognition of a state's responsibility to ensure the essential conditions of personal liberty (security, safety, sustenance, etc.) than in states where it does not. None of the other mainstream theories offers anything like the protection against arbitrary and unjust acts of government that judges have been able to deliver with the proportionality principle. As we saw in Chapter 1, with only rare exceptions[50] originalists, proceduralists, and moralists alike are generally unwilling and/or unable to create any space for social and economic rights unless they are written out explicitly in the text.[51] All three insist that positive and negative rights are different concepts even though both are drawn from the same ethical principle of equal liberty and both are structured around the same framework of analysis. All of them miss the logical connection that holds between the positive obligations states have in virtue of their guaranteeing traditional rights of liberty and equality and the negative obligations of non-interference. Certainly none has laid out a right to fair shares as generous as that which has been derived from the principle of proportionality.

Originalists, proceduralists, and moralists also do relatively poorly when it comes to traditional rights and freedoms, such as religious liberty and the anti-discrimination principle. Religious freedom of any kind is something of an anomaly for procedural theories of judicial review and is either recognized as such or just conveniently ignored.[52] As well, John Hart Ely has said that judges who adhere to a procedural account of judicial review will have great difficulty finding ways to provide relief to women who are victims of discrimination that is inflicted or tolerated by the state. For Ely, because women are typically a majority of the population, they cannot claim to be a discrete and insular minority that is in need of protection from the courts. Their numerical superiority, Ely thinks, is usually enough to ensure that women can look after their interests in the ordinary processes of politics.[53]

Theorists who read constitutional texts from the perspective of those who were part of the original act of creation, or through the lens of some overarching theory of political justice, generally have been able to do more for religious minorities than their colleagues who think of constitutions in purely procedural terms. However, on issues of equality and discrimination they too come up short. In the United States, for example, originalists struggle with the issue of sex discrimination[54] and even Ronald Dworkin, whose theory professes to guarantee that states show everyone equal concern and respect, thinks the American approach of extending some groups more protection against discrimination than others is attractive. As well, on Dworkin's theory, people who are victims of

---

[50] The most notable being Jürgen Habermas, *Between Facts and Norms*, 123, 125, 247, 263, 415–17.

[51] See e.g. R. Bork, 'The Impossibility of Finding Welfare Rights in the Constitution' [1979] Wash. UL Rev. 695; J. Ely, *Democracy and Distrust* (Cambridge, Mass.: Harvard University Press, 1980), 162; P. Monahan, *Politics and the Constitution* (Toronto: Carswell, 1987), 126; R. Dworkin, *Freedom's Law* (Cambridge, Mass.: Harvard University Press, 1996), 11, 36.

[52] See e.g. Ely, *Democracy and Distrust*, 94; Monahan, *Politics and the Constitution*, ibid.

[53] Ely, *Democracy & Distrust*, 164–70.

[54] Bork, *Tempting of America*, 326–31; cf. 'Neutral Principles . . . ' (1971) 47 Indiana LJ 1.

arbitrary and discriminatory acts of government that are not intentional or malicious cannot expect any relief from the courts.[55] So for example, courts can do nothing for women who are excluded from jobs because they don't meet height or weight qualifications, even if they are strong enough, if the restrictions were adopted as a matter of administrative convenience and not for misogynous motives. Only a theory of review that recognizes that proportionality and equality are synonyms, that the former is the fullest and most complete expression of the latter, has the capacity to treat all forms of discrimination as arbitrary and unjust and beyond the lawmaking powers of all states.

Proportionality makes the legal concept of rights the best it can possibly be. Its understanding that rights are based on, and give expression to, a universal principle of distributive justice ensures arbitrary and discriminatory acts of government are kept to a minimum. Proportionality puts all the emphasis on the duties governments owe to those who are subject to their rule rather than marking off spheres of personal autonomy where the sovereignty of the individual is absolute and unconditional. For many, the superiority of proportionality in protecting basic human rights will be seen as its greatest achievement. For others, however, its rigorous constraints will not be an unambiguous good. Populists and ardent democrats will worry about the extent to which the sovereignty of the people will be diminished if courts strictly scrutinize every act of government against the very tough standards of proportionality. Conventional wisdom holds that there is a strong correlation between the strict enforcement of basic human rights and limits on what the people can and cannot do. An activist judiciary and democracy are seen as pulling in opposite directions like competitors in a 'zero-sum' game. Whatever gains and advantages accrue to one come at the expense of the other. When people can claim rights to equality and religious freedom, governments lose the power to tell them what they must believe and what they can aspire to be.

Although it is common to think of rights interfering with the sovereignty of the people to mould the characters of the communities in which they live, that is not the case, as the comparative jurisprudence has shown, with proportionality. It is, perhaps, the most remarkable feature of a model of judicial review that is structured around this principle that it is able to do so much to ensure governments respect the rights of people without seriously limiting the choices they can make about the sorts of societies they want to create. Proportionality provides a metric on which both rights and democracy, law and politics, can do better. The only politics that proportionality prohibits is the politics of extremism and hate. Laws can't be passed that label some as inferior to others. The formal equality of each person's autonomy means everyone's rights are the same. States owe the same duty to each person who is subject to their rule. Except for that one constraint, proportionality leaves it entirely to the people to decide what their

---

[55] R. Dworkin, *Sovereign Virtue* (Cambridge, Mass.: Harvard University Press 2000), 456–65; *A Matter of Principle* (Cambridge, Mass.: Harvard University Press, 1985), 66.

projects and priorities will be. Once it is established that a law doesn't directly challenge the equal moral authority each person possesses over his or her life, politicians can pursue just about any purpose they please. Every ambition and motivation that accepts everyone's equal moral status as a self-governing individual will pass the test. The principle of proportionality takes all benign purposes as given and evaluates the means by which they are pursued and their effects and the relationships between all three. It is a universal ideal in large part because it is so solicitous of local rule.

By comparison with other theories, proportionality leaves as much room for government to manœuvre as any and a good deal more than most. Rival theories typically impose significant restrictions on the sovereignty of the general will and the lawmaking powers of the state. Originalists in the United States, for example, say that except in rare cases affirmative action programmes that are intended to remedy systemic discrimination are unconstitutional because all racial classifications, whatever their purpose, offend the Fourteenth Amendment's guarantee that everyone receives the equal protection of the law.[56] Although Dworkin believes that, on the best moral reading of the equal protection clause, affirmative action programmes are legitimate, he says the legal status of a foetus, one of the central moral and political issues of our time, is for the courts, not the people, to decide.[57]

Judges who analyse affirmative action and abortion laws through the prism of proportionality think about the rights of vulnerable groups and the status of a foetus very differently. Proportionality separates the powers of the judiciary and the elected branches of government by making the latter responsible for the decisions that express the moral values of the people. So, for example, India's Supreme Court endorses affirmative action programmes being passed for the purpose of helping those who are least advantaged because they make the principle of equality the best it can possibly be.[58] Similarly, when it was asked for its opinion on the issue of abortion, Hungary's Constitutional Court took a hands-off approach to the question whether foetuses are entitled to the same constitutional rights as humans who have been born. The moral and legal status of the foetus, it ruled, was something only the people, through their elected representatives, could decide. It was not a decision that courts were authorized to make.[59] As a prescription for political behaviour that is constitutionally

[56] See e.g. Antonin Scalia's opinions in *Grutter* v. *Bollinger* (2003) 539 US—; *Richmond* v. *J. A. Crosson Co.* (1989) 488 US 467; *Metro Broadcasting* v. *FCC* (1990) 497 US 547; *Adarand Contractors* v. *Pena* (1995) 515 US 200; cf. Bork, *Tempting of America*, 149–50.

[57] Dworkin, *Law's Empire*, 381–9; *Sovereign Virtue*, ch. 12; *Life's Dominion*, 164–5; *Freedom's Law*, 102–10.

[58] The Court's jurisprudence on what are known in India as 'reservation' cases is vast. As an introduction see *Indra Sawhney* v. *Union of India*, AIR 1993 SC 477; AIR 2000 SC 498; *Deepak Sibal* v. *Punjab University* AIR 1989 SC 903; *State of Kerala* v. *Thomas*, AIR 1976 SC 490; *Chitra Gosh* v. *Union of India* AIR 1970 SC 35. For a balanced assessment of the Court's work, see Marc Galanter, *Competing Equalities* (Berkeley: University of California Press, 1984).

[59] *On the Regulation of Abortion*, Decision 64/1991.

correct proportionality says to aspiring politicians: 'virtually anything in moderation but nothing to excess.'

Although it would seem to count in favour of the proportionality principle that it satisfies Dworkin's twin criteria of 'fit' and 'value' better than any rival theory, some may worry that its empirical and moral claims leave it open to a fundamental, potentially fatal objection. Because, it might be said, the instruction to judges to exercise their powers of review within the framework set by proportionality has been drawn from the way courts actually go about their work, the whole theory rests on very shaky foundations. It looks like an attempt to draw an 'ought' from an 'is'; something philosophers have been telling the world for hundreds of years is impossible to do. The principle of proportionality and the theory of review it recommends, however, are not the products of such 'naturalistic' reasoning. Although in *our* research, *we* discovered the principle in the cases, that was not the method of the courts. For the judges, proportionality is grounded in the words and structure and purposes of constitutional texts, not in the jurisprudence they write. The lesson of the cases is that proportionality is a constitutive, immutable part of every constitution. It allows, as we have seen, rights and democracy to flourish simultaneously. As guardians of the constitution, judges have a duty to ensure the rights and freedoms it guarantees get as much protection as possible. Logically, legally, and morally they have no other choice.[60] Proportionality has priority over all of its rivals because it is able to reconcile both democracy and rights in a way that optimizes each.[61] Proportionality alone has the capacity to ensure constitutions are the best they can possibly be. None of the others comes close.

5. PROPORTIONALITY AND PRIVATE SCHOOLS

Testing the model of constitutional adjudication that the jurists have constructed around the principle of proportionality against the conventional criteria of constitutional theory makes a very compelling case for the practice of judicial review. As powerful as it is, however, it still may not resonate with people who find it foreign to their political and legal culture. In the United States for example, asking judges (to say nothing of legal academics), to stop trying to make sense of words on a page, events in the past, and/or earlier opinions of those who sat on the Bench undoubtedly will be seen by some as un-American. For them, the idea of the Supreme Court adopting a rule of strict scrutiny in every case would amount to a legal revolution. To suddenly abandon what are universally accepted as the cornerstones of American constitutional law will be beyond their legal imagination.

---

[60] See G. Vlastos, 'Justice and Equality', in R. Brandt, *Social Justice* (Englewood Cliffs, NJ: Prentice Hall 1962), 31.

[61] The German legal theorist, Robert Alexy, has highlighted the optimizing nature of proportionality, in his work *supra* n. 19, as has the German Constitutional Court in its description of the principle of 'practical concordance' that it uses in cases of religious liberty as we saw in Ch. 2, 44–9.

To overcome such scepticism and xenophobia, there are two things a person might do. One can continue to read cases on the theory that the more familiar one gets with the comparative jurisprudence, the less alien it will seem. Alternatively, one might turn inward and reflect on what a group of philosophers, legal scholars, and judges, known as pragmatists, have been saying about law in their country for the past hundred years. Any judge who does either or both conscientiously and in good faith should, sooner or later, come to see that the core idea of the rule of law is a universal, not a local, idea.

Those who choose to stay with the jurisprudence face the familiar problem of what volume of the law reports to take off the shelf next. The possibilities are unlimited. Many of the most important rights and freedoms—expression, association, privacy—remain unexplored. Even before heading off into new territory, there are a lot of cases in which issues of religious freedom, sex discrimination, and social and economic rights are raised simultaneously that will be of particular interest. This jurisprudence, which cuts across all three areas we have studied, abounds with important cases: lawyers[62] and accountants[63] denied the right to work because of the religious practices they follow; Muslim girls told they cannot attend state schools if they cover their heads with a scarf;[64] religious organizations refusing to allow people who do not share their faith[65] or the same ideas as to what constitutes sin[66] to work in their hospitals or schools. The list could be extended indefinitely.

At this stage of our inquiry, it is too late to embark on another major review of more cases. We have digested enough jurisprudence for one sitting. Before closing the books, however, there is one narrow but important issue—state funding of private (usually religious) schools—that raises questions about religious freedom, equality, and positive rights, which merits a brief last look. A state's responsibility for funding the education of people who refuse to attend its schools implicates all three areas of jurisprudence we have been examining and it remains a controversial issue in many parts of the world. The cases also provide a window on how judges behave when the claims that are made for state support are put forward on a collective or group basis and so provide a fitting point on which to bring our study of the cases to a close.

The jurisprudence on the right of religious and other minorities to claim public support for the construction and operation of their own schools is, like everything else we have read, rich and revealing. At one end of the spectrum, Hungary's Constitutional Court has ruled that a state must fund private schools 'in

---

[62] *Prince* v. *President Cape Law Society* [2002] 2 SA 795; [2002] 12 BHRC 1 (SACC); *Re Chichwe* [1995] 2 LRC 93 (ZSC).

[63] *Thlimmenos* v. *Greece* (2002) 31 EHRR 411.

[64] See S. Poulter, 'Muslim Headscarves in School: Contrasting Legal Approaches in England and France' (1997) 17 Oxford Journal of Legal Studies 43; see also *Sumayyah Mohammed* v. *Moraine* [1996] 3 LRC 475 (T and THC); *X* v. *Canton de Genève* 1997 BGE 123 I 296.

[65] *Corporation of Presiding Bishop of Church of Jesus Christ of Latter Day Saints* v. *Amos* (1987) 483 US 327.

[66] *Vriend* v. *Alberta* [1998] 1 SCR 493; (1998) 156 DLR (4th) 385.

proportion to their undertaking the state's programmes'.[67] The Hungarian rule which calls on church and state to co-operate where their interests overlap is followed by most states in western and central Europe. In Germany and Japan state funding is considered to be a constitutional duty.[68] At the other extreme, the American Supreme Court, favouring its historical and doctrinal methodology, has traditionally taken the position that not only is most public support not required, it is not even allowed.[69] Canada, where assistance can be given but not claimed, falls somewhere in between.[70]

No one has been tempted to draw the line between church and state as sharply as the Americans and it is not hard to see why. The Hungarian approach guarantees more religious freedom, greater popular sovereignty, and ultimately less judicial politics in the adjudication of this controversial and difficult question. Religious freedom is obviously enhanced wherever the rule of proportional funding governs. Everyone receives the same support from the state for their children's education. Parents who want to send their children to schools that reflect their religious ideas can do so without having to bear a special tax. By comparison, Americans and many Canadians who believe education and religion should not be separated are forced to support a school system that offends them. They are made to pay twice—like a fine—for their faith. First, they have to bear the entire cost of the education of their own children and then they have to pay taxes to support the public, secular system which they cannot, in good conscience, use.[71]

Democracy and the sovereignty of the people do better as well. The traditional American rule and theories that insist on limiting contact between the church and the state as much as possible impose substantial restrictions on the kinds and the character of laws the people can enact. Because of the way the US Supreme Court has interpreted the First Amendment, Americans have not had the power to shape their most important public institutions according to their deepest and most vital beliefs. The principle of proportionality, by contrast, allows each community a lot of freedom in deciding for itself the type of relationship between religion and education that suits its values and circumstances best. It also permits great flexibility at the level of policy design. The only obligation is to ensure that all schools—public and private—that follow the curricula and deliver the pro-

---

[67] *Resettlement of Church Property Case*. Decision 4/93 (1994) 1 EECR 57; also reproduced in Sólyom and Brunner, *Constitutional Judiciary*, 246.

[68] John E. Coons, 'Educational Choice and the Courts' (1986) 34 Am. J Comp. Law 1.

[69] *Everson v. Board of Education*, 330 US 1, 15 (1947), per Hugo Black, 'Neither [a state government nor Congress] can pass laws which aid one religion, aid all religions or prefer one religion over another.' More recently the Court has been less categorical in its thinking and various forms of government aid that benefit religious schools indirectly have been approved. See e.g. *Agostini v. Felton* (1997) 521 US 203; *Zelman v. Simmons-Harris* (2002) 122 S. Ct. 2460.

[70] *Adler v. Ontario* (1996) 140 D.L.R. (4th) 385; *Waldman v. Canada*, U. N. Human Rights Committee, Communication II 694/1996, 29/02/96 para. 9:2.

[71] M. McConnell, 'The Selective Funding Problem: Abortions and Religious Schools' (1991) 104 Harv. L Rev. 989.

grammes approved by the state are funded on the same basis. There is no requirement that the state should actually establish schools that cater to the religious beliefs of its minorities nor provide exactly the same amount of funding that it does for its own, non-sectarian schools. Each state can also decide for itself whether to pay the subsidy to the students and their parents or whether to provide direct support to the schools. Both have their advantages.[72] It is ultimately up to the people to decide whether a programme of group or individual rights works best for them. In constitutional law, there is no difference between the two. Whatever its choice, the only thing the state cannot do is force those whose spiritual beliefs are different than the majority's to bear a disproportionate burden educating their children.[73]

The principle of proportional funding does not oblige the majority to compromise an ambition of fostering a common culture and value system for the whole community. Quite the contrary. Everywhere the principle is applied it is accepted that the state may make funding conditional on religious schools agreeing to teach the same curriculum that is used in state-run schools. The logic that underlies proportional funding is based on the assumption that religious schools provide their pupils with an education that meets the standards set by the state. On a principle of fair shares, if both religious and secular schools are essentially doing the same job, neither ought to receive preferential treatment from the state.

India's Supreme Court has had more occasions to think about the educational rights of religious and linguistic minorities than most courts and even though these rights are expressly provided for in the text of the constitution,[74] it has always taken the position that the state is entitled to lay down reasonable conditions for the way the funds it is obligated to pay are used. According to the judges in Delhi, not only can the state insist that the educational institutions they support 'maintain and facilitate the excellence of its standards', it is also entitled to require that its interests in combating intolerance and bigotry in Indian society be reflected in admissions policies as well. So, for example, in one landmark ruling the Court insisted that while religious minorities were entitled to preserve the religious character of their schools, and reserve 50 per cent of the seats for members of their communities, the other half of the students had to be drawn from the society at large in order to ensure sectarian schools did not pose a threat to the secular, pluralistic character of the state.[75]

---

[72] M. J. Trebilcock, R. Daniels, and M. Thorburn, 'Government By Voucher' (2000) 80 Boston UL Rev. 205; M. McConnell, 'Multiculturalism, Majoritarianism and Educational Choice . . . ' (1991) U Chic. L Rev. 123; see also R. Posner, *Law, Pragmatism, and Democracy* (Cambridge, Mass.: Harvard University Press, 2003), 123–4.

[73] *Resettlement of Church Property Case.* Cf. *Adler* v. *Ontario,* per l'Heureux-Dubé dissenting.

[74] Article 30(1) provides that all religious and linguistic minorities have the right to establish and administer educational institutions of their choice, in Blaustein and Flanz, *Constitutions of the World.*

[75] *St Stephen's College* v. *University of New Delhi* AIR 1992 SC 1630; (1991) Supp. 3 SCR 121.

Economists examining the question of state support for religious schools would describe proportional funding as a 'Pareto superior' method of reconciling the secular interest of the state in ensuring its children get a proper education and the religious imperatives of groups trying to follow the most important precepts of their faith. There is a lot of evidence that proportional funding can do everything that a rule of strict separation can do and more. The state can realize all the objectives it has for its system of education and support the freedom of religious minorities simultaneously. The fact that in the Netherlands, which is among the most tolerant and best-educated countries in Europe, more students attend publicly funded private (and usually religious) schools than those operated by the state puts the lie to the claim that community values can only be conveyed in common schools which everyone is forced to attend.[76] In Canada, there are no discernible differences in the levels of tolerance and standards of excellence between those provinces (roughly half) of the country where religious schools are supported by the state and those where they are not.[77] Studies in the United States confirm religious schools can be just as successful in achieving academic excellence and inculcating values of tolerance and respect for others as secular public schools.[78]

Not only does a rule of proportional funding give more support to religious liberty and recognize a wider mandate for democracy than one that tries to cut all connections between church and state, it is also less vulnerable to judicial politics. The American approach of trying to keep church and state as separate as possible is, by comparison, wholly partial and partisan for one point of view. It privileges secular and assimilationist values over the aspirations of religious groups to organize their communities around the most important tenets of their faith. Consistent with everything we observed in Chapter 2, the American approach means the question of whether states must provide aid for religious schools is answered according to the political philosophy of each judge.

By contrast, proportional funding remains scrupulously neutral as between the competing pedagogical philosophies of secular majorities and religious minorities. Like any positive duty a state owes to its people, its obligation to fund their education can be drawn from any of the traditional rights. Proportional funding is logically entailed by standard guarantees of liberty and equality. Even in Hungary, where the constitution explicitly provides for the separation of church and state, religious freedom is understood to guarantee more than non-interference. Hungary's Constitutional Court, like Germany's and the Supreme Court of Japan, thinks religious freedom should be interpreted so as to make it the best expression of its underlying purposes. From that perspective, states fail to live up to their constitutional obligations when they do not ensure that the

[76] John E. Coons, 'Educational Choice and the Courts'.

[77] A point emphasized by Claire L'Heureux-Dubé in her dissenting opinion in *Adler* v. *Ontario* and conveniently ignored by the majority in its ruling against requiring the state to treat everyone equally in the funding of its schools.

[78] McConnell, 'The Selective Funding Problem', 1004, 1013–14.

conditions that are necessary for religious freedom to be meaningful are adequately protected. As László Sólyom, the first President of Hungary's Constitutional Court, has stressed, there is no neutrality in a policy of passivity and inactivity.[79]

Refusing to provide the same (proportional) subsidies to secular and religious schools that meet the general standards set by the state is a flagrant inequality that is impossible to defend. The differential treatment of the two types of school constitutes a serious injustice to those who favour integrating rather than keeping religion and education separate and apart. Moreover, it is wrong to think that those who want their children educated in schools that reflect their religious values are not discriminated against because they have the same (i.e. equal) opportunity as everyone else to take advantage of whatever educational programme is offered by the state. It is false to say that what they are demanding— support for their schools—is really a claim for something 'extra'.[80] As a factual description of how common, secular schools are perceived in society, it simply isn't true. The fact is secular schools do not provide the same opportunities for everyone. Depending on the nature and extent of a person's religious faith, publicly supported secular schools present radically different opportunities. Civic republicans and socialists may love them, but those who believe that religion should play an important part in the education of their children do not see secular schools as a good. For them, they are bad, something to be avoided, whatever the cost.

To say everyone is treated equally because public secular schools are formally open to all, denies those who believe that religion is an important part of everything they do, the respect they are entitled to receive. As in every other case we have considered so far, to retain their neutrality judges must accept the best evidence of how those most affected feel about whatever law or act of state is before them. Substituting a single, universal evaluation of secular schools for the actual assessments of those involved constitutes an illegitimate intrusion of politics into what is law's domain. It repeats the mistake Anthony Kennedy made in the very first case we read.[81] Empirically, it amounts to a wholesale rewriting of the facts. Morally, it dismisses the perceptions of those who claim they are not being treated fairly by the state as unworthy of any respect.

Considering the question of what rights people have to demand the state's support in the education of their children brings us back full circle. Whether the issue of school funding is analysed as a question of religious freedom, discrimination, or positive rights, the answer is the same. Once again we observe courts giving their best answers when they make proportionality the ultimate test of legitimate state activity and stick to the facts of the case. For some, this will

---

[79] *Resettlement of Church Property* case; a conclusion that Cass Sunstein—who thinks the American rule can be justified on other grounds—is also inclined to accept. See Cass Sunstein, *The Partial Constitution* (Cambridge, Mass.: Harvard University Press, 1995), 307, 317, 341.

[80] W. Sadurski, *Moral Pluralism and Legal Neutrality* (Dordrecht: Kluwer, 1990), 184–5.

[81] *Lee v. Weisman* (1992) 505 US 577, *supra* Ch. 2, 38–40.

signal that it is time to head back to the library and decide which volume of the law reports to read next. For others, however, more cases are not what is needed. Lots of people believe that regardless of how well the jurisprudence of one country compares with another, the *legitimacy* of any system of adjudication, and especially constitutional review, is specific to particular societies.[82] They belong to the school that teaches that the style and substance of legal reasoning in every country varies with its particular history and traditions and cannot be expected to embrace ideas and concepts that are foreign to its way of thinking. For those among them who are American, no matter how emphatically the cases show proportionality's superiority over rival theories, they also emphasize just how alien it is to the way they think about and practice constitutional law. The fact that America finds itself offside again will only confirm their instinct that proportionality has no place in the way judicial review works in the United States.

To think this way is natural, even understandable, but it is, in the end, a mistake. Proportionality has more connection with American law than is often appreciated. The word itself is part of the Court's standard tests when it reviews remedial legislation enacted under Section 5 of the Fourteenth Amendment[83] and in its assessment of whether punishment is 'cruel and unusual' and so in violation of the Eighth.[84] As well, the Court uses the same basic framework of analysis whenever it 'strictly scrutinizes' the ends, means, and effects of a law it is asked to review.[85] It is also, increasingly, the subject of comment by individual justices and academics.[86] Perhaps most importantly, its pragmatic methodology has deep and distinguished roots in America's legal past.

6. PROPORTIONALITY AND PRAGMATISM

As the jurisprudence we have examined in this and the last three chapters has shown, proportionality transforms judicial review from an interpretative exer-

---

[82] See e.g. Steven Burton, *An Introduction to Law and Legal Reasoning* (Boston: Little, Brown, 1985), ch. 10. See also Philip Bobbitt, *Constitutional Fate* (New York: Oxford University Press, 1982); Antonin Scalia in *Prinz* v. *United States* (1997) 521 US 898, 921 n 11; *Thompson* v. *Oklahoma* (1988) 487 US 815, 868. Cf. M. Tushnet, 'The Possibilities of Comparative Constitutional Law' (1999) 108 Yale LJ 1225; Vicki Jackson, 'Narratives of Federalism: of Continuities and Comparative Constitutional Experience' (2001) 51 Duke LJ 223.

[83] *City of Boerne* v. *Flores* (1997) 521 US 507.

[84] *Lockyer* v. *Andrade* (2003) 123 S Ct. 1166; *Ewing* v. *California* (2003) 123 S Ct. 1179.

[85] Tribe, *American Constitutional Law*. The close connection between strict scrutiny and proportionality is especially vivid in the Court's affirmative action jurisprudence. See e.g. *Grutter* v. *Bollinger* (2003) 123 S.Ct. 2325. The major difference between the two is that where proportionality generally allows the elected representatives of the people to determine what the aims and ambitions of their communities will be, strict scrutiny seriously restricts which purposes lawmakers can legitimately pursue.

[86] See e.g. *Nixon* v. *Shrink Missouri Government PAC* (2000) 528 US 897 per Breyer J; Vicki Jackson, 'Ambivalent Resistance and Comparative Constitutionalism: Opening up the Conversation on "Proportionality" Rights and Federalism' (1999) 1 U Pa. J Const. L 583; P. Gerwitz and J. Cogan

cise, giving meaning to the words of a constitutional text, into a very focused factual inquiry about the good and bad effects of specific acts of the state. Cases are decided on their individual merits, one at a time, rather than on the basis of categorical definitions divined by textual exegesis. In directing judges to undertake practical, factual investigations of specific state activity, proportionality reflects a pragmatic conception of law that has had a long and influential history in the United States. Indeed, pragmatism can fairly be thought of as America's own, home-grown, philosophical tradition and some of its most famous jurists, including Oliver Wendell Holmes, Benjamin Cardozo, and Richard Posner, have been guided by its central tenets in their thinking as to how judges should go about their work.[87]

The way pragmatists tell judges to analyse cases parallels very closely how courts proceed when they apply the principle of proportionality to distinguish assertions of state power that are legitimate from those that are not. 'Think things not words' is how Holmes famously put it in 1899 in an address to the New York State Bar.[88] This is a philosophy of law that is sceptical of grand theories. Pragmatists such as Holmes aim more modestly at finding the best solution possible in each case.[89] For John Dewey, one of the early high priests of pragmatism in the United States, the logic of law is not a process of formal concepts and rigid demonstration but rather a method of 'reaching intelligent decisions in concrete situations'.[90] The welfare of society, Cardozo—another of America's great pragmatic jurists—once wrote, was law's 'final cause'.[91] For him the goal, not its origin, was the important thing.

The way pragmatists think about the legal principles judges use to decide cases fits proportionality like a glove. Dewey described general principles as the 'means of intellectual survey, analysis and insight into the factors of the situation to be dealt with'.[92] Holmes regarded them as 'instruments of inquiry', 'intermediate premises'[93] designed as practical aids to guide judges to decisions that

(eds.), *Global Constitutionalism* (New Haven: Yale Law School, 2001), Pt. IV. See also Richard Posner, *The Problematics of Moral and Legal Theory* (Cambridge, Mass.: Harvard University Press, 1999), 258.

[87] Robert Summers, *Instrumentalism and American Legal Theory* (Ithaca: Cornell University Press, 1982) Although it has been characteristic of pragmatic jurists to reflect on their understanding of law in extra-judicial writing, unquestionably the most prolific has been Richard Posner. See e.g. *Law, Pragmatism and Democracy*; *Problematics of Moral and Legal Theory*, ch. 4; *Overcoming Law* (Cambridge, Mass.: Harvard University Press, 1995), ch. 19; *The Problems of Jurisprudence* (Cambridge, Mass.: Harvard University Press, 1990), ch. 15. For a delightful introduction to the early history of pragmatism in the USA see L. Menand, *The Metaphysical Club* (New York: Farrar, Straus, & Giroux, 2001).

[88] O. W. Holmes, 'Law in Science and Science in Law' (1899) 12 Harv. L Rev. 443, 460.

[89] Summers, *Instrumentalism and American Legal Theory*, 45; Posner, *Law, Pragmatism and Democracy*, ch. 2

[90] John Dewey, 'Logical Method and the Law' (1925) 10 Cornell L Quarterly 17, 21.

[91] Benjamin Cardozo, *The Nature of the Judicial Process* (New Haven: Yale University Press, 1921), 66.

[92] Dewey, 'Logical Method and the Law', 26.

[93] Thomas Grey, 'Holmes and Legal Pragmatism' (1989) 41 Stanford L Rev. 787, 819.

were sound and in the public's best interest. This, as we have seen, is precisely the role that proportionality has played in defending religious freedom, stopping sex discrimination and guaranteeing everyone a general measure of well-being. Like all legal principles pragmatists endorse, proportionality directs rather than supplants a close and careful evaluation of the facts.[94]

In the same way that the principle of proportionality can produce very different answers to a question such as whether women have a right to procure an abortion depending on where it is asked, pragmatists too believe all judgments are contextual and contingent and relative to the particular circumstances in which they are made. Pragmatism, like proportionality, privileges the perspective of those who are actually party to a dispute.[95] As a practical matter, for both, purposes and goals are evaluated in terms of their means and effects rather than on the basis of whether, against some master value, they are inherently good or bad.[96]

American judges who reason pragmatically should feel more than just a sense of familiarity and a comfort level with the principle of proportionality. It should be apparent that pragmatism's account of adjudication is stronger with a principle of proportionality than without. Proportionality provides an answer to critics, such as Dworkin, who reject pragmatism's mantra of 'focusing on facts' as empty and unhelpful because it doesn't tell judges which facts are important and so allows them to do whatever *they* think is best.[97]

In responding to the charge of being unprincipled, consider what pragmatists can say about *Lochner*,[98] *Brown* v. *Board of Education*,[99] and *Roe* v. *Wade*[100] if they made proportionality part of their vocabulary. They could tell a more consistent, less political story about what are widely regarded as the three most important decisions of the US Supreme Court in the twentieth century than anyone has offered so far. Division of opinion among constitutional theorists about the quality of the Court's rulings on the rights to work, attend integrated schools, and procure an abortion has typically (although not always) split along party lines.[101] Liberals such as Dworkin tend to loathe *Lochner* because it seems to say it is outside the bounds of legitimate lawmaking for people to establish basic labour standards in their communities and love *Brown*

[94] Posner, *Law, Pragmatism and Democracy*, 75.

[95] Summers, *Instrumentalism and American Legal Theory*, Introduction; Thomas Grey, 'Freestanding Legal Pragmatism' (1996) 18 Cardozo L Rev. 21, 30–3.

[96] Posner, *Law, Pragmatism and Democracy*; Thomas Grey, 'Holmes and Legal Pragmatism', 789, 798–805. Of course, in philosophical terms, pragmatism does evaluate human behaviour against an ideal of equal liberty.

[97] Dworkin, *Law's Empire*, ch. 5; 'Reply' (1997) 29 Ariz. St. LJ 431.

[98] *Lochner* v. NY (1905) 198 US 45.

[99] *Brown* v. *Board of Education*.

[100] *Roe* v. *Wade* (1973) 410 US 113.

[101] Notable exceptions would include Wechsler's critique of *Brown* v. *Board of Education* in 'Toward Neutral Principles', John Ely's attack on the Court's decision in *Roe* v. *Wade*—'The Wages of Crying Wolf . . . ' (1973) 82 Yale LJ 920, and Robert Bork's disavowal of *Lochner* in *Tempting of America*, 46–9, 158.

and *Roe* because they are seen to further the emancipation of blacks and women.[102] Conservatives, like liberals (and practically everyone else), applaud the Court's ruling in *Brown* but on *Lochner and Roe* they have different ideas. Conservatives have no difficulty identifying with the Court's defence of free market values in *Lochner* but they believe the Court abused its powers in *Roe* by taking sides in the abortion debate and imposing its values on the country.[103]

Proportionality offers a way to overcome the partisanship that has plagued so much of what has been written about these three great landmarks of American constitutional law. Rather than testing whether these cases were resolved in ways that are perceived to be politically correct, pragmatists, looking at them through the lens of proportionality, would say the Court got it right every time. From a pragmatist's perspective, on each of these occasions, when the country asked the justices for their opinion on the most controversial and challenging issues of the day, the great majority of them remained faithful to the constitution and the ultimate rule of law.[104]

With the principle of proportionality in hand, pragmatists can tell a story about what are arguably the three most influential cases in all of American constitutional law that makes them the best they can possibly be.[105] As we saw in the last chapter, proportionality can bring about a complete redemption of *Lochner*. If, as the evidence seemed to suggest,[106] this was a case of crude collusion and self-dealing between big business and organized labour to enlist the support of their political cronies to put their less (politically) powerful competitors out of business, then, on a test of fair shares, the restriction on the number of hours people could work in a bakery was grievously flawed. In contrast with other, early pieces of labour legislation that were upheld by the Court, the law that was under review in *Lochner* really was regressive and perverse.[107] No matter what one's politics, if the act of the legislature in Albany was a political fix, it was an abuse of power that should never have been certified as having the status of valid law.

In *Brown* v. *Board of Education* proportionality provides the principle Herbert Wechsler thought was missing in the Court's own opinion. It offers a neutral basis on which the competing freedoms (of association) of blacks and whites can be resolved in the way the Court proposed. Wechsler's mistake was in thinking

---

[102] Dworkin, *Law's Empire*, 374–6, 397–9; *Life's Dominion*, 102–17, 168–72; *Freedom's Law*, ch. 3.

[103] See e.g. Richard Epstein, 'Toward a Revitalization of the Contract Clause' (1980) 51 U Chic. L Rev. 732; Bernard H. Seigan, 'Constitutional Protection of Property and Economic Rights', 29 San Diego L Rev. (1992) 161; Bork, *Tempting of America*, 74–84, 112–16.

[104] Ironically, Holmes, who dissented in *Lochner* ((1904) 198 US 45), was not always one of them.

[105] John Hart Ely, who thinks both *Lochner* and *Roe* were wrongly decided, undoubtedly shows them in the worst light: *supra* n. 51.

[106] Richard Epstein, 'The Mistakes of 1937' (1988) 11 Geo. Mason UL Rev. 517.

[107] For good discussions of the Court's overall approach to labour and employment standards legislation see Epstein, ibid., and David Currie, 'The Constitution in the Supreme Court: The Protection of Economic Interests 1889–1910' (1985) 52 U Chic. L Rev. 324, 381–2.

the rights of association of the two groups were completely the same. As a factual matter, from the perspective of the parties, they were not. Forced segregation is much more destructive of human freedom than forced integration precisely because of the deep psychological wounds it inflicts. Telling black children they cannot be educated in the same schools as white students is brutally offensive to their dignity and self-worth in a way that forcing whites to share their classrooms is not. Segregationists may be deeply offended by having to mix with people with whom they want no association, but their stature and status in the community is not diminished by their forced integration. Although the Court's order to desegregate American schools 'with all deliberate speed' favoured the (positive) right of association of African Americans over the (negative) rights of whites who were opposed to interracial associations of all kinds, the principle of proportionality provides a rational and just explanation of why the competing freedoms had to be prioritized in that way. Where *Plessy* v. *Ferguson*,[108] the case that *Brown* overruled, dismissed the complaint that segregation was demeaning to blacks by saying that would only be the case if they chose to regard it in that light (a very early example of a court 'blaming the victim'), the way proportionality works, it is precisely because that was their reaction that they were entitled to succeed.

Roe v. *Wade*, the third really pivotal decision of the twentieth century, is regarded by many people as the worst the US Supreme Court has ever made. When it ruled that the state must respect a woman's freedom to decide whether to terminate a pregnancy at least in the first few months after conception, they say the Court gave its approval to the wholesale murder of unborn children. Even some who like the result condemn the judgment as more the product of judicial politics than a requirement of the law.[109] Looked at through the lens of proportionality, however, the Court's 'trimester solution' appears as an impartial, even-handed assessment of the competing conceptions of life that collided in the case. The evidence the Court highlighted in its judgment showed that no American state had ever recognized that foetuses have the same rights and legal status as humans after birth. For much of its history, abortion was legal in America and even when it wasn't it was never punished as severely as the killing of humans who had been born. Nor, as William Douglas pointed out, did states ever issue death certificates to foetuses who miscarried, even when they were viable and fully developed.[110]

Against the uncontradicted evidence that the life of a foetus had never been accorded the same legal status as a born human being, it would have been wrong for the Court to have imposed its own, stricter definition of human life on women. The trimester solution holds the state to its own standards in defining the meaning of life by tracking the biological development of a foetus. When a foetus is furthest from being what the state treats as a legal human person, when

---

[108] (1896) 163 US 537, 551.   [109] Ely, 'The Wages of Crying Wolf . . . '.
[110] *Doe* v. *Bolton* (1973) 410 US 179, 218.

it is in a purely vegetative state and insensitive to all feeling, the life of the woman, for whom an unwanted child may result in great suffering (including death) for herself and her child, has priority. At the other end of its gestation, when it is only a matter of days between an act of abortion and infanticide, the state is perfectly entitled to treat behaviour that is so contemptuous of human life as a crime. The woman who fails to act early on in her pregnancy, when her interests have priority, has little cause to complain. Initially she maintains complete control of her body and the longer it takes to terminate a pregnancy the harder it gets to tell a story of ruin and enduring unhappiness that starts with the birth of her child.

Contrary to its natural instinct, in *Roe* v. *Wade* the Court resisted categorical, all-or-nothing solutions. Like the Supreme Court of Canada[111] and Hungary's Constitutional Court,[112] it did not take sides on the intractable moral question of when life begins. Instead, it focused on the legal and factual circumstances of foetuses and women who do not want to give birth and tried to show equal respect to both. Reasoning in this way allowed the Court to effect a solution that was true to America's own understanding of the issue. Tested against the principle of proportionality, *Roe* v. *Wade* got it right. In a country that has never treated foetuses as having the same moral status as human beings who have been born, no government has the right to force any woman to give birth to an unwanted child.

Proportionality's account of the Supreme Court's decision in *Roe* v. *Wade*, like its understanding of *Lochner* and *Brown*, is as American as apple pie. It shows the principle is as much a part of the rule of law in America as anywhere else. It tells a story that at the really big moments in constitutional adjudication in the last century, the US Supreme Court consistently handed down judgments that meet the most rigorous standards of justice and constitutional legitimacy. Regardless of what other mistakes they may have made, or how poorly they may have explained themselves, they did do the right thing when it counted the most.

American jurists, with an instinct to be pragmatic should embrace the principle of proportionality unconditionally and without reservation. Proportionality makes pragmatism the best it can possibly be. By directing judges to the evidence that best describes the parties' own evaluation of their situation, proportionality encourages judges who find themselves leaning to one side of a case to listen more carefully to the other.[113] Proportionality permits pragmatic judges to attain a level of objectivity and impartiality beyond anything they have achieved so far.[114] Consciously to turn one's back on what in every other constitutional democracy is regarded as the most important criterion for

---

[111] *R.* v. *Morgentaler* (1988) 44 DLR (4th) 385.   [112] *On the Regulation of Abortion.*

[113] Thomas C. Grey, 'What Good is Legal Pragmatism?', in M. Brint and W. Weaver (eds.), *Pragmatism in Law and Society* (Boulder, Colo.: Westview, 1991), ch. 1.

[114] For a critique of contemporary pragmatic theory, see Stanley Fish, 'Almost Pragmatism: The Jurisprudence of Richard Posner, Richard Rorty and Ronald Dworkin', in Brint and Weaver (eds.), ibid. ch. 3.

distinguishing laws that are constitutional from those that are not would be inconsistent with the pragmatist's commitment to find the best solution in every case, and it would be unpatriotic to boot. Every time a court rules that a government need not prove that the purposes and effects of what it proposes to do are measured and proportional, it makes it possible for some people to behave arbitrarily and abusively towards others. By shrinking the area of community life where law is the king, it breaks faith with Thomas Paine and the spirit of the revolution.[115] It betrays a legal tradition in which its highest judges have generally shown a heightened vigilance when the great freedoms to work, procreate, and be free from invidious discrimination were at stake. At a time when a majority of Americans believe the slogan 'might makes right' is a valid axiom of dispute resolution,[116] only the pragmatic judge can guarantee that the rule of law will always be sovereign in the land that paid homage to it first.

---

[115] Thomas Paine, *Common Sense*, in B. Kurlick (ed.), *Political Writings*, rev. student edn. (Cambridge: Cambridge University Press, 2000), 27–8.

[116] Indeed, for some, the ultimate source of all law. See e.g. Posner, *Law, Pragmatism and Democracy*, 260–1.

Index